GENRE NETWORKS
AND EMPIRE

Genre Networks
and Empire

Rhetoric in Early Imperial China

Xiaoye You

SOUTHERN ILLINIOS UNIVERSITY PRESS : CARBONDALE

Southern Illinois University Press
www.siupress.com

Copyright © 2023 by Xiaoye You
All rights reserved
Printed in the United States of America

26 25 24 23 4 3 2 1

Cover illustration: Elegant retro Chinese style background template with ocean wave and fog cloud. Image from Phoebe Yu on Shutterstock.

Library of Congress Cataloging-in-Publication Data
Names: You, Xiaoye, 1974– author.
Title: Genre networks and empire : rhetoric in early imperial China / Xiaoye You.
Identifiers: LCCN 2022044197 (print) | LCCN 2022044198 (ebook) | ISBN 9780809338979 (paperback) | ISBN 9780809338986 (ebook)
Subjects: LCSH: Chinese language—Rhetoric—History. | Chinese language—Rhetoric—Political aspects. | Chinese language—To 600.
Classification: LCC PL1271 .Y68 2023 (print) | LCC PL1271 (ebook) | DDC 808/.04951—dc23/eng/20221121
LC record available at https://lccn.loc.gov/2022044197
LC ebook record available at https://lccn.loc.gov/2022044198

Printed on recycled paper ♻

Southern Illinois University System

獻給
游明鏗和劉梅香
To my parents Mingkeng You and Meixiang Liu

CONTENTS

Illustrations and Tables	ix
Abbreviations	xi
Dynasties of Early China	xiii
Preface	xv
Introduction	1
CHAPTER 1 Genre Networks as a Political Institution	25
CHAPTER 2 Reading the Heavenly Mandate	52
CHAPTER 3 Regulating the Inner Court	75
CHAPTER 4 Weighing the Ways of Government	97
CHAPTER 5 Defending Imperial Integrity	120
CHAPTER 6 Praising and Criticizing as Entertainment	143

viii *Contents*

Conclusion: 165
Limits of the Genre Network

Appendix: 175
Genres Discussed in the Book

Notes 177

Works Cited 191

Index 205

ILLUSTRATIONS AND TABLES

Illustrations

1.1 Chang'an, the capital city of   45
the Western Han dynasty.

1.2 Imperial edict of the fifth year   48
of Yuankang unearthed in Juyan.

5.1 The Middle Kingdom during   123
the late Warring States period.

5.2 Revolting kingdoms and their   134
military incursions in 154 BCE.

Tables

2.1 Key Discourses on   54
Natural Anomalies

3.1 Key Discourses Concerning   78
the Inner Court

4.1 Key Court Discussions in   99
the Western Han

5.1 Key Discourses on   122
the Integrity of the Han

6.1 Stories, Poetry,   147
and Rhapsody

ABBREVIATIONS

BH: *Book of Han* 漢書

BLH: *Book of the Later Han* 後漢書

DS: *Discourses of the States* 國語

GSR: *The Grand Scribe's Records* 太史公書, 史記

ZT: *Zuo Tradition* 左傳

DYNASTIES OF EARLY CHINA

PREIMPERIAL

Xia c. 2070–c. 1600 BCE

Shang c. 1600–c. 1046 BCE

Zhou c. 1046–256 BCE

    Western Zhou 1046–771 BCE

    Eastern Zhou 770–256 BCE

        Spring and Autumn 771–476 BCE

        Warring States 475–221 BCE

IMPERIAL

Qin 221–207 BCE

Han 202 BCE–220 CE

    Western Han or the Former Han 202 BCE–9 CE

    Xin 9–23 CE

    Eastern Han or the Later Han 25–220 CE

PREFACE

Studying non-Western rhetoric is, among other things, a process of unlearning. The unlearning starts from a recognition that scholars inhabit in the legacies of European colonialism, including racism, capitalism, structuralism, monolingualism, linear temporality, and academic disciplinarity. For scholars of color, it is also a process of reconciling with their cultural allegiance.

I learned about Chinese rhetoric through reading Western scholarship. Like many, I was inducted into the fields of rhetoric and writing studies through my encounter with Robert B. Kaplan's doodles. I ran into them when researching for my master's thesis in China. Kaplan described the preferred thought patterns in the Anglo-American expository writing as linear while those in other traditions as circular or zigzagging. The doodles not only helped me understand the expectations of the native English reader but also gain a nascent idea of Chinese rhetoric. During my PhD studies at Purdue, I read George Kennedy's book *Comparative Rhetoric* and was intrigued by his "General Theory of Rhetoric that will apply in all societies" (1998, 1). Through the Greco-Roman terms, which Kennedy claimed as "the only fully developed system of rhetorical terminology" (5), I learned about classical Chinese rhetoric. Now, I know Kaplan's doodles and Kennedy's General Theory of Rhetoric were products of modern Western epistemology, which corroborated with European colonization; these rhetorical schemes racialized non-Western peoples and their rhetorical traditions.

Meeting with these White rhetorical schemes inspired me to study Chinese rhetoric on its own terms. Previously, I examined the history of English composition in China, and I suggested that in their pursuit of decolonization, the Chinese negotiated with and appropriated Western conventions for their own voices. I also studied English use in China, Japan, and the United States and proposed that we understand English as a cosmopolitan (rather than Anglo-American) and transliterate (rather than monolingual) practice and teach English literacy from this perspective. Studying ancient Chinese rhetoric in

xvi *Preface*

this book, I decided to take a decolonial stance and to consider what studying a non-Western tradition on its own terms means.

This decision has opened up a can of worms. On the one hand, it raises methodological questions dealing with what and how: With a colonial and antiracist stance, what aspects of ancient Chinese rhetoric are worth examining? Can I be critical of a tradition that I identify with deeply? What exactly does this critical stance entail in terms of analytic methods? On the other hand, this decision raises political questions. I am working in a predominantly White institution in the middle of Pennsylvania, the ancestral lands of the Erie, Haudenosaunee, Lenape, Shawnee, Susquehannock, and Wahzhazhe Nations. English and Asian Studies, the two areas in which I work, were historically reticent about the settler colonial state and complicit in US imperialism in the world. How will my work evade imperialism inherent in area studies? How will my work transcend feeding new data into the Western knowledge system? While taking a decolonial approach, can my work be truly decolonial (such as helping with the repatriation of land to Indigenous people) rather than being an example of a new settler's move to innocence? I have wrestled with these questions while writing the book.

This book has resulted from my efforts to learn and unlearn about Chinese rhetoric over the last two decades. Like the Western tradition, the Chinese tradition is rich and complicated; it evolved with a long history of geopolitical control and conquest. To understand this tradition, I have conversed with many scholars. In graduate school, I was mostly indebted to Janice Lauer, who introduced me to classical Western rhetoric, which spurred my curiosity about its Chinese counterpart. Over the years, stimulating conversations with Andy Kirkpatrick, Dwight Atkinson, Ulla Connor, Robert Caserio, LuMing Mao, Keith Gilyard, Jan Swearingen, Hui Wu, Arabella Lyon, Huiling Ding, and Huatong Sun further encouraged me to study classical Chinese rhetoric, a tradition often misrepresented in the West. While working on this book, I benefited from the feedback given by Steve Fraiberg, Damián Baca, Richard Enos, Zhaozhe Wang, Erica Brindley, Jack Selzer, and two anonymous reviewers. Students taking my graduate seminar Rhetoric and Mobilities in spring 2021 commented on the book manuscript as well. I learned much about decoloniality from coteaching the graduate seminar Decolonizing Rhetoric and Composition with Suresh Canagarajah in fall 2021. I am very thankful to my research assistants Su Young Lee and Rebecca Corinne Haddaway, who not only copyedited my writing but also commented on my ideas.

Preface

I am also thankful to the Southern Illinois University Press staff for their professionalism. Acquisition editor Kristine Priddy made the peer review process immeasurably beneficial. EDP manager Linda Jorgensen Buhman, and project managers Khara Lukancic and Lisa Stallings, and the copyeditor Ann Boisvert all helped improve the book in one way or another.

I want to thank my family for their unfailing support. I am most grateful that my parents, Mingkeng You and Meixiang Liu, aroused my interest in the Chinese literary and rhetorical tradition at an early age by introducing me to the four classical novels. My father performed Chinese calligraphy for the cover illustration. I am also thankful to my wife Hsiao-Hui Yang and children Joy Tianhuan and Felix Tianle for their understanding and encouragement of my work. With a solid training in Chinese classics, Hsiao-Hui helped me understand the specificities of certain ancient texts.

The book project was supported by a sabbatical leave generously awarded by the College of the Liberal Arts at Pennsylvania State University.

Early versions of portions of this book were previously published in *Ancient Non-Greek Rhetorics* edited by Carol Lipson and Roberta Binkley ("Reading the Heavenly Mandate: Dong Zhongshu's Rhetoric of the Way (*Dao*)," 153–75, copyright @ 2009 by Parlor Press, adapted by permission) and *College English* ("Building Empire through Argumentation: Debating Salt and Iron in Western Han China," 72 (4): 367–84, copyright @ 2010 by NCTE, adapted by permission).

GENRE NETWORKS
AND EMPIRE

INTRODUCTION

The new-democratic revolution is not any other revolution, but can only be and must be a revolution against imperialism, feudalism and bureaucrat-capitalism waged by the broad masses of the people under the leadership of the proletariat. 無產階級領導的, 人民大眾的, 反對帝國主義、封建主義和官僚資本主義的革命, 這就是中國的新民主主義的革命。

—Mao Zedong (1961)

This book explores the decolonial option in studies of non-Western rhetoric. The decolonial option seeks to expose how the colonial and imperial matrix of power operated in the past and continues to operate in a series of interconnected structural modes; further, it works to liberate people from the mirage of modernity and the trap of coloniality by building a foundation of local knowledges and meaning-making practices (García and Baca 2019; Mignolo 2011; Ruiz and Sánchez 2016). While these goals have been most visibly articulated by Indigenous and Latinx intellectuals and activists (Mignolo and Walsh 2018; Tuck and Yang 2012), they resonate with comparative rhetoricians, who study non-Western rhetoric. Aligned with decolonial scholarship, comparative rhetoricians have long argued that non-Western rhetoric needs to be examined on its own terms rather on those of the Greco-Roman tradition and they are wary of any attempt to build a universal theory of rhetoric. They also warn that emic studies of a non-Western rhetoric are inadequate. Rather, rhetorical practices need to be studied in dialogue with other traditions and with ongoing sociopolitical concerns serving as frames of reference (Hum and Lyon 2008; Mao 2013), moving toward what Walter Mignolo (2011) calls "border epistemology" (20).[1]

The paths to the border epistemology hold both challenges and promises. Some of the challenges are already manifest in the opening paragraph of this introduction.[2] The use of terms "West" and "non-West" risks reinforcing colonial binaries such as the "civilized" West versus the "barbaric" rest and reifying the dominance of the Western rhetorical tradition. The use of the term "rhetoric" easily evokes speechmaking and civic education in ancient Greece and Rome. The use of English, one of the Euro-American imperial languages, for scholarly writing has exacerbated the difficulty of decolonization. Nevertheless, border epistemology offers promise, including humanizing non-Western peoples, centering "other" ontologies and epistemologies, and ultimately building a more inclusive foundation of meaning making, feeling, and living.

In efforts to decenter Western epistemology, however, there exists a tendency to usher non-Western concepts and practices into rhetorical studies without fully attending to the oppressive social structures from which these concepts and practices emerged. This book argues that in studies of a non-Western rhetoric, the decolonial option must include an exposition and critique of the imperial, colonial, ethnic, racial, and sometimes feudal matrix of power residing in that tradition.[3] This move can benefit comparative rhetoric in a number of ways. First, it reminds us that people in non-Western contexts have suffered and continue to suffer injustices not only caused by colonialism, imperialism, and capitalism, but also by feudal, gendered, ethnic, racial, and linguistic hierarchies of local origins. As cited in the epigraph, for instance, Mao Zedong pointed out, in 1948, the entanglement of domestic and foreign forms of oppression amid China's struggle for decolonization (Mao 1961, 235). Second, this move serves to foreground the problematics of a dualistic thinking frequently found in comparative rhetoric, such as viewing the non-West as an exterior to the West. In doing so, it helps us recognize resistance and oppositionality as "rhetorical traps of a coloniality and modernity/rationality grid" (García and Cortez 2020, 103). Third, this move encourages scholars to further interrogate how rhetoric has enabled the West to sustain an imperial matrix of power from the past (the Greek and Roman empires) to the present (North Atlantic nations).

In order to make the decolonial move, this book examines rhetoric in early imperial China, a period rendered invisible by Western biases, and does so by centering Chinese theories of genre. Specifically, this book focuses on how an imperial matrix of power was established through what ancient Chinese called *wenti jingwei* (文體經緯), or genre networks. Owing to liberal democratic ideologies, the field of rhetorical studies has paid much attention to rhetorical theories and practices in preimperial China, especially during the

Introduction

Warring States period (475–221 BCE), when hundreds of schools of thought vied for political power. This book argues for the importance of moving away from this period and into the imperial era for its affordance of understanding rhetoric and other ways of government such as autocracy. To explore rhetoric and autocracy, this book argues that Chinese networked theories of genre are essential, as a distributed use of genres was instrumental for imperial government. While networked approaches to genre studies have been employed in the West to study scientific and organizational communications (Bazerman, 1999; Spinuzzi, 2003, 2008), this book will demonstrate that the ancient Chinese developed such approaches for understanding textual relations and imperial government and for writing history.

Central to the ways that genre networks regulated the activity of the imperial government was a range of texts and codes. The technology of writing was underscored by court historians. After the first emperor of China, Qin Shi Huang, united the Middle Kingdom in 221 BCE, as recorded by historian Sima Qian, he tightened control over his subjects by regulating their use of writing. He did this in a number of key ways: by imposing a script with standard orthography (seal calligraphy), burying literati alive, and burning books from the Hundred Schools of Thought. In addition to these violent measures, he strengthened empire-wide communication by imposing a unified legal code and bureaucratic procedure, standardizing a system of weights and measures, systematizing the axles of wheels and the widths of state roads, and formalizing bureaucratic genres. Serving as the nerve system, the codes, procedures, roads, and genres connected the central government and its distant bureaus. While the Qin dynasty (221–207 BCE) was short-lived, only lasting fifteen years, it laid a foundation for its successor, the Han dynasty (202 BCE–220 CE), to develop a sophisticated semiotic system to manage ethnic diversity and geopolitical complexities.

Regulating the use of writing was a crucial policy for ruling a large, diverse population over a vast land. The policy suggests that the state was not only aware of the utility of written language in its bureaucratic government but also deeply wary of the pernicious nature of certain discourses. Government is both an activity and an art, aiming at shaping, guiding, or affecting the conduct of some person or persons. The sense and object of governmental acts have to be thought out, to be invented. To govern, the ruling class of the Qin and Han dynasties discussed what government meant and the best strategies to achieve it, manifesting the imperial logic. While Lydia H. Liu suggests that the

4 *Introduction*

movement to widespread use of the Chinese script is a technology of "spatial rationality and political control" in the empire (377), I would argue that genre activities gave rhetorical form and substance to imperial government. To arrive at some knowledge of what government consisted of and how it was conducted in these dynasties, we must consider how genres mediated government and helped to materialize its rationality.

Genres are dynamic ritualistic and rhetorical forms in ancient China. Developed in response to recurring situations, they evolve over time in response to genre users' needs. Through the use of institutional genres, bureaucrats constitute social structures and reproduce them by drawing on genre rules. As the Middle Kingdom transitioned from city-states to a territory state in the third century BCE, the state consciously formulated genre rules, particularly for bureaucratic genres. Further, it archived, categorized, and regulated the form of genres as a technology for both political control and participation. Thus, genre networks were both a political institution and an epistemic construct. How did genres function as a tool for generating and reproducing the imperial matrix of power? What opportunities did genre networks create for political participation? How did they mediate in policy decisions that impacted the far reaches of the empire? How did court historians portray and theorize genre networks as a political institution?

While studies of rulership in early China have previously analyzed the modes, media, and materiality of political rhetoric, few have examined genre networks as a form of government or an epistemic construct. Genre networks are systems of words in motion, in which the ruler and scholar-officials managed to address sociopolitical exigencies by drawing on their favored ontological, epistemological, and discursive forms. Genre networks mediated governmental decisions and acts, giving form to government regularities, logics, and strategies. Genre activities harnessed political, economic, and military power and generated novel political power through humans, texts, transportation systems, and other material objects. This book will examine key genre networks crucial for the operation of the imperial matrix of power. It argues that genre networks, mobilized by political deliberation and supported by exegesis of the classics, provide a central means for understanding epistemology, rhetoric, and government in early China.

Studying genre networks as both a political institution and an epistemic construct constitutes a decolonial move in comparative rhetoric. In addition

Introduction   5

to introducing a rhetorical and epistemological system from the Global South, the book critiques rhetorical studies as historically being complicit in relations of domination and for having centered the Greco-Roman tradition. Influenced by this tradition, logocentricity has functioned as the most prominent comparative lens, which views words as representation of an external world and holds logical discourse as epistemologically superior. Influenced by logocentrism, ancient Chinese rhetoric has been studied mostly prominently as a cognitive capacity, hence terms such as *xiuci* (修辭), *ming* (名), and *bian* (辨) being called out as meaning "rhetoric." Further, Chinese rhetoric is sometimes exoticized as a racial *différance*.[4] By focusing on genre networks, this book calls attention to a neglected part of the Chinese tradition. This part sees discourse as living, bodily, and ritualistic practice.[5] It creates meaning as it interacts with human and nonhuman actors across space and time. Following the recent shift toward examining the manuscript culture in Chinese Studies (Kern 2005; Lai and Wang 2017; Meyer 2012),[6] which departs from logocentrism, this book calls for a networked approach to studying ancient Chinese discourse.

To study the genre networks of empire requires both a decolonial and a transnational perspective. The decolonial perspective means centering ancient Chinese theories of genre and examining the role of rhetoric in establishing the imperial matrix of power. The transnational perspective means developing a hybrid framework to genre studies by merging ancient Chinese and contemporary Western theories of genre, tracing texts across genre events and sometimes geopolitical borders, and exposing the national, racial, and linguistic hierarchies invented and fortified by ancient Chinese and European imperialism. In the reminder of the introduction, I will first offer a decolonial critique of scholarship on ancient Chinese rhetoric. Influenced by Western values, much of the scholarship has been devoted to the preimperial era, focusing on the rhetorical and philosophical thinking of various intellectual schools and the oratory adroitness of traveling persuaders. I suggest that political disputation continued in early imperial China and was extended and complicated by genre networks. Next, I will chart a brief genealogy of genre studies in ancient China to identify two indigenous network theories of genres. Finally, I put these theories and contemporary Western theories into dialogue with each other to develop a transnational framework for the study. The introduction concludes with an overview of the chapters.

A Decolonial Critique of Studies of Ancient Chinese Rhetoric

Studies of non-Western rhetoric have been deeply shaped by Western perspectives and values (Hum and Lyon 2008; Ruiz and Sánchez 2016; Baca and García 2019). As part of the liberal democratic order orchestrated by North Atlantic nations after World War II, the field of rhetorical studies has focused on the Greco-Roman tradition, hailing it as the cornerstone of Western civilization. Out of that tradition, Aristotle's theory of rhetoric has received special attention because it focuses on how an individual may gain political power in a democracy. With the dominance of his theory, the field has not only ignored the dark side of the Greco-Roman civilization but also the colonial and imperial nature of modern Western nations. The pernicious impact of these disciplinary tendencies on studies of ancient non-Western rhetoric manifests in valuing written texts over other modes of representation, theory over practice, Aristotelian concepts over other rhetorical systems, persuasion over other modes of discourse, and democracy over other forms of government.

In early studies of ancient Chinese rhetoric, scholars examined how the Chinese conceptualized language use and practiced persuasion using Western logocentric constructs. In an early study, *An Introduction to Chinese Rhetoric* (修辭學發凡; 1932), for instance, Chen Wangdao was influenced by American rhetoric textbooks to adopt a narrow definition of rhetoric, perceiving it as mainly dealing with arrangement and style in written discourse.[7] In the Cold War era, Robert T. Oliver published *Communication and Culture in Ancient India and China* (1971) where he examined key texts associated with Confucian, Moist, Legalist, and Daoist schools during the Warring States period. Resorting to the Aristotelian categories of ethos, pathos, and logos, he analyzed both the politico-philosophical thinking and the rhetorical methods that the key figures of these schools advocated for or exemplified in their speeches.[8]

Along with Western logocentric constructs, Western scholars often fetishized or exoticized the non-West. Western perspectives and values, especially those associated with liberal democracy,[9] have fueled scholars' fascination with political persuasion in non-Western societies. In studies of ancient Chinese rhetoric, for instance, scholars have focused on the tactics employed by itinerant scholar-officials when they engaged rulers and ranking officials during the Warring States era. In *Intrigues: Studies of The Chan-kuo Ts'e* (1964), for

Introduction   7

example, James Crump offered an English translation of *Chan-Kuo Tse*, or *Zhanguo Ce* (戰國策), a collection of 497 anecdotes filled with speeches delivered by the *shi* (士), or the scholar-official. Crump identified key persuasive strategies adopted in these speeches and suggested that the text reveals the extent to which the art of persuasion dominated political discourse during the period. Also focusing on *Zhanguo Ce*, Mary Garrett and Sharon Bracci Binn examined Chinese rational thinking as manifesting in the diverse Aristotelian topoi used by the *shi*.

By fetishizing and exoticizing the Warring States period, the West has rendered other periods almost invisible. For example, in comparison, rhetorical studies dealing with early imperial China, such as the Qin and Han dynasties, are few and far between.[10] Scholars seem to assume that political wrangling among the city-states during the Warring States era provided a fertile ground for political and philosophical disputation, and that when Qin Shi Huang buried scholars alive and burned their books, the centralized state no longer permitted political disputation. This lack of attention to the imperial period attests to what Mary Garrett has claimed as a Western bias: a false belief that rhetoric, or persuasion, is germane to a democracy where cacophonous voices are heard and negotiated (1999).[11] More profoundly, this belief and the concomitant scholarly work have continued the colonial and imperialist attempts of Western nations to dominate the world in knowledge making (Connell 2007; Pratt 1992).

While the Warring States allowed combative voices of the Hundred Schools and the Qin and Han appeared to suppress these voices, upon scrutinizing textual materials from these two dynasties, one would uncover a much different picture. In philosophy and religion, as Hall and Ames have noted, "the intellectual geography of the Hundred Schools in the pre-Qin period gives way to a syncretic Confucian-centered doctrine which absorbs into itself and to some degree conceals the richness of what were competing elements" (1995, 243–44). In statecraft, like during the Warring States era, the state allowed political disputations in its imperial court. For instance, a well-known court debate on salt, iron, and liquor policies took place in 81 BCE, in the Western Han, and lasted several months. The debaters drew on rhetorical concepts and strategies from several schools of thought traceable to the Warring States era (You 2010a). As David R. Knechtges and others have also discovered in their studies of *fu*, or rhapsody, in the Han dynasty, political remonstration took place not only through practical but also literary genres that place emphasis on aesthetics. Knechtges demonstrates, through his studies of Yang Xiong, one of the renowned *fu* writers, that Han rhapsody continued the legacy of the itinerant persuaders from the Warring States era and their art of conveying things by indirection (1976, 21).

Recent years saw a concerted effort to decolonize rhetorical studies by searching for and dialoguing with Indigenous perspectives. Critiquing Robert T. Oliver's heavy reliance on Western constructs as inadequate, other scholars have turned to explore Chinese constructs (Garrett 1993a, 1993b; Kirkpatrick 1995, 2005; Lu). For instance, in *Rhetoric in Ancient China, Fifth to Third Century B.C.E.: A Comparison with Classical Greek Rhetoric* (1998), Xing Lu identifies terms such as *ming* (名) and *bian* (辨) as the native ways of understanding rationality and disputation as practiced by the major intellectual schools. By examining these schools' rhetorical precepts and their key figures' discursive strategies, Lu has discovered major differences between ancient Chinese and ancient Greek traditions in areas such as rhetorical education, sense of rationality, perceptions of the role of language, approach to the treatment and study of rhetoric, and expression of emotions. Recently, Hui Wu rendered an English translation of *Guiguzi* (鬼穀子), a treatise allegedly representing the Vertical-Horizontal school's rhetorical thinking. Like Lu's work, this translation further unveils the rhetorical precepts developed by the ancient Chinese in educating students about political suasion. As Wu notes, the school's rhetorical thinking is dominated by *yin-yang* philosophy, which provides a foundation for the school's rhetorical strategies and concepts, "particularly listening, analogy, and reflection for the purpose of establishing human connections in the process of persuasion" (Wu and Swearingen 2016, 24).

Further, scholars of Chinese rhetoric recently moved away from logocentrism to an understanding of rhetoric as also a medium and material. The Warring States era saw a transition from an oral, commemorative, and ritualistic use of text to a culture where manuscript texts were increasingly used for communicating ideas.[12] After studying the types of writing, or genres, employed by the state and society to command assent and obedience during this transition, Mark Edward Lewis (1999) argues that writings in the Warring States era created a textual double that claimed to depict the entire world. He shows that government documents such as legal codes, population registers, and records of legal cases or administrative decisions were the primary means of holding the state together and carrying the ruler's intent to the far reaches of his realm. In another study, Charles Sanft (2014) examined the role that multimedia communications played in generating and exercising political power in the Qin dynasty. His analysis reveals that early Chinese thinkers recognized the importance of communication and perceptions for the function of government. In the Qin dynasty, the perceptions of the genral public about the empire were created by the standardization of weights and measures, the national tours conducted by the emperor, the elevated roads in the capital and the empire-wide highway system, the national population registration, and the national practice of law. These activities not only enabled the government to communicate to the masses an imperial myth and a myth of cultural uniformity but also to realize them.

In the meantime, scholars have underscored the materiality of rhetoric and imperial government.[13] In his studies of the legal practice in the Qin and Han dynasties, for instance, Oba Osamu (1988, 2017) used excavated materials to reconstruct the ways laws and regulations were formulated and practiced and to understand the operation of specific posts in the bureaucratic system. After examining written materials recovered in military and communication posts in the Han empire's western regions, Tomiya Itaru (2010) argued that imperial government was actualized through the very form of wooden strips and tablets. These artifacts reveal the temporal-spatial dimensions of government documents as they moved within the bureaucratic system. Specifically, his study has unveiled features of particular genres used in government, the literate training of the bureaucrats, and the practice of local government, transportation, and granary management. While studies of unearthed materials have provided insights on how government, specifically laws and regulations, was practiced locally, they reveal relatively little about the decision-making processes in the upper-level government.

Paying attention to the media and the materiality of rhetoric, scholars of early imperial China have invariably pointed to one defining feature of the period: that a sophisticated and distributed use of a dozen oral and written genres emerged out of the bureaucratic government. This feature was noted as early as in the Eastern Han dynasty when scholar-official Cai Yong (蔡邕, 133–192 CE) depicted court rituals. According to Cai, the emperor would issue four types of edicts. When reporting to the throne, his subjects would submit memorials of four types (Cai 1985; Giele 2006). Recently, scholars examined these genres in addition to a variety of others that were used in the remonstrance of the monarch.[14] However, these studies tended to view genre as a text type and analyzed each genre's rhetorical and political features without attending to their materiality. I argue that instead of single genres, genre networks would provide the central means to attending to the materiality of genres and to understanding epistemology, rhetoric, and imperial government. To study genre networks and government from a decolonial perspective, next, I will trace ancient Chinese genre studies in search of Chinese perspectives on genre. This genealogy intends to demonstrate that the ancient Chinese had a fairly sophisticated understanding of genre, including a network approach. Studying genre networks in the Chinese rhetorical tradition can help decenter the field of rhetorical studies and move away from Western notions of genre.

A Genealogy of Genre Studies in Early China

Genre practice was central to government and to the relations of dominance in the early Shang dynasty (1600–1046 BCE). In excavated animal bones and tortoise shells dating from that period, inscriptions were found that both recorded and were a part of ritual practices, such as the divinations performed before tribal wars or during sacrificial ceremonies. In the early Zhou dynasty, passages were also cast into bronze vessels, often commemorating events of stately significance, such as winning a war, relocating the capital city, or conferring titles to royal family members and generals. Gradually, the Zhou court saw the rise of a small, literate group called *shi* (史), who served multiple roles in the government: master of event, religious consultant, political advisor, scribe, and diplomat.[15] Thanks to their work, the government practices of Zhou were recorded in texts, including those that later formed the Confucian canon.

These classics not only embody government practice but also the *shi*'s rising genre awareness. Of the classics at Confucius's time, four have survived: *Documents* (*shu* 書), *Odes* (*shi* 詩), *Changes* (*yi* 易), and the *Spring and Autumn Annals* (*chunqiu* 春秋). While surviving as books, they are better viewed as prototype genres in the Zhou dynasty. These books functioned like loose-leaf folders in which the *shi* would keep adding new texts. When doing so, they would have to consider a text's context of production—the communicative purpose, the interlocutors, and the sociopolitical exigencies. The *Documents* currently contain twenty-eight political texts, falling into six genres: *dian* 典, *mo* 謨, *xun* 訓, *hao* 誥, *shi* 誓, and *ming* 命. The genre with the largest number of texts, called *hao* (誥), includes twelve oral pronouncements either during state sacrificial ceremonies held in the royal family shrine or ceremonies for conferring titles. The master of event, often the ruler, issued a statement to inform

Introduction 11

the attendees about the royal family history or to remind family members of their responsibilities. The genre second largest in number was made up of five war declarations, *shi* (誓), in which the ruler calls upon his followers to make an oath, enumerates the crimes of their enemy, issues demands, and declares punishments for the enemy. The *Odes* now contains three hundred and five poems, selected from more than a thousand, that circulated in the Spring and Autumn era. These poems were composed in the voices of ordinary people for describing their lives and expressing feelings, the voices of officials for recounting their work and feelings about the government, and in the voices of the *shi* and musicians for praising the royal ancestral gods. The core of *Changes* is a Western Zhou divination text called the *Changes of Zhou* (*Zhou yi* 周易), assembled into the current form sometime between the tenth and fourth centuries BCE. The basic unit of this ancient text is the hexagram (*gua* 卦), a figure composed of six stacked horizontal lines, each being either broken or unbroken. The text contains all sixty-four possible hexagrams, along with the hexagram's name, a short hexagram statement, and six-line statements used to determine the results of divination. In the process of its canonization, a set of ten commentaries called the Ten Wings was added in the Warring States era. These commentaries describe the text as a microcosm of the universe and a symbolic description of the processes of change. They suggest that, by partaking in the spiritual experience of the text, the individual can understand the deeper patterns of the universe. The *Spring and Autumn Annals* records major events in the state of Lu between 772 BCE and 481 BCE. Allegedly edited by Confucius, the four classics were in wide circulation during the Warring States era.

Efforts to theorize these classics and other genres did not emerge until the Han dynasty.[16] Signifying such efforts, the Chinese word used to discuss genre, 體 (*ti*), was in wide use then. However, carrying the notion of normative style, the word was not only used for genres but also for periods, authors, topics, or occasions.[17] The efforts to theorize genres could be attributed to the government sponsorship of classical studies and the emergence of new genres. Emperor Wu (157–87 BCE) endorsed Confucianism as the state orthodox and appointed experts of different lineages to teach the classics in the imperial academy. The first extensive treatment of a genre comes from a preface to the *Odes* written by a literatus with the family name "Mao." The author explicates the odes in terms of their personal and sociopolitical functions as well as their literary strategies. The interest in genre was also spurred by the formation of new genres in the Han. As mentioned earlier, Cai Yong introduced eight bureaucratic genres formalized in the Eastern Han. He presented them as part of the court rituals, alongside, for example, codes for how the emperor and his officials were to address each other, for naming the emperor and his family members' residences, for clothing, and for charioting. Another genre that rose to prominence in the Han was *fu*. It was theorized by a court historian and a *fu* writer of the Eastern Han, Ban Gu, in the *Book of Han* (*han shu* 漢書) when he introduced the poetic collections stored in the imperial library. Ban traced *fu* to the Odes, surveyed the *fu* pieces composed by writers during the Warring States era, and delineated the features of *fu* in the Han (Ban 2007, 342).

The scholarly interest in genre finally gave rise to *The Literary Mind and the Carving of Dragons* (*wenxin diaolong* 文心雕龍) in about 500 CE, the magnum opus in genre studies.[18] Displeased by a pretentious and hollow style prevalent in his times, the author Liu Xie (劉勰) hoped to cure this literary disease by seeking an antidote in classical writings. Before embarking on this endeavor, Liu had spent over a decade studying and cataloging Buddhist sutras. This experience gave him both inspiration and insights for mapping out Chinese writings, making his genre theory a product of intercultural dialogue.[19] His studies of genre in turn gave him an opportunity to discuss strategies of writing, construct a history of Chinese literature, and assess Chinese writers. In this grand treatise, Liu devotes five chapters to his theory of Chinese writing, twenty to more than sixty genres, nineteen to strategies of writing, and six to literary history and criticism.

In theorizing Chinese writing, Liu proposed a *jing-wei* (經緯, network) theory of genre, not only creating a hierarchy among genres but also solidifying an aesthetic order in the imperial matrix of power. *Jing* refers to warp, a path going north and south, or scriptures and sutras. Liu first proposes that *dao*, or the Way of the patterned, ordered, and interconnected world, reveals itself through acoustic, visual, and emotive patterns. These patterns were captured in the works of ancient sages. Thus, to understand *dao*, one needs to study the sagely texts, in his case, Confucian classics. Liu then proposes that the sages used their writing to educate the people, thus they kept records of government and education, historical events, and personal acts and remarks. Their writings provide a means of illuminating *dao*, largely the Confucian *dao*, which is the way of benevolent ruling (Liu Hsieh 2015, 10). Liu further suggests that one needs to study the classics conscientiously because they are the fountainheads for the several dozen genres, and because they provide a student with a repertoire of writing styles for imitation. *Wei*, or weft, refers to a particular group of texts that were supposed to complement the Confucian classics. In the Han dynasty, a large number of apocryphal texts were written, sometimes in the name of Confucius and his disciples. These texts often appealed to mysterious, supernatural powers rather than taking a moral approach. Liu suggests that they did much harm to the classics, though they could still benefit the development of written discourse (29). Thus, in his network theory, Liu celebrated *jing* as headed by the Confucian classics (*zongjing*, 宗經) and rectified *wei* embodied by some apocryphal texts (*zhengwei*, 正緯). By celebrating *jing*, Liu not only affirmed the prestige of the Confucian classics but also elevated literature to a canonical status.[20]

Liu's network theory came to inform his approach to genre studies, resembling Plato's dialectic of collection and division.[21] Accentuating a historical perspective, his approach includes such steps as definition, sampling, analysis, and synthesis. First, he divides the written corpus into the rhymed versus the unrhymed and then sorts them into genres. Second, he traces a genre to its origins to understand its evolution. Third, he examines the literary terms associated with a genre and clarifies their meanings. Fourth, Liu identifies and comments on representative texts that fall under a genre, assessing their historical roles and literary features. Fifth, to provide guidance for writers, he generalizes the thematic and textual requirements for each genre. Thanks to his systematic approach, for the first time in history, Liu was able to present "a general outline" of classical Chinese genres (Liu Hsieh 2015, 4).

While Liu's approach has continued to inform genre studies in China today,[22] it is inadequate for a study on genre networks and government. First, Liu has focused on written genres, hence *wen* (文) in his book title, and overlooked oral ones, which were crucial for governmental practice. Further, by treating texts as artifacts uprooted from their genre events, Liu has deprived them of much of their sociohistorical agency. In his ontology, he views genre as a text type consisting of a set of formal features. A scholar's task is to understand these features in relation to the sociopolitical contexts of their production. Thanks to this ontology, Liu and later critics have slighted the power of genres in enabling and regulating personal and institutional actions.

To examine the networked use of genres in imperial government, Chinese court historians developed useful theories. While Liu Xie regarded genres as textual artifacts, dynastic historians viewed them as agentive actors. In *The Grand Scribe's Records* (*Taishigong shu* 太史公書 or *Shiji* 史記), Western Han historian Sima Qian (司馬遷 145–86 BCE) invented a host of strategies that shaped the writing of future dynastic histories. His agentive ontology of genre first manifests in his keen interest in constructing biographies in history writing. When narrating the life of an individual, Sima often contrived scenes of conversations or inserted that person's written discourses in part or in full, a strategy that accentuates genre activities. This strategy, also a genre invention, has blended the strategies of three prototypes of history writing before him: the *Spring and Autumn Annals* offers a year-by-year account of events (deaths, official visits, battles, and sacrifices); the *Documents* gathers standalone discourses issued at certain political moments; and histories written in the Warring States period, such as *Discourses of the States*, *Zuo Tradition*, and *Intrigues of the Warring States*, feature rulers and scholar-officials conversing on state affairs. By juxtaposing discourses with events in biographies, Sima Qian assigned agency to genres, which shaped the direction of sociopolitical events.

Sima's agentive ontology further manifests in the innovative structure of his history writing: an assemblage of genres for constructing a Confucian moral universe. The *GSR* contains twelve basic annals (*benji* 本紀), ten chronological tables (*biao* 表), eight treatises (*shu* 書), thirty hereditary houses (*shijia* 世家), and seventy categorized memoirs (*liezhuan* 列傳). This microcosmic model can be traced to earlier texts, such as *Changes* and *Mr. Lü's Spring and Autumn Annals* (*Lüshi chunqiu* 呂氏春秋). Through this genre invention, Sima sought to create a Confucian moral-social order based on a cosmological model.[23]

In his authorial notice included within the *Records*, he attributed his desire for completing this voluminous work, hence his ontology of genre, to shoring up a historiographic tradition established by Confucius. The latter allegedly composed the *Annals* to uphold the spirit of the classics *Documents*, *Music*, *Rites*, and *Odes*. Collectively, these classics provided political and moral guidance for the ruler and his officials. As a court historian, Sima vowed to write a history similar to the *Annals* and complementary to the classics. Further, he located his role in a cosmological order widely accepted in the Han. He compared the ministers serving the ruler to the heavenly bodies revolving around the Pole Star: "The twenty eight lodges surround the north polar star, and thirty spokes share one common hub, they revolvingly wander without an end, and the supporting servants who act as legs and arms match this, they practice the right way with loyalty and trustworthiness in order to serve the ruler and sovereign. So I created the thirty Hereditary Houses" (Ssu-ma 2019, 360). The analogy of the hub compares court officials, including Sima, to spokes upholding the hub of the carriage wheel (the ruler) and moving the carriage (the state, or the moral universe) forward. In ancient Chinese astronomy, constellations were called heavenly lodges (*tiangong* 天宫), which circumvolved the Pole Star (see more about ancient Chinese astronomy in chapter 3). The dukes and ministers honored in the "Hereditary Houses" and other genres in Sima's history supported the ruler crucially through their work with words. Thus, inserting the ministers' and scholar-officials' oral or written texts in their biographies, Sima viewed genres as having enabled these individuals to score remarkable governmental achievements.[24]

Indeed, the political role of genres was a major concern in Sima's biographies. He portrayed many historical figures as skilled in assisting the ruler with words, and he often commented on the political and moral functions of their discourses. Thus, their biographies can be viewed as his attempt at historicizing and theorizing genres. For instance, in the biographies of Su Qin and Zhang Yi, two renowned political persuaders during the Warring States era, Sima noted their ability in brokering powers ("權變") with words and the danger they created in ruining a state ("傾危之士"; Ssu-ma 1994b, 142). In the biographies of those skilled in witty and humorous speech, Sima commended them for solving political or social problems through the use of analogies and metaphors ("談言微中, 亦可以解紛";2019, 186). In the biography of Sima Xiangru, a literary attendant in the Han court, Sima justified the inclusion of his *fu* works by comparing their functions to those of the *Annals, Changes,* and *Odes,* which all sought to enlighten the ruler in ways of achieving benevolent rule ("言雖外殊, 其合德一也"; 2020, 217). Blending strategies of historical writing from the past, Sima emplaced discourses in unfolding events featuring genres as key actors mediating and shaping the events through genre networks. Thus, Sima proposed a network theory of genre different from Liu Xie's. In Sima's theory, if we follow his cosmological model, historic figures and their discourses acted within a specific constellation (in reality, a hereditary house or a government office) forming what Western genre scholars now call an "activity system."[25] As their discourses interacted with other discourses and individuals, they generated a resultant force, setting the moral universe in motion.[26]

While developing their networked theories of genre, like Confucian literati of their times, both Sima Qian and Liu Xie were not immune to an imperial ideology imbued with ethnocentrism. In studying Chinese imperial discourse, not only a decolonial but also a transnational orientation is imperative. These

16   *Introduction*

orientations would highlight ethnocentricity in the imperial discourse and alert us—rhetoricians—to our own nationalist or Western impulses.

Toward a Transnational Approach to Genre Studies

Taking a decolonial stance necessitates a transnational approach to genre studies. One of the consequences of European colonialism was the rise of modern nation-states. This political formation has translated into a method-ological nationalism in rhetorical studies. It often treats nation-state culture as discrete and examines its rhetoric from a monolingual and monocultural lens. Thus, to decolonize rhetorical studies means to unsettle methodolog-ical nationalism and embrace a *multi* or *trans* perspective to language and culture. While centering non-Western epistemologies, the transnational approach requires putting them in dialogue with one another and with Western epistemologies. Delinking from Western modernist knowledge and relinking with pluriversal knowledges for a just social future, the two central tasks of decoloniality, should not exclude dialogues across epistemological traditions. For this book, the transnational approach means developing a hybrid framework for genre studies by merging ancient Chinese and con-temporary Western theories, tracing texts across genre events, and critiquing ethnocentricity in scholarship.

As part of the transnational approach, this book develops a hybrid frame-work for genre studies by breaking temporal, spatial, and national bound-aries. Sima Qian's agentive ontology of genre aligns with, and thus can be merged with, the contemporary Western understanding of genre as social action (Bazerman 1997; Quint 1993; Miller 1984). Rather than sets of lin-guistic and textual features, genres have been viewed by US rhetoricians as "typified rhetorical actions based in recurrent situations" (Miller 1984, 31). Specifically, as Berkenkotter and Huckin (1993) explain, genres are dynamic rhetorical forms, developed in response to recurring situations, that evolve over time in response to genre users' needs. One's knowledge of genre comes from participating in communicative activities in daily and professional life. Through the use of institutional and disciplinary genres, humans constitute social structures and reproduce them by drawing on genre rules. Genre con-ventions reflect a community's norms, epistemology, ideology, and social ontology. In the meantime, genres are cultural artifacts that can tell us things about how a particular culture configures situations and ways of acting. Taking

Introduction 17

this hybrid framework to genre studies, this book will examine genre networks by focusing on the dynamic relations between texts and situated government practices and structures.

In studying the dynamic relations between texts and situated government practices, the transnational approach will focus on tracing the movement of texts across genre events. This approach views texts as agents traveling in and interacting with a network or an ecology of human and nonhuman actors, often crossing geopolitical borders.[27] As they move, they translate and move meanings across space and time, often in unexpected ways. Central to the transnational approach is looking at the flow of this movement and the ways texts are recontextualized as an ongoing struggle. The approach entails examining those moments of struggle, of friction. This, in other words, is where the acts of dominance and resistance were played out in early imperial China. In these "meaning-making trajectories" (Kell 2013, 9), it is crucial that we follow the author and the text in order to trace the thread and the nodes where the text translates, recontextualizes, and amplifies meanings. Originating from literacy studies, this mobile method has now been adopted in studies of communication networks among the elite class in Song China (960–1279 CE; De Weerdt 2015; De Weerdt, Ming-Kin, and Hou-Ieong 2016), epistolary networks among the Jesuits in deliberating controversial missionary practices in India in the early seventeenth century (Zaleski 2020), and human relation networks among Chinese international studies enacted by their mobilities and literacy practices recently (Fraiberg, Wang, and You 2017).

Tracing texts across genre events is made viable in the present study thanks to the rich records left from the Han dynasty, including dynastic histories, individual works, and archaeological finds, although some networks could be traced in a more detailed fashion than others. In the Western Han, for instance, a genre network centering on territory issues could be traced by following court discussions to Emperor Wu's edicts, to a memorial submitted by Liu An (a prince of Huainan), and then finally the emperor's response to Liu's memorial (see chapter 5). Or, in the beginning of the Eastern Han, a genre network on imperial integrity could be reconstructed by tracing the epistolary exchanges among Emperor Guangwu and leaders in the western regions; this genre network gradually led to the collapse of these regional forces and the reunification of the empire.[28] Although this tracing might not be as detailed as that performed in ethnography, it will reveal how genre generates meanings and political power at each node of the network.

Finally, the transnational approach critiques ethnocentricity not only in rhetorical studies but also in both Chinese imperial discourses and the Chinese scholastic tradition. Throughout early China, the monarchs categorized other peoples based on geographic distance, often calling those living beyond their sovereignty uncivilized, barbarians, or animals (Takao 2014). As part of the imperial discourse, traditional Chinese scholarship was imbued with ethnocentrism. In modern Chinese scholarship, this ideology is folded under nationalism, in which scholars construct narratives of Chinese language, literature, and culture by centering ethnic Han and erasing the voices of non-Han peoples.[29] To counter ethnocentrism while valuing ancient Chinese perspectives on genre, ethnocentrism first needs to be exposed in the Chinese imperial discourse. Rhetorical studies provides a critical tool for observing how ethnocentric language and cultural policies were developed and sustained. Second, in breaking away from ancient Chinese and European colonial emphasis on lingua-cultural and racial boundaries, the book highlights the translingual and transcultural realities of the empire. Ancient Chinese and other ethnic languages are neither discrete nor stable but rather are dynamic and negotiated. Genre activities necessarily involve the negotiation of language and cultural differences. Genre networks will be examined with an eye toward the ways multilingual or multidialectal and multicultural resources were mobilized.[30]

With the transnational approach, this study has taken three steps in examining genre networks and government. First, the broad political concerns of the dynast and his officials are identified, such as the Heavenly Mandate, regulating the harem, ways of government, territory integrity, and entertainment. These concerns prompted the ruling class to engage in epistemological, political, and cultural activities. Through rhetoric and genre networks, they created and sustained an imperial matrix of power intersected by religious, sexual, ethnic, politico-military, aesthetic, and linguistic hierarchies.[31] Specifically, this book will examine the following hierarchies:

- A metaphysical order that recognized the omnipotence of an anthropomorphic Heaven and claimed the ruler as His son and the legitimate leader of His earthly subjects.
- A gender hierarchy that privileged males over females.
- A politico-military organization that includes the commanderies, the kingdoms, and vassal and foreign states.

Introduction 19

- An ethnic hierarchy that positioned the Han people as culturally superior to other peoples.
- An aesthetic hierarchy that privileged certain forms of literature and art.
- A linguistic hierarchy that privileged the written over the oral and the state-sponsored writing system over regional and foreign ones.

Derived from Western epistemology, these categories of hierarchy are used to construct a critique on how a matrix of power was established by rhetoric in early imperial China.[32] The hierarchical concerns of the ruling class fall squarely under government construed in Confucianism, which, according to the *Record of Rites* (*liji* 禮記), involves cultivating the self, managing the family, and governing the state.[33]

Second, under each broad concern, representative genre networks are identified and traced. A genre network is defined as an array of connections and meanings that unfold as a discourse, or a series of discourses, is produced and circulated in response to a sociopolitical exigency. In reading the Way of Heaven, for instance, the emperor would be stirred by a natural anomaly and then would issue an edict (*zhao* 詔), which would solicit commentaries (*yi* 議) and exam essays (*dui* 對) submitted by scholar-officials. In regulating the inner court, edicts turn into laws, biographies (*zhuan* 傳) establish paragons of virtue, and admonitions (*jie* 戒) impart lessons for women. In the way of entertainment, songs or poetry (*shi* 詩) and street talk or stories (*xiaosuo* 小說) would be fused into rhapsody (*fu* 賦), which would then be recited or sung at state banquet to praise and admonish the ruler and, by extension, the government. Dynastic histories are read closely with an eye toward discourses participating in or responding to the same political concern or event. The discourses are then threaded chronologically or spatially.

Third, each genre network is examined to understand not only the key genres, but also how the network generated meanings and political power. Specifically, the following questions are considered. What was the political philosophy, or "governmental rationality," that undergirded the rise and expansion of a network? In policy debates, for instance, it was often the binary thinking of the Kingly Way and the Despotic Way of government. In reading the Heavenly Mandate, it was the correlative thinking that viewed natural occurrences as Heavenly judgments on the royal family and on government. Next, what were the rhetorical features of the genre networks? The features include political exigencies, interlocutors, discursive strategies, and the ways of textual circulation. Finally, how did the circulating genres generate political power and mobilize bodies? It was persuasion and identification enacted jointly by authority, rationalism, and affect in specific nodes of the network. By answering questions related to governmentality, the features of genre networks, and persuasion and identification, we may unveil the imperial government practice in terms of its specific regularities, logic, strategy, self-evidence, and reason.

Genre networks to be examined in the book are those the dynastic historians wanted to foreground. The standard histories of the Han, *The Grand Scribe's Records* (*GSR*), *Book of Han* (*BH*), and *Book of the Later Han* (*BLH*), will constitute the major corpus. The corpus also includes individual works such as *Luxuriant Gems of the Spring and Autumn* (*Chunqiu fanlu* 春秋繁露), *Debating Salt and Iron* (*Yantielun* 鹽鐵論), and *Biographies of Eminent Women* (*Lienü zhuan* 烈女傳). All these texts were written by men and approved by the state; therefore, they upheld the men's values and perpetuated their version of history. The male authorship and state sponsorship bear implications for the present study. First, as the historians aspired to provide guidance for rulers through their work, it is important to consider how historical narratives informed by their agentive ontology of genre might have shaped government practice. Second, it is imperative to listen to marginalized voices and values in historians' selective archival work. Even when these histories included women's voices, for instance, as chapter 3 will reveal, they were selected based on male perspectives.

Centering local histories and knowledges in the pursuit of pluriversal episteme makes translation a crucial methodological issue. Boaventura De Sousa Santos (2016) has urged those who are committed to intercultural translation to answer a series of questions: What to translate? To translate from what into what? When to translate? Who translates? How to translate? And why translate? In studies of Chinese rhetoric, Hui Wu has pioneered in this effort, articulating her response to these critical questions and translating classical texts such as *Guiguzi* (*The Master of the Ghost Valley*) and post-Mao literary works by women (*Once Iron Girls*, Wu 2010) into English. Much of the corpus produced in early imperial China has not been translated into English yet, such as the voluminous *Book of Han* and *Book of the Latter Han*, the primary texts on which this study has been based. I have translated passages from both of these texts into English using editions published by Zhonghua shuju, an authoritative publisher in Chinese classics. For texts that

Introduction 21

are available in English translation, I have cited the editions that reflect the most recent scholarship.

The book has taken a transnational approach to citation practice. First, it has not only cited Western scholarship but also Chinese and Japanese scholarship, representing both Western and indigenous perspectives. Second, the book has included original Chinese phrases and passages parallel to their English translations to disrupt and challenge the reading habit of monolingual Anglophone readers. These moves, on the one hand, exercise "epistemic delinking" in rhetorical studies, moving away from European modernist epistemology and monolingual nation-state ideology. On the other hand, these moves recognize a multilingual scholarly community and celebrate a translingual citation practice that is well-established in Chinese Studies.

I will end with a note on the names of the genres used in this book. Like any classification, a genre conception is limiting and reductive. Many genres discussed in this book were not formalized or named until the Eastern Han dynasty. I will use a specific name for a text if historians have named it in the dynastic histories. Otherwise, I will use "edicts" as a general term to refer to imperial commands and "memorials" for letters to the throne. I will only use the names of the bureaucratic genres spelled out by Cai Yong when I discuss texts produced in the Eastern Han dynasty.

Book Overview

Chapter 1 will examine transmitted and archaeological sources to understand how a court-centered, multigenre activity system was supported through education, theorization, and institution as the Middle Kingdom transitioned from city-states to a territory state. I will first consider how the ruler was trained to become a competent listener and arbiter and how scholar-officials were trained to serve as his entertainers, advisers, and remonstrators. Textual evidence suggests that their training program was structured based on the classics and filled with exegetic activities. These classics provided a literary and cultural foundation for new genres to emerge in the empire. Next, I will consider the ways political suasion was conceptualized in early China by examining two technical treatises produced in the Warring States era. Representing distinct visions for state relations, they portrayed different ruler-adviser relations and suggested discourse strategies to be employed therein. Finally, I shall survey the government structure, bureaucratic genres, and the postal relay system built to mediate control and deliberation in the early empire. Working together, they made genre networks a crucial political institution.

Chapter 2 will focus on a type of imperial edict that invited discussions and debates, which in turn reproduced a metaphysical order and legitimated an emperor's ruling. Responding to natural anomalies and omens, these edicts and the responses they solicited from scholar-officials strengthened the imperial power by generating theories about Heaven-human relations, expanding political participation, and encouraging self-cultivation in the governing body. The genre networks that were thus formed—involving imperial edicts, queries, exam essays, and commentaries—helped to sustain an ontology, a view of the world as transcendental, transactional, and translingual. As Confucian literati participated proactively in the epistemological work, Confucianism received state sponsorship. The sponsorship in turn encouraged the school to expand its theoretical apparatus, moving from a secular to a metaphysical focus.

Chapter 3 will examine genre networks on regulating the inner court. The inner court refers to the living quarters designated for the imperial consorts and their support staff; by extension, it signifies the domestic sphere traditionally relegated to elite women. While the narrative of progress of civilization and religion growing out of European imperialism has erased women's voices, as a decolonial move, this chapter seeks to demonstrate that women's voices were also marginalized if not completely erased by men in early Chinese imperialism. I will first examine the efforts of elite men in the late Western Han, who endeavored to establish legal and moral codes for the court ladies. Next, elite women's voices will be considered, focusing on the edicts issued by two empress dowagers of the Eastern Han. These edicts reveal their own philosophy and approach to regulating the inner court, particularly the emperor's maternal family. Finally, I will examine the genre events in which Ban Zhao, one of the court ladies, participated to understand further what role an elite woman outside the immediate royal family could play in the Han rulership. Although the dynastic histories portrayed these women from a Confucian male perspective, their genre activities demonstrate their variegated ways of negotiating patriarchy and gaining political power.

Chapter 4 will examine how court discussions worked to establish ethnic and epistemic hierarchies crucial for the imperial control. I will first trace the concepts of the Kingly Way and the Despotic Way in early China. With philosophical roots in Confucianism and Legalism, they often stood as polarized orientations to government, each drawing on its adherents during the

Introduction

preimperial era. After an introduction to these two orientations, arguments for or against them across several court discussions in the Western Han will be examined, focusing on one that was arguably the most expansive in topical coverage. In these court discussions, debaters drew on different intellectual schools to substantiate their arguments dealing with labor, ethnic and racial, and epistemic hierarchies. In constantly shifting grounds, the Kingly Way and the Despotic Way both served as heuristics to accommodate diverse voices and interests in the imperial government. By focusing on the case of court discussions, we will recognize that while a genre network may consist of multiple genre events, a genre event such as the court discussion could involve a heavy traffic of texts and genres; and that the court discussion is not only written but also oral, embodied, performative, and ritualistic.

Chapter 5 focuses on the discourse styles employed in court discussions on politico-military organization and ethnic relations in the Western Han. In particular, it examines genre networks—involving what were later called "dissenting opinions" addressed to the emperor or regional rulers and the "sovereign answers"—dealing with defending the integrity of the Han empire. First, I will survey the argumentative style of the Vertical-Horizontal school and that which is associated with the *Spring and Autumn Annals*. Next, dissenting opinions submitted by two literati to the king of Wu dissuading him from revolting against the central government will be examined to understand how the Vertical-Horizontal school shaped politico-military organization in the early Han. Finally, dissenting opinions submitted to Emperor Wu and Emperor Yuan dealing with the Yue peoples will be analyzed to demonstrate the rhetorical power of Confucian classics in constructing ethnic relations in the mid–Western Han. Moving from the revolt of the seven kingdoms to the issues of the Yue peoples, we observe the rising prominence of the Confucian classics in the genre networks dealing with imperial integrity. At the same time, temporal-spatiality of the court debates was enlarged by the postal system, connecting government personnel thousands of *li* away and enjoining oral and written genres.

In chapter 6, I argue that treating texts as literary artifacts by extracting them from genre networks as Sima conceived, Liu Xie's genre theory has deprived texts of much of their sociohistorical agency. In making a decolonial move, thus, I will put literary genres, such as stories, odes, and rhapsody, back into their genre networks and examine how the networks helped to establish aesthetic and linguistic hierarchies in the Han. I will first survey the practice of storytelling that flourished in the Warring States period. Performed in the palace, certain narrative forms were elevated from street art to courtly art. Next, I will consider the odes, the verses of Chu, and the rhapsodies. Depicting the lives of the commoners and the ruling class, the odes of the Zhou dynasty were often sung along with music, dance, or ritual practice in state events. Widely presented and quoted in political gatherings and used for the education of the elite, the odes became a prized literary form of the northern aristocracy. The verses of Chu, appearing in the late Warring States period, and *fu*, popularized during the Han dynasty, provided the literati with new forms for political participation and self-expression, in effect making *fu* the genre of the empire. Finally, I suggest that the elevated status of *fu* popularized its writing style, making it instrumental in translating imperial lives in that it allowed the literati to relate meaningfully to political, gendered, cultural, religious, and linguistic difference.

In the conclusion, I will reflect upon what the study reveals about the nature of genre networks in the Han dynasty in terms of imperial government, political deliberation, and epistemology. Further, I offer thoughts for decolonizing studies of ancient rhetorics as I address key questions about engaging in a genre network approach, historiography, border thinking, and the recovery of non-Western epistemologies for decoloniality.

Chapter 1

Genre Networks as a Political Institution

Head musicians and historians will sing odes, other musicians recite cautionary notes, ministers submit advice, and scholar-officials pass on words of the commoners. 瞽史誦詩, 工誦箴諫, 大夫進謀, 士傳民語. —Jia Yi

Early Chinese texts portrayed political suasion as ritualistic and theatrical. In a memorial submitted to the emperor, for instance, a Western Han scholar-official Jia Yi (賈誼 200 BCE–168 BCE) discussed political reforms and the education of the princes. He invoked a scene depicted in pre-Qin texts such as the *Record of Rites*, *Discourses of the States* (*DS*), and *Zuo Tradition* (*ZT*).[1] As quoted in the epigraph, surrounded by musicians, historians, ministers, and scholar-officials, the monarch receives words of great value to his government (Ban 2007, 491). He sits in the center of the entourage, acting as a listener, an arbiter, and a decision maker. The other parties are there to influence him through entertainment, advice, and remonstration. Of equal significance are their titles—*gu* (瞽 master musician),[2] *shi* (史 historian), *gong* (工 musician), *dafu* (大夫 minister), and *shi* (士 scholar-official)—which signify the long-established division of labor in political suasion.

Imaginary as it is, this scene has captured the workings of a multigenre activity system; these court officials drew on and enacted a series of genres. The head musician and court historians sang songs drawn from a collection of ancient odes. Other musicians recited maxims and remonstrations derived from ancient political documents. Ministers submitted memorials by borrowing expressions and textual forms from the classics. Scholar-officials presented folk sayings and opinions culled from outside of the court. Close proximity to the ruler gave these individuals discursive power enviable to others that were kept at a distance. To make the multigenre system work, all parties, including the monarch, needed training in speaking and listening. In early China, such training programs were prescribed and practiced, theories of political suasion developed, and communication channels established to include distant parties.

With a glimpse of this classical scene, this chapter will examine transmitted and archaeological sources to understand how the multigenre activity system was supported through education, theorization, and institution amid the Middle Kingdom's transition from city-states to a territory state. As a decolonial move, this chapter will demonstrate that ancient China has its own tradition of rhetorical education, thus lending support to the argument that the rhetorics of ancient civilizations should be placed on a continuum rather than in a hierarchy with Greco-Roman rhetoric resting at the top.[3] I will first consider how the ruler was trained to become a competent listener and arbiter, and how scholar-officials were trained to serve as his entertainers, advisers, and remonstrators. Textual evidence suggests that their training program was structured based on the classics and filled with exegetic activities. Solidified as written genres, these classics provided a literary and cultural foundation for new genres to emerge in the empire. Next, I will consider the ways political suasion was conceptualized in early China by examining two technical treatises produced in the Warring States era. Representing distinct visions for state relations, *The Master of the Ghost Valley* (*Guiguzi*) and the *Works of Master Han* (*Hanfeizi*) portrayed different ruler-adviser relations and suggested discourse strategies to be employed therein. Finally, I shall survey the government structure, bureaucratic genres, and the postal relay system built to mediate control and deliberation in the early empire. Working together, they made genre networks a crucial political institution.

Rhetorical Education and Classical Genres

While in ancient Greece and Rome, rhetorical training was devoted to elite men who were trained in order to persuade their peers in public forums; this training, also available to the elites in ancient China, focused on guiding the ruler. This feature came from the Chinese autocratic tradition in which the ruler was entitled to absolute power but also with tremendous responsibility.[4] Any recklessness could cost his ruling, his life, or worse, his entire household. Playing a delicate game, he needed his officials to watch over his shoulder, attend to his concerns, and protect him in case of danger. Chinese texts featured competing curricula for rhetorical training as early as the Spring and Autumn era. These curricula used texts of different genres to teach students about history, morality, and speech. In turn, widely used texts were reified and turned into canons.

A curriculum, focused on ritualization, about becoming a gentleman (*junzi* 君子) can be found in the *Analects*. Confucius (551–479 BCE) sees the training as primarily submerging the ruler or the gentleman in established rituals. For Confucius, man is a special being with a unique dignity and power derived from and embedded in rites. He places tremendous faith in the agency of the gentleman for achieving what is Good, that is, the moral power. When his student Yen Hui inquired about the moral power or authoritative conduct (*ren* 仁), Confucius remarked: "Through self-discipline and observing ritual propriety (*li* 禮) one becomes authoritative in one's conduct. If for the space of a day one were able to accomplish this, the whole empire would defer to this authoritative model" (*Analects* 1998, 152). Clearly, Confucius believes that ritualization starts from inside the self. It initiates when the self tries to probe and identify moral goodness within. Yen Hui inquires further about submission to ritual. The master explains, "Do not look at anything that violates the observance of ritual propriety; do not listen to anything that violates the observance of ritual propriety; do not speak about anything that violates the observance of ritual propriety; do not do anything that violates the observance of ritual propriety" (152). In other words, to comply with the ritual code, a gentleman needs to guard his acts of looking, listening, speaking, and gesturing because these acts carry profound and powerful symbolic meanings.

Confucius views learning from the past as key to his ritual training. Ritualization is a life-long process of adjusting one's mind and heart to approach the *dao* (the Way) and exemplify it through proper acts in both private and public spheres. It is first and foremost a process of constant learning and investigation of the self. Revealing his own ritual practice, Confucius confides to his students: "I am not the kind of person who has gained knowledge (*zhi* 知) through some natural propensity for it. Rather, loving antiquity, I am earnest in seeking it out" (*Analects* 1998, 115). To learn from the past, ancient songs, rites of previous dynasties, and music constitute the subjects of investigation. Confucius expresses this need in saying, "I find inspiration by intoning the songs, I learn where to stand from observing ritual propriety, and I find fulfillment in playing music" (122). These subjects were supported by the classic *Odes* passed down from earlier generations.

As recorded in the *Analects*, the *Odes* was extensively used in Confucius's teaching for its ritual and rhetorical power. The first anthology of Chinese songs, the *Odes* depicted the simple, everyday lives of the multitude, lives of the rich and the powerful, and ritual performance in the court. Confucius explicates the ritualizing power of the odes to his students: "My young friends, why don't any of you study the *Songs* [*Odes*]? Reciting the *Songs* can arouse your sensibilities, strengthen your powers of observation, enhance your ability to get on with others, and sharpen your critical skills. Close at hand it enables you to serve your father, and away at court it enables you to serve your lord. It instills in you a broad vocabulary for making distinctions in the world around you" (*Analects* 1998, 206). In other words, studying the odes enables one to sharpen their skills in handling situations both at home and in office rhetorically—to incite people's emotions and observe their feelings while expressing their own. Therefore, for Confucius, these ancient odes serve as "a guide to manners and morals, a record of antiquity, and a storehouse of elegance in language" (Saussy 1995, 50).

Confucius's ritual-based pedagogy appears to have reflected the widely shared thinking on nurturing a ruler in his times. A compatible design comes from the *DS*, another pre-Qin text filled with political events and conversations that took place during the Western Zhou and the Spring and Autumn eras. Despite differences in authorship and context, the *DS* example comes close to Confucius' thoughts on educating a gentleman. A conversation occurred in the reign of King Zhuang of Chu (613–591 BCE). The king sent Shi Wei to instruct one of the princes because Shi was reputed for his moral and intellectual strengths. Shi went on to consult one of his colleagues Shen Shushi on how to conduct mentoring. Like Confucius, Shen suggests a training supported by classical texts:

> You teach him history (春秋) to make him see the importance of celebrating kindness and condemning wickedness, to alert him. You review the royal family lineage (世) with him to show that virtuous forefathers prevailed but the muddle-headed was dethroned, to make him act with caution. You teach him odes (詩) so as to unveil the former kings' benevolence, to inspire him. You explain the court rites (處) so that he understands the distinction between the high and the low class.

You instruct him music (樂) so as to cleanse his mind and to bring him peace. You teach him the laws (令) passed down from the former kings to familiarize him with the officials' duties. You explain the discourses on self-cultivation and state governance (語), so he can enhance his moral power and perceive that the former kings ruled with humanity and virtue. You instruct him about past events (故志), so he knows why things rose and fell and therefore takes extreme precaution in his behaviors. You explain to him the former kings' instructions (訓典) so that he understands his kinship with the people and use such to measure and handle affairs. (*Guoyu* 2014, 328)

Shen's curriculum resembles Confucius's but surpasses it in complexity. In addition to Confucian subjects, such as history, odes, music, and rites, Shen also suggests the study of the royal family lineage, laws, and discourses of the states. Shen's curriculum, especially the inclusion of laws and discourses of the states, suggests not only an expansion of the ritual-based training but also the rise of rationalism in government practice in the Spring and Autumn era (771–476 BCE).

Shen's list of subjects could be viewed as a taxonomy of ancient Chinese genres, some of which were not valued in the Confucius curriculum. As the composition of the *DS* testifies, the genre *yu* (語; discourse) had matured during the Warring States era. Court historians used it to record or reconstruct conversations critical to the development of a political event. It is puzzling that Confucius made no mention of the discourses, a genre that appears to have formed in his time. This omission may suggest that he, or his disciples who authored the *Analects*, disdained the teaching of argument as a technique divorced from the cultivation of one's moral being. This neglect may suggest that Confucians distanced themselves from government bureaucrats (*li* 吏), who needed to study laws and discourses of the states in order to handle bureaucratic routines.[5]

While the conversation between Shi and Shen may be discredited as fictional, unequivocally the author of the story valued suasion in the curriculum. The purpose was not to make the prince glib but to expose him to the types of suasive discourse in which he would partake in the future. As the conversation unfolds, Shen proposes that if the prince does not attend to the above teachings or rectify his shortcomings, he ought to be remonstrated with indirect words and virtuous individuals be sought to shepherd him (*Guoyu* 2014,

328). Here, the author paints the psyche of the prince as complex and resilient but possibly being unable to stand on a high moral ground. His place in the power relation, however, allows his mentors and officials to influence him with indirection. Indirect words expose the prince to ways in which messages are coded in seemingly insignificant topics. He gradually learns how to decipher the subtleties of words. The author of the story, through his alter ego, Shen, affirms the place of studying artful words in the royal curriculum.

If Confucius and the author of the *DS* proposed two distinct approaches, one centered on ritualization and the other tilted toward dialogical persuasion, respectively, Jia Yi of the early Han embraced that of Confucius. An imperial erudite (*boshi* 博士), Jia served as a teacher for the kings of Changsha and Liang. In a memorial submitted to Emperor Wen on political reforms, as introduced in the beginning of this chapter, he detailed his vision for nurturing future rulers. He held that a ruler must be a practitioner of such virtues as ritual propriety, righteousness, honesty, and shame ("禮義廉恥"; Ban 2007, 491). Like Confucius, Jia appeals to antiquity and places ritualization at the center of his curriculum. For instance, he cites the following passage verbatim from the *Record of Rites*:[6]

> After their sons were born, former kings nurtured them with rites by having scholar-officials carry them around to observe ritual practice. When worshiping Heaven in the southern suburbs, officials cleansed themselves and wore clean clothes and caps to show solemnity. When going through the palace entrance, they descended from their horses. When passing by the royal family temple, they lowered their upper body and walked briskly to show filial piety. Thus, the education of the princes started in their infancy. (Ban 2007, 491; Huang Huaixin)

In addition to involving the princes in ritual practice, as Jia suggests, the former kings of the Zhou dynasty also selected officials to teach, entertain, and protect them. Those officials were screened based on their moral standing, filial piety, fraternity, and intellectual strengths. Accompanied by these individuals, "the prince beholds virtuous behaviors, hears benevolent words, and treads on the right path" (491). Consequently, he will develop the habit of reasoning and speaking in the righteous way. To strengthen his argument, Jia then cites Confucius as saying, "The habit cultivated when one is little would seem like an innate character" (491). In his emphasis on rites, like Confucius, Jia views speaking, or speaking benevolently, as a natural outcome of one's ritualization.

As the prince reaches school age, rhetorical training is added in Jia's curriculum. The prince does not have to argue against his inferiors but learns to become a judicious listener and fair judge. In the royal academy, he studies how to govern the state; at home, he practices the principles of statecraft. Checked by his teachers, he will be punished if he fails. Once the prince is capped as an adult, he will be freed from his mentors. His training will continue, though, because he is then placed in the political center of the state, engaged in various governmental genre events. Citing from the *Record of Rites* again, Jia describes the prince's training in this stage: "The prince will be accompanied by historians who record his faults and officials who remonstrate him by controlling his food intake. Flags will be raised to call for suggestions, wooden boards erected on major roads to record his errors, and drums installed in front of the palace to solicit criticisms. Head musicians and historians will sing odes, other musicians recite cautionary notes, ministers submit advice, and scholar-officials pass on the words of the commoners" (Ban 2007, 491). The training charted by Jia can be understood as part of ritualization—the fault-picking and critical practices seem rather ritualistic. Installing flags, wooden boards, and drums for soliciting public opinions, ministers submitting advice, and scholar-officials passing on words of the commoners were staged ways through which a ruler communicated with his subjects. These channels exposed the prince to social woes and issues.

Configured as a listener, however, the ruler or the ruler-to-be was not passive. He was supposed to listen attentively and speak strategically. The need for listening rhetorically was first spelled out by *The Master of the Ghost Valley* (see the next section). It was rehearsed by Liu An (179–122 BCE), a prince of Huainan in the Western Han, and his patrons in *Huainanzi* (淮南子), a collection of essays traditionally labeled as Daoist.[7] Liu presented these essays to the court of Emperor Wu in 139 BCE hoping to enlighten the young sovereign on statecraft. Liu does not deny the centrality of ritualization; he devotes more than one essay to self-cultivation. In terms of handling issues in the court, he proclaims that the ruler needs to master the art of listening. He says:

> The ruler's techniques (consisting of) establishing non-active management and carrying out wordless instructions. . . . Therefore, though his mind knows the norms, his savants transmit the discourses of the Way; though his mouth can speak, his entourage proclaims his words; though his feet can advance, his master of ceremonies leads; though his ears can hear, his officials offer their admonitions. Therefore, his considerations

are without mistaken schemes; his undertakings are without erroneous content. His words [are taken as] scripture and verse; his conduct is [taken as] a model and gnomon for the world. (Liu An 2010, 295)

In Liu's concept of the supreme listener, the ruler actively participates in the decision-making process. He listens to his officials' daily briefings, attends to diplomatic issues, and partakes in ritual ceremonies. However, conscious of the power of his words—once he talks, his words become the law—he relegates the job of speaking and debating to his officials. The critical issue for the ruler is finding the right moment to speak, or to end the officials' quibbling by making a decision. The burden of making a sound decision is fully placed on him. Speaking strategically, he can prevent government errors, which would otherwise erode his authority and political power.

For the listener, the art of speaking required him to understand the *dao* while staying peaceful, calm, and unwavering. The *dao* here refers to the properties of the natural world and the way things work. Self-cultivation that Confucius, Shen, and Jia envisioned in their curricula focuses on acquainting the ruler with the natural way of human society. Liu sees the ruler as a master of the *dao*, who acts accordingly: "His advancing and withdrawing respond to the reasons; his movement and rest comply with [proper] patterns. His likes and dislikes are not based on ugliness or beauty; his rewards and punishments are not based on happiness or anger" (Liu An 2010, 296). To act according to the natural way, the ruler has to resort to rationalism rather than ever-changing feelings and emotions. Therefore, Liu suggests that the ruler concentrate on crucial issues and leave the rest to his officials, and that his five senses be censored and protected, not to be distracted from the issues at stake; "[If] his eyes looked recklessly, there would be profligacy; if his ear listened recklessly, there would be delusion; if his mouth spoke recklessly, there would be disorder" (296). Listening rhetorically centers on the ruler's rationalism, requiring both knowledge of the *dao* and a peaceful state of mind. He speaks solely after his mind has worked without distraction.

While the ruler was positioned as a quiet listener and a strategic speaker, his officials were portrayed as quarrelsome debaters in the early texts. Since the Spring and Autumn era, there seems to be little disagreement on how to train court debaters but more disagreement on how they could execute remonstrance in fluid situations. Skimming through texts of different intellectual schools, one would be awed by the abundant oral wrangling between

Genre Networks as a Political Institution

masters and their disciples as well as between rulers and their advisers. The reader will encounter moments where a master would contrive scenarios that would call for oratory acumen. A student would practice basic oratory skills through discoursing with his master and his fellow classmates and then go on to perfect his skills in real-life circumstances. Private tutoring under a master seems to have been the norm until the middle of the Warring States era. In the Jixia (稷下) Academy, established by the State of Qi in the fourth century BCE, for instance, erudites of different schools were recruited to teach there and accorded official titles. By allowing students and teachers to select each other freely, the academy encouraged intellectual wrangling and cross-pollination of discourses and ideas. In addition to teaching, the masters, such as Mencius and Chun Yu Kun, also advised the rulers on state matters. Therefore, students learned oratorial skills not only from interacting with their masters but also from observing intellectual debates and counseling activities. In what follows, texts of different intellectual schools will be examined to glean both the training methods and the masters' favorite argumentative strategies.

Confucius was seen as an influential master by Han scholars, therefore his pedagogy and oratory strategies deserve our attention. A first-time reader of the *Analects* tends to conclude that Confucius despised excessive use of words, or that he undervalued the use of argumentative discourse. The master repeatedly connected the use of excessive words to the base person (*xiaoren* 小人), whom he shunned. However, Confucius viewed argumentative speech as necessary in one's counsel with a ruler on the condition that the speaker cultivate himself and become a practitioner of the *dao*, one who embraces values such as humanity, fraternity, ritual, knowledge, and trust. Once, someone asked Confucius whether he considered himself a clever talker like the others of his days; Confucius disagreed: "It is not that I aspire to be an eloquent talker, but rather that I hate inflexibility" (*Analects* 1998, 179). The clever talker was sophistic and made a living by advising rulers without committing to any value system. Seeing himself as a defender of the idealized Way of the Zhou court, Confucius wanted his disciples to be adaptive in their speech and to nudge rulers toward benevolence.

One scenario in the *Analects* illustrates what Confucius perceived as the proper realm of argumentative discourse. The story took place as the Chi family was about to launch an attack against another family in the state of Lu, Confucius's home state. Two disciples working as retainers for the Chi family came to debrief Confucius on the upcoming event. When they excused themselves from the morally unjustifiable attack, Confucius repudiated: "If when one's lord encounters danger his ministers do not support him, or when he is about to fall his ministers do not catch him, then what on earth are his ministers for? And besides, what you say is not so. When a tiger or a rhinoceros escapes from its cage, or when a precious tortoise shell or piece of jade is destroyed in its case, who is to blame for this?" (*Analects* 1998, 195). In his rebuttal, Confucius portrayed the ruler in several metaphors—a tiger, a rhinoceros, a precious tortoise shell, and a piece of jade. In accordance with these metaphors, the advisers were supposed to support, contain, and protect the ruler. In the rest of the story, as often happens in the *Analects*, Confucius seized the moment to lecture on the importance of ruling a state through benevolence and culture rather than militancy. This episode helps to illustrate an archetypical case in which court advisers were supposed to, through admonition, contain a ruler's unreasonable desires and to avert any dangers to the state.

Court advisers' voices were often cacophonous. When different voices fought for the ruler's attention, the righteous ones could be buffered and ignored. This seems to have caused major anxiety for Mencius, a member of the Confucian school who once taught at the Jixia Academy. The book *Mencius* contains his speeches delivered in front of kings, demonstrating his relentless striving for their attention. When asked by one of his disciples why he is so keen on combative speeches, Mencius emphasizes advice giving as a fierce struggle between righteous and unrighteous advisers. The latter were often informed by vicious doctrines. Mencius claims: "If the ways of Yang and Mo are not stopped, and the way of Confucius is not made known, the people will be deceived by these deviant views, and the path of humaneness and rightness will be blocked. When the path of humaneness and rightness is blocked, animals are led to devour people, and people will be led to devour one another" (*Mencius* 2009, 70). Mencius's defense reflects the challenges facing a court adviser. Constant fighting among the states created an expanding cadre of itinerant advisers who roamed from state to state seeking employment. Trained in different intellectual lineages, they upheld different doctrines or committed themselves to none. The increasing presence of these individuals created excruciating anxiety for Mencius, who worried that Confucian political ideals would be crowded out. In answering the disciple's query, his defense was mounted as a justification for training in argumentative discourse.

The training for court debaters seems to have converged on a similar approach across intellectual lineages. The masters would contrive a scenario in which a ruler would rally his officials for consultancy, allowing the disciples to improvise speeches. Examples of such are replete in the records of these schools. The hundreds of conversations between the rulers and advisers contained in the *Intrigues of the Warring States* are now viewed by some as practice speeches construed by students of the Vertical-Horizontal school (Crump 1996). *Zuo Tradition* and the *Discourses of the States* provided numerous imitable examples of clever and virtuous eloquence for students of any school. In the *Analects*, Confucius once created a highly plausible situation in which a ruler asked his disciples what government offices they would like to take. The contrived scene in fact called for the disciples, based on their aptitude and political interests, to spell out their visions for state governance (*Analects* 1998, 149–51).

When the contexts of these early texts are considered, we begin to gain a glimpse of the rhetorical training that the rulers and scholar-officials received. For example, living almost in the same period, Shen Shushi appears to agree with Confucius on the subjects that a prince or a gentleman should study. Poetry, music, rites, and history seem to have constituted the curricular core across states in the Spring and Autumn era. In the early Western Han, after years of turmoil, court rites were neglected and forgotten. Consequently, imperial erudite Shusun Tong (叔孫通) argued for their importance and taught them to other officials. Living in the same period as Shusun, Jia Yi also saw the urgency of restoring rites in the Han political life, and he viewed the training of the princes as part of the restoration efforts. Liu An presented his essays to Emperor Wu decades later. However, Liu did not focus on training the prince but on the ruler perfecting his art of listening, a new focus which suggests that Liu probably viewed Jia's design of integrating oratory training into ritualization as a given by his time.

The texts examined above also suggest that genre networks formed in parallel with elite education. The systematic training of royal heirs and the *shi*, who coveted officialdom, started in Confucius's time if not earlier. Their training required the frequent use of texts such as the *Odes*, the *Documents*, and the *Spring and Autumn Annals*, which were not only gradually reified as canons but also solidified as genres. Used in conjunction with lectures, dialogues, and storytelling, these texts interacted with human and nonhuman actors within and outside of educational settings. Initially in oral form, the use of these texts in education and political discourse, as suggested by the sources examined, gave rise to written genres and a manuscript culture. In turn, as Liu Xie observes

36   *Genre Networks as a Political Institution*

in his mapping of genre networks in *The Literary Mind and the Carving of Dragon*, these classics would provide a literary and cultural foundation for several dozens of genres that flourished in early medieval China.

Theories of Political Suasion

While one has to sift through early texts to glean the practice of oratory training, two technical treatises produced in the Warring States era have theorized political suasion. Their theories would reverberate and compete for relevance in governmental genre networks in the early imperial period. The fourth and third centuries BCE saw the emergence of a body of technical literature in China—treatises on divination, medicine, agriculture, logic, military science, and so forth. In addition to the Confucian texts *Analects* and *Mencius* discussed earlier, two treatises clearly demonstrate their authors' investments in political suasion. While the Confucian texts emphasized benevolence and ritual as the premises of persuasion,[8] *The Master of the Ghost Valley* (*Guiguzi* 鬼穀子), allegedly authored by members of the Vertical-Horizontal school,[9] focuses on how the ruler and his advisers should interact with each other through schemes and calculation. The *Works of Master Han* (*Hanfeizi* 韓非子), allegedly written by the Legalist Han Fei (280–233 BCE), devotes several sections to advising both the ruler and advisers on how to speak.[10] Underscoring a rivaling and fluid relationship between the ruler and his advisers, both texts address ruler-adviser relations, audience, subject matter, style, and strategies of discourse.

Written at different times, the two treatises expressed distinct visions for state relations. While *The Master of the Ghost of Valley* assumed a loose alliance of states, the *Works of Master Han* imagined a strong, centralized state. Living in the middle of the Warring States era, the authors of the former were concerned about how an itinerant persuader (*youshi* 遊士) could win the favor of a ruler through eloquence. In contrast, Han Fei once worked as an adviser for the king of Qin, who later became the first emperor of Qin. Composing his work at the end of the Warring States era, Han Fei shared a similar vision with the king, who harbored an ambition for establishing a centralized nation. With disagreement over visions for state relations, these two treatises thus support two distinct modes of advice to the monarch identified by Su-Ching Chang and illustrated by Yuri Pines (2013) that emerged in succession during the Warring States era. *The Master of the Ghost Valley* was aligned with the "confrontational" mode throughout the era, in which the *shi*, in a more fluid relation with the monarch,

Genre Networks as a Political Institution 37

tended to offer cutting criticisms. *Hanfeizi* embodies an "authoritarian" disposition found among the Legalist adherents toward the end of the era, where the advisor desisted from attempting to cajole or challenge the ruler; instead, he depended on manipulating the ruler's predilections.

The Master of the Ghost Valley

The Master of the Ghost Valley conceptualizes a fluid relationship between the adviser and the ruler. It adamantly promotes regime change if the state interests call for it. It teaches that when social conflicts and problems cause fractures (*xi* 巇) in the state, casting away the incumbent and establishing a new political order is a solution. *The Master of the Ghost Valley* teaches metaphorically: "Before a fracture begins, it shows some sign. It can be filled in to mend; it can be withheld to mend; it can be stopped to mend; it can be concealed to mend; it can be replaced to mend" (Wu and Swearingen 2016, 53–54). In this framing, the monarch is both fallible and replaceable. Sometimes replacement is even mandatory; he could be replaced by someone who is able to amend the fractures. Not only is the ruler-subject relationship never fixed, the text suggests that one's loyalty to a monarch can be weak. One is free to serve a state if the monarch trusts him and allows him to use his ability to its fullest extent. He is also free to desert the ruler, all depending on his calculation of various factors.[11] What drives him to pursue government service is the lofty personal and social ideals shared by the traveling persuaders: "[Dwell] between Heaven and Earth like the sages to establish oneself, serve the world, profess education, promote the reputable, and practice intelligent naming" (60).

The Vertical-Horizontal school idealized the sage as a master of the *yin-yang* approach. The sage was portrayed as someone who truly understands the Way, or the way in which the natural world operates, and acts with such enlightenment. He observes the world and perceives the workings of the opposite and complementary forces of *yin* and *yang*. Then he applies the *yin-yang* approach to understand the matrix of human desires and behaviors, using this understanding to guide his participation in political oratory. In speech making, the *yin-yang* approach is concretized through two everyday motions, opening (*bai* 捭) and closing (*he* 闔). Opening one's mouth to speak is designated as *yang*; closing it to remain silent is designated as *yin*. One modulates his expression—when and what to speak—by controlling and coordinating these motions. The text goes on to mark the various themes in political discourse with *yin* and *yang*:

It is said that longevity and birth, peace and happiness, wealth and prestige, prominence and glory, fame and honor, hobby and interest, fortune and benefit, pride and ambition, and likes and desires are *yang*, which is called beginning. It is said that death and destruction, worry and anxiety, poverty and disadvantage, suffering and humiliation, abandonment and damage, loss, disappointment, harm, torment, and punishment are *yin*, which is called ending. All speeches that employ *yang* are "beginning." This sort of speech talks about positive things and is used to launch business. All speeches that employ *yin* are "ending." This sort of speech talks about negative things and is used to get a plan cancelled. (Wu and Swearingen 2016, 41–42).

By designating these themes as either *yin* or *yang*, the text encourages the speaker to grasp the nature of a topic and use the knowledge for constructing arguments. In addition, it reminds the speaker of the fluid nature of life experience: what are considered desirable qualities of life (*yang*) can metamorphose into something negative or harmful (*yin*).

The *yin-yang* approach was also evoked to characterize the interlocutor and to guide stylistic choice. The text suggests that one uses *yin* and *yang* to gauge the nature of the interlocutor and to speak in a corresponding style. For example, when conversing with those who are stern and aggressive, one should focus on positive, inspiring topics; when conversing with those who are gentle and defensive, one could talk about trivial and daily matters. When speaking with those who show little aspiration for life, one should tone down his speech; when speaking with those with great aspirations, one should use an inspiring, upbeat tone.[12] Clearly, the text views speech as constitutive of natural dynamics and the joint work of *yin* and *yang* forces. Not only are discourses subject to the two forces, so are the interlocutors and their stylistic choices.

The text also generalized discourse strategies that could be widely found in speeches recorded in pre-Qin texts. Two of them can be highlighted here. One is the use of symbolism and metaphor to engage the interlocutor while gauging his thoughts and feelings. The text says, "When the other person speaks, he is in motion; when you listen, you are motionless. Hear what he says based on his speech. When his statements are inconsistent with what you observe, inquire in response, and you surely can evoke a reaction. All spoken words represent images of things; all things are comparable. With images to compare, you can foresee what comes next" (Wu and Swearingen

2016, 43–44). When one is not acting, he quietly observes the actor's words and gauges his thoughts and feelings. Symbolism and metaphor are viewed as strategies of nonaction. However, the *yin-yang* perspective can also render a reversal of the discourse dynamics. Once the listener starts to speak, he is acting; he shifts from the *yin* position to the *yang* position, becoming subject to the other's gaze and gauge.

The other discourse strategy focuses on mastering political topoi and appropriating canonical texts in speech and writing. This strategy is recommended when one probes the ruler's likes and dislikes to win his trust: "Follow the doctrines on the *Dao* and virtues (道德), compassion and the loyalty (仁義), rites and rituals of entertainment (禮樂), and sincerity and integrity (忠信) for plans and strategies (忠信). Start with the Book of Poetry (詩) and the Book of History (書) and alternately deliberate on advantages and disadvantages to discuss what should be adopted and what should not" (Wu and Swearingen 2016, 51–52). The passage suggests that the traveling persuaders shared a similar rhetorical repertoire with Confucian literati in the Warring States era. These topoi and texts connected the *shi* and provided them with a shared cultural and linguistic repertoire for fashioning their arguments.

Works of Master Han

Han Fei unapologetically portrays the ruler-minister relation as rivalry. The ruler seeks to withhold his power and guard his sovereignty; his ministers covet the throne and bide their time to usurp state power. Han Fei warns the ruler: "Never enrich a man to the point where he can afford to run against you; never ennoble a man to the point where he becomes a threat; never put all your trust in a single man and thereby lose your state" (*Han Feizi* 2003, 39). The ruler needs to keep a suspicious eye not just on his ministers but everyone around him. His officials will form cliques and plot schemes against him; his consorts and concubines will wish his early death so that their sons can ascend to the throne and so they can enjoy relations with other men while still young. Exposing these ulterior motives in court discourse aligns with Han's negative view of human nature. Influenced by his teacher Xunzi, Han saw humans as innately evil. Thus, the ruler finds himself besieged by perpetual dangers, far from the peaceful scenes depicted by Jia Yi in the epigraph. Distrust and constant vigilance characterize the ruler's psyche.

This psyche comes to mold the ruler's behavior, including the ways he handles political consultation. When advising the ruler on how to act, authors of the major Chinese classics often appeal to the Daoist notion of nonaction. Likewise, Han Fei evoked the *dao* and nonaction. Staying reticent, the ruler should refrain from revealing his temperament, sentiments, preferences, and dislikes. Failing to detect them, his officials can hardly plot any schemes against him. Being observant and calculating while concealing what he does helps the ruler to perform his role: "See but do not appear to see; listen but do not seem to listen; know but do not let it be known that you know. When you perceive the trend of a man's words, do not change them, do not correct them, but examine them and compare them with the results. Assign one man to each office and do not let men talk to each other, and then all will do their utmost" (*Han Feizi* 2003, 17). Although the ruler does not indulge his ministers in debate, he clearly sees what they say and what they achieve. Han Fei urges the ruler to wield reward and punishment as "two handles" of the government. When a minister's achievements match his words, he will be rewarded; otherwise, punished. Although the ruler is reticent and nonparticipatory, his officials will get the job done. In a shadowy role, the ruler participates in the deliberative process by resorting to his highest power and the reward-and-punishment mechanism.

Han Fei's repeated calls for detachment only suggest the daunting challenges that a ruler faces when making a decision. The ruler is not always enlightened, his temperament and weaknesses are hardly concealable, and he often compromises his supreme power and misuses rewards and punishments. Therefore, Han Fei enumerates ten faults that rulers often commit and draws on historical anecdotes to illuminate each. The faults include practicing petty loyalty, fixing eyes on petty gains, behaving in a base manner, being obsessed with music, being infatuated with women, and so forth. In each anecdote, there is a conversation between a ruler and his advisers. Often the former fails to heed the latter's words and commits a costly mistake. As many of the anecdotes show, when offered advice, the ruler does not always have the propensity to make a wise decision.

Despite his fallibility, the ruler occupies an advantaged position in the deliberation. He wields his supreme power and the "two handles" of government to exercise his rhetorical authority. Low in the ranks, his ministers have to play the game with extreme caution. A misstep may cost them their lives. To advise the ministers, Han Fei wrote his renowned chapter, "Difficulties of Remonstration" (說難).

The difficulties of remonstration come from the challenge of speaking in tune with the ruler's transient state of mind. It was neither the knowledge needed for a speaker to make his case nor the audacity to exercise his full abilities. Instead, "[o]n the whole, the difficult thing about persuasion is to know the mind of the person one is trying to persuade and to be able to fit one's words to it" (*Han Feizi* 2003, 73). Han Fei muses on the challenges of reading and speaking to the ruler's mind in five sections of his treatise: (1) a speaker's seven missteps that will put his life in danger; (2) eight things that a speaker does that may cause the ruler's suspicion and disregard; (3) ways of sounding pleasant to the ears of the ruler; (4) the supreme state of persuasion; and (5) the importance of ascertaining the ruler's loves and hates before delivering speeches.

The ruler's mind is hard to decipher. One cannot easily tell whether he is interested in virtue or profit. He can pretend to favor one thing while secretly desiring the other. For some undertakings, the ruler needs to guard his secrecy; it is to his advantage to create some confusion and vagueness. However, when one approaches the ruler to consult him, he may inadvertently discover and disclose the latter's secrecy. Han lists seven possible missteps that may put an adviser's life in danger. These missteps, in one way or another, may result in the unveiling of the ruler's hidden motives.

In addition to heeding the ruler's intention and secrecy, the speaker has to take good care of the substance and style of his speech. In the political game, the ruler cannot afford to be anything other than observant, sensitive, and suspicious. He has to remind himself that his ministers and consorts will constantly plot against him. They seek government office largely for their own benefit rather than for that of the state or of the royal family. His suspicion creates difficulties in persuasion for a speaker. Han enumerates eight of them:

> If you talk to the ruler about men of real worth, he will think you are implying that he is no match for them; if you talk to him of pretty men, he will think you are attempting to use your influence to get your friends into office; if you talk to him about what he likes, he will suspect you of trying to utilize him; and if you talk about what he hates, he will suspect you of trying to test his patience. If you speak too bluntly and to the point, he will consider you unlearned and will shun you; if you speak too eloquently and in too great detail, he will consider you pretentious

and will reject you. If you are too sketchy in outlining your ideas, he will think you a coward who is too fainthearted to say what he really means; if you are too exuberant and long-winded in stating your proposals, he will think you an uncouth bumpkin who is trying to talk down to him. (*Han Feizi* 2003, 75)

What Han Fei suggests here is taking a detour and using a moderate style. One should avoid topics that will draw the ruler's suspicion, a suspicion that the speaker is withholding insidious, self-interested motives. A moderate style is needed to paint a positive image of both the ruler and the speaker. Han goes further to suggest that the speaker emphasize aspects that the ruler is proud of and downplay aspects that he is ashamed of.

The pain of persuasion can be alleviated when one has won the ruler's trust. As per his natural psyche, the ruler will remain dubious and sensitive, but a minister's long-tested relation with the ruler can convince the latter of his devotion and loyalty. Supported by the trust, his communication with the sovereign can grow more forthright: "If you are able to fulfill long years of service with the ruler, enjoy his fullest favor and confidence, lay long-range plans for him without ever arousing suspicion, and when necessary oppose him in argument without incurring blame, then you may achieve merit by making clear to him what is profitable and what is harmful, and bring glory to yourself by your forthright judgments of right and wrong" (*Han Feizi* 2003, 77). This is the supreme state of persuasion that a minister can enjoy. There is a sense of integrity, but never equality, between the two. All warnings pertaining to speaking with the ruler continue to apply. But by being skilled in reading and speaking to the ruler's mind, the minister has internalized the warnings. This trust, growing out of years of commitment and service, is a rarity for most ministers.

Han Fei's theory emphasizes the cultivation of both the listener and the speaker, which characterizes the theories of suasion across different intellectual schools. The ruler needs to know how to listen and how to wield his supreme power while abiding by the laws that sustain his rhetorical authority. His ministers have to listen carefully, reading his mind and pursuing his full trust. For Han Fei, both parties share the burden of deciphering each other's words and hidden motives. They are perpetually entangled in a tense and dangerous mind reading game. What they actually say is consequently subsumed under the vigorous mind reading of the speaker or the listener.

What divides *The Master of the Ghost Valley* and the *Works of Master Han* lies in their different ideals for the ruler-adviser relation. The former affords the *shi* liberty to roam among the city-states; they could even replace an incompetent ruler. The latter locks the *shi* in a heavily centralized polity, which they could hardly transform or leave behind. The different ruler-adviser relations envisioned come to affect how these texts have viewed the interlocutors and their discourse strategies. *The Master of the Ghost Valley* seems to have assigned all parties with equal discursive power with the ruler and his ministers being positioned dynamically in a *yin-yang* relation. They alternate between the *yin* (listening) and the *yang* (speaking), gaining different kinds of discursive power at different times. Therefore, reward and punishment, the "two handles" of government wielded by the ruler and emphasized by Han Fei, are notably missing in *The Master of the Ghost Valley*. Moreover, the two discourse strategies highlighted in *The Master of the Ghost Valley* also come to strengthen the advisers' discursive power. They can use symbolism and metaphors as detours to solicit the ruler's thoughts and feelings without arousing suspicion, and they can resort to topoi and canonical texts to shore up their arguments.

Composed amid the wrangling among the city-states, *The Master of the Ghost Valley* represents the worldview of the itinerant persuaders who spoke for and between these states. The liberty to break out of the confines of a polity and roam among the states gave them a sense of freedom. Despite playing subservient roles in a state, they constructed a transcendent sage as their ideal persona, a master of the *dao* who understood the workings of *yin* and *yang*. They relied on sagely wisdom to navigate political structures diplomatically. However, after the central states were conquered and annexed by the state of Qin in 221 BCE, they soon found their roaming space drastically narrowed. With the emperor enjoying unchallenged power, the *shi* would find resonance in Han Fei's musings on the difficulties of remonstration. However, the teachings of *The Master of the Ghost Valley* remained relevant, and even prominently visible, in genre networks dealing with gender relations and imperial integrity (see chapters 3 and 5).

Imperial Government and Communications

Anyone who worked in the imperial government participated in decision-making in one way or another, with those who had direct access to the emperor's consultation meetings possessing the greatest discursive power. The following chart shows the key posts in the Western Han central government, traditionally called "the outer court," and their responsibilities:[13]

Ministers in the Western Han Central Government

Royal Teachers (*Shang Gong* 上公)
  Taishi (太師), *Taifu* (太傅), *Taibao* (太保), *Sifu* (四傅),
  Shiyou (師友)
Head Ministers (*San Gong* 三公)
  Chengxiang (丞相), Chancellor
  Taiwei (太尉), Supreme Commander
  Yushi Dafu (御史大夫), Imperial Counselor
Ministers (*Qing* 卿)
  Taichang (太常), managing ceremonies in the royal family temple
  Boshi (博士), royal erudites specialized in the classics
  Guanglu (光祿), guarding and managing the palace
   Dafu (大夫), managing court consultations
   Lang (郎), court servants and charioteers
   Yezhe (謁者), managing court ceremonies
   Qimen (期門), managing military transportations
  Tingwei (廷尉), managing law enforcement
  Weiwei (衛尉), managing palace guards
  Taipu (太僕), managing horses and husbandry
  Honglu (鴻臚), managing kingdoms and ethnic minorities
  Zongzheng (宗正), managing the extended royal family
  Shinong (司農), managing agricultural matters
  Shaofu (少府), managing tax collection

The ministers heavily participated in the court discourse and shaped its practice. In addition, thousands of bureaucrats joined in indirectly. For example, in the Western Han, there were sixteen offices under *Chengxiang* (Chancellor) and eleven under *Yushi Dafu* (Imperial Counselor; Xu Tianlin 1963b, 288–90). Although most officials lacked the opportunity to directly engage the emperor, they could chime in through their superiors and through writing. Officials who worked inside the emperor's palace, such as those in *Dafu, Lang, Yezhe,* and *Qimen* positions under the minister of *Guanglu,* made direct contact with the emperor and the ministers and could conveniently pass on words.[14] The emperor could be also swayed by the court

Genre Networks as a Political Institution

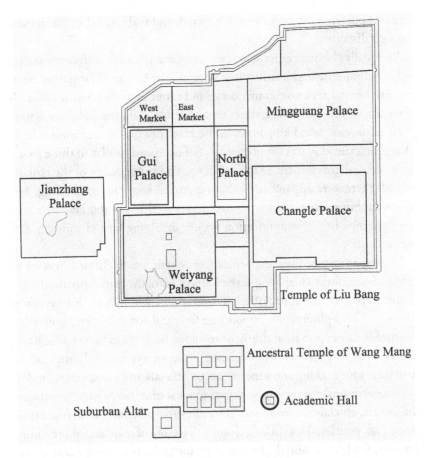

FIGURE 1.1 Chang'an, the capital city of the Western Han dynasty. The layout of the city Chang'an is drawn and annotated by the author based on the image in Li Yufang (1997, 72).

ladies—empress dowager, empress, concubines—and eunuchs, who added up to over five thousand at a certain point in the Eastern Han.[15] Roaming across two courts—the outer court consisting of government offices and the emperor's palace (Weiyang Palace) and the inner court consisting of the court ladies' palaces, Changle, Gui, North, and Mingguang Palace (see the layout of the city Chang'an in figure 1.1)— the Western Han emperor interacted with different groups in distinct genre networks.[16] At these palaces, particularly Weiyang Palace (the sovereign's residence and workplace), bodies of different bureaucratic ranks met, interacted, and realigned their allegiances through discourse.

An equally elaborate bureaucratic structure was placed in each commandery and kingdom, creating local discourse systems. The Qin and Han governments divided the country into commanderies and counties, and dispatched officials to monitor or to lead local governments. Ranking officials and princes were given territories, called kingdoms, in the Han for semi-autonomous rule. In a kingdom, the king was supported by staff positions similar to those found in the central government (An and Xiong, 2:227–65). Some of the ranking officials there were dispatched by the emperor to keep tabs on the king. The enormous but relatively efficient bureaucracy in the Qin and Han dynasties was sustained by a communication system involving tens of thousands of bureaucrats.

The expansion of the communication system was facilitated by a set of genres. According to Cai Yong of the Eastern Han, the Han formalized eight genres as part of the court ritual. The emperor would issue four types of edicts: *ce* (策 diplomas) for appointing fiefs and top ministers, conferring honorable titles upon their death, or revoking titles upon them committing crimes; *zhi* (制 decisions) for declaring an amnesty; *zhao* (詔 imperial instructions) for making announcements to officials and commoners; and *jie* (戒 admonitions) for issuing warnings to local officials. When reporting to the throne, officials and commoners would submit memorials of four types: *zhang* (章 petitions) for making clear one's feeling of gratitude or presenting a report, *zou* (奏 memorials) for investigating and impeaching, *biao* (表 presentations) for expressing one's feelings, and *boyi* (駁議 dissenting opinions) for maintaining a difference of opinion.[17]

These genres were ritualized on both material and discursive terms. The court stipulated the lengths of the bamboo or wooden strips, the expressions to be used, and the way to formulate a text. For example, as Cai Yong (1985) notes, *ce* is written, in alternating order, on a long strip that measures two *chi* (尺; 46 cm) and a short one that measures one *chi* (23 cm). They are connected with two strings, one at the upper and one at the lower end of the shorter strip. Below the strings, one writes in seal script. The body text starts by announcing the year, month, and day and using the expression "The August Thearch says . . ." (皇帝曰). The court also prescribed the language and format of texts submitted by officials and commoners. For instance, in *zhang* and *zou*, to show respect to the emperor, the writer needs to use the expression "I bow my head (to the floor)" (稽首) and indent the text across all the strips. While *zhang* does not need to be sealed in a silk sack unless it contains confidential information, *zou* always needs to be.

In addition to these genres, bureaucratic communications were supported by a sophisticated postal relay network. The network took shape across the central states during the Spring and Autumn era and was strengthened in the Qin and Han dynasties. The Han laws on government document delivery prescribed the establishment of relay stations and their staffing (Zang). Every ten *li* (about 5 km), a station called *you* (郵), *chuan* (傳), or *zhi* (置) would be built in areas north to the Yangtze River; south to the Yangtze River, a station would be built every twenty *li*; in less populated northern and western commanderies, a station would be built every thirty *li*. Each station was served by twelve to twenty-four families depending on its size. These families maintained the station and served as messengers. They were rewarded with a piece of arable land that could be passed down to their offspring. Depending on the urgency of a document, the messenger would ride a horse or walk. Each document was marked by a delivery deadline. Missing it, the messenger would be penalized. Built along main roads, a station typically included bedrooms, a kitchen, and a stable. In addition to delivering documents, the staff provided food and lodging for bureaucrats passing by.

When texts circulated in the bureaucracy, genre networks came into being. Broadly, the texts circulated in three directions. First, the central government would publish edicts and send them down to kingdoms and commanderies, which might move them down the chain to counties, towns, and villages. Second, a text might initiate from the lowest level, such as a village, and travel all the way up to the central government. Third, a text might move horizontally across government branches. The rise of a genre network can be illustrated by a government document created in 61 BCE and recovered in the 1930s in Juyan (居延), a northwestern outpost of the Han empire. As a common practice of its day, this document was written on eight wooden strips, each measuring about 23 cm (one *chi*) long and 1.5 cm wide. Originally strung as a bundle, these strips were loose when unearthed, and mixed with strips from other bundles. Oba Osamu was able to reconstruct the bundle in the 1960s based on the location of discovery, the theme, and the calligraphic style (1988). (See figure 1.2 for the reconstructed document.) Reading from right to left, the first three strips show the upward movements of a document in the bureaucracy; the next five strips show downward movements.

48 *Genre Networks as a Political Institution*

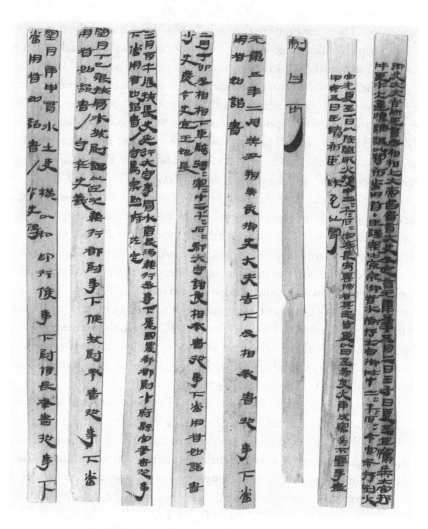

FIGURE 1.2 Imperial edict of the fifth year of Yuankang unearthed in Juyan. The image is created by the author by compiling open-source image files from Zhongyang yanjiu yuan.

The first two strips constitute a memorial submitted to the emperor by the Imperial Counselor Bin Ji. Bin reports that based on another memorial that Chancellor Wei Xiang forwarded from the minister of ceremony, a calendar officer recommended a series of ritualistic events related to the summer solstice. The two strips show the upward movement of texts: a proposal from a calendar officer went up to his supervisor, the minister of ceremony, who then forwarded it to the chancellor. Passing through the hands of these officials and their offices, one memorial then metamorphosed into another memorial for the emperor.

御史大夫吉昧死言垂相相上太常昌書言大史垂定言元康五年五月二日壬子夏至宜寢兵太官抒井更水火進鳴雞偶移以聞布當用者臣謹案比原宗禦者水衡抒大官禦井中二千石令官各抒別火

Risking his life, Imperial Counselor (Bin) Ji reports to Your Majesty: Chancellor (Wei) Xiang forwarded a memorial from the Minister of Ceremony Chang. According to the calendar officer Chuiding, summer will arrive on the second day of the fifth month in the fifth year of Yuankang (61 BCE). He recommended that soldiers take a vacation and that the imperial dining service clean wells and change the water and firewood. They report to the court at daybreak. Ji notes, charioteers and officials of forestry and waters will clean the wells in the dining quarters. Officials of two thousand bushels of grains will order their officials to clean their own wells and change the firewood.

官先夏至一日以除賺取火授中二千石官在長安雲陽者其民皆受以日至易故火庚戌寢兵不聽事盡甲寅五日臣請布臣昧死以聞

The day before the Summer Solstice, firewood officers will obtain new fires by drilling wood, and pass them to officials of two thousand bushels of grains residing in Chang'an and Yunyang areas and their subjects, who will then replace the old fires on the Summer Solstice. On the same day, soldiers will begin a five-day recess without performing any duties. Please make this announcement. Risking his life, Ji humbly presents the report to Your Majesty.

The memorial was then turned into an executive order by the third strip, which recorded the emperor's terse response, "Granted" (制曰可). The expression transformed the first three strips into an imperial edict called *zhao* (詔), or announcement for the officials and commoners, to be circulated across the empire.

The circulation of the edict was made possible through the next five strips in the bundle and, importantly, through the hands of five scribes. The fourth strip says that "On the eleventh day of the second month in the fifth year of Yuankang, Imperial Counselor passed the edict to Chancellor. Implement the order upon receiving the edict. Request other officials to implement it as directed" (元康五年二月癸醜朔癸亥御史大夫吉下丞相承書從事下當用者如詔書). This strip suggests that the Imperial Counselor's office prepared the edict and sent it down the bureaucratic structure. The fifth strip then says, "On the fifteenth day of the second month, Chancellor Wei Xiang passed the edict to General of Carriages and Horses, officials of two thousand bushels of grains, governors, and chancellors of kingdoms. Implement the order upon receiving the edict. Request other officials to implement it as directed." The directive "Implement the order upon receiving the edict. Request other officials to implement it as directed" (承書從事下當用者如詔書) produced an illocutionary force that sent the executive order across a great terrain. One of the edict's destinations was Jianshui county of Zhangye commandery located in the northwestern frontier, two thousand *li* (about six hundred miles) away from the imperial center. Nearly two months later, as indicated by the eighth strip, the edict reached Jianshui before it was further passed on to local villages and fortresses. As the eight strips were written in the same calligraphic style, it can be deduced that at least five scribes at different locations copied the edict and each added a strip to enable its travel.

It is worth noting that this edict was not archived nor mentioned in the dynastic history. Working with numerous government documents, court historians such as Ban Gu had to be selective. In their history writing, it is conceivable that they only recorded what they viewed as worthy. The rituals of cleaning wells, changing water and firewood, and soldiers taking recess on the Summer Solstice might seem so mundane that Ban Gu did not care to mention the edict. This neglect indicates that much about bureaucratic communications was left out in official histories. While these histories inform us about how bureaucratic genres generally worked in the Han, the discovered document reminds us that how they actually worked was far more complex.

Conclusion

This chapter suggests that genre networks were a political institution in early imperial China and that they were institutionalized through educational, theoretical, and bureaucratic means. Repeatedly, early Chinese texts have pointed to the functioning of a multigenre system in service of the state. To make the system work, the ruler and his advisers studied state histories and speeches, bureaucratic documents, rites, and odes. Their training was structured by a set of classics passed down from early generations, which would provide a literary and cultural foundation for new genres to emerge in the empire. In theorizing political suasion during the Warring States era, the authors of *The Master of the Ghost Valley* and the *Works of Master Han* harbored different visions for state relations. The former assumed that the central states, despite wars and intrigues, would coexist as they had in the past. Thus, its rhetorical theory was more dialogical. In contrast, the latter imagined a unified state and a ruler with unchallenged power. Hence, its theory was more psychological. The rise of the centralized state drastically expanded the scope of political deliberation. The Qin and the Han established a sophisticated bureaucratic system, formalized a series of genres, and built a postal relay network. Working jointly, these measures made genre networks a crucial political institution.

CHAPTER 2

Reading the Heavenly Mandate

The *Odes* says, "The sun and moon portend calamities, by means of their anomalies." I shall always remember my negligence, which pains me profusely.
《詩》雲:"日月告凶,不用其行。"永念厥咎,內疚於心。

—Emperor Guangwu

The edicts issued by the imperial court embodied power and demanded to be heard. The edicts were, as revealed in both received histories and archaeological finds, more than stand-alone orders but links in a chain of discussions, debates, and responses. While embodying the Han emperor's authority in orchestrating these actions, the edicts sometimes revealed his submission to other authorities, such as Heaven and the Confucian classics. Emperor Guangwu (25–57 CE) of the Eastern Han, for instance, bowed to these authorities in an edict after a solar eclipse in the fall of 30 CE. He portrays the eclipse as a Heavenly warning delivered in response to social unrest under his reign. As quoted in the epigraph, he cites from the *Odes* to corroborate his interpretation of the "anomalous" behaviors of this celestial body (Fan 2007, 20). The strategy of a ruler negotiating power with other authorities began well before the Han dynasty. What is remarkable about this strategy is that the imperial court mobilized a metaphysical order to argue for the legitimacy of the ruler and to consolidate power at an unprecedented scale.

As a symbol of the emperor's power, the edicts conveyed his evolving administrative foci and concerns. Some performed seemingly ritualistic, epideictic functions, such as executive clemency, assignment of peerage, establishment of heirs, certification of posthumous titles, or promotion of agricultural work. The founders of the Western Han and the Eastern Han, Liu Bang and Liu Xiu, for instance, focused on these rituals as ways to assert their power and to garner support. In contrast, as responses to sociopolitical exigencies, such as relief work after natural disasters, correction of social woes, or promotion of filial piety, other edicts were more deliberative. While some edicts were end products of prolonged deliberations, others extended an invitation for discussions and debates.

In order to make a decolonial move, this chapter will focus on a type of edict that invited discussions and debates, which in turn reproduced a metaphysical order and legitimated an emperor's ruling. Responding to natural anomalies and omens, these edicts and the responses that they solicited from scholar-officials strengthened the imperial power by generating theories about Heaven-human relations, expanding political participation, and encouraging self-cultivation in the governing body. The genre networks thus formed—involving edicts, queries, exam essays, and commentaries—helped to sustain an ontology, a view of the world as transcendental, transactional, and translingual. While Heaven-human relations were developed as a prominent philosophical discourse in a manuscript culture in preimperial China (Meyer 2012), this chapter argues that this discourse was crucially mediated by genre networks in the Han dynasty. As Confucian literati participated proactively in the epistemological work, Confucianism received state sponsorship. The sponsorship in turn encouraged the school to expand its theoretical apparatus, moving from a secular to a metaphysical focus.

This chapter will first examine the earliest edict of this kind and explore the epistemology and ontology that it embodied by considering Confucius's and Dong Zhongshu's theories of *dao*, Heaven, rites, and historical knowledge. This epistemology and ontology undergirded the genre networks that were set in motion by this type of edict. In fact, Dong articulated his theory in a series of exam essays written in this network. Next, another genre in the network, officials' commentaries, will be examined for its rhetorical features. Finally, the chapter will demonstrate that as genre networks on natural anomalies kept growing, the Confucian theoretical apparatus became syncretic; and it will deomonstrate that the networks widened political participation and strengthened government. The following is a list of key discourses on natural anomalies to be examined in this chapter (see table 2.1).

54 · *Reading the Heavenly Mandate*

TABLE 2.1 *Key Discourses on Natural Anomalies*

Author	Discourse
Emperor Wen 文帝	An edict inviting officials and the literati to help him interpret natural anomalies (178 BCE)
Emperor Wu 武帝	Inquiries on natural anomalies, the Heavenly Mandate, and government in a court exam (134 BCE)
Dong Zhongshu 董仲舒	Three exam essays responding to Emperor Wu's inquiries (134 BCE)
Gu Yong 穀永	A commentary that connected natural anomalies with unruly court ladies (15 BCE)
Xiang Kai 襄楷	A commentary that interpreted natural anomalies by drawing on astrology, mathematics, the Huang-Lao school, and Buddhism (166 CE)

Edicts on Natural Anomalies and Disasters

Imperial edicts were not only a way for an emperor to exercise his power, but they were also the emperor's way to garner support from his subjects. Edicts were issued throughout the Han to assign peerage, particularly during the respective reigns of the founders of the Western and the Eastern Han. Soon after they ascended to the throne, they issued edicts to assign kings, marquises, and fiefdoms. These founders were all portrayed in the *BH* and *BLH* as fearless leaders skilled in quelling military conflicts in tumultuous times. They seemed uninterested in the throne initially but were then persuaded by their followers to accept the Heavenly Mandate (*tianming* 天命). Used in political discourse since the Zhou dynasty, the concept signified the ruler's power being endowed by Heaven.[1] Take Liu Xiu (5–57 CE), future Emperor Guangwu, as an example. He was cajoled by his followers onto the throne in the middle of a military campaign. His generals made a series of arguments: the need of a ruler in chaotic times; his excellence over his rivals in military power, culture, and morality; and his followers wanting to benefit from his ascension (Fan 2007, 8). Liu finally gave in when a scholar contrived a prophetic text, called *chen* (讖), in which he was confirmed as the chosen emperor. The edicts issued thereafter on assigning kings and fiefdoms, called *ce* (策), were results of shifting power and of a network of arguments made locally and from afar. *Ce* functioned as covenants signed between the newly ordained ruler and his loyal followers. The generals pledged their allegiance, and in return they earned honor and fiefdoms.

Reading the Heavenly Mandate   55

As an emperor was established through arguments and intrigues, his legitimacy became a perpetual question. In one type of edict called *zhao* (詔), or imperial announcements, the emperor sometimes confessed his confusion over the legitimacy question and actively sought the assistance of his officials. *Zhao* of this type were issued after natural anomalies or disasters, such as solar eclipses, earthquakes, landslides, floods, and famine. As shown by Emperor Guangwu in the epigraph, troubled by these events, the ruler would be forced to review his governance. He would invite high-ranking officials to join him in this effort. This type of edict was issued throughout the Han. Some emperors issued them multiple times during their reign. These orders took on the emperor's voice and followed similar rhetorical moves. The ruler first cites a piece of wisdom related to Heaven and government. Second, he connects natural anomalies or disasters to the failings of his governance. Third, he confesses that he is puzzled by the message of the natural anomalies or uncertain how he can improve his governance. Finally, he calls the executive offices at the central and local government for assistance, including recruiting morally and culturally superior individuals for consultation.

These rhetorical moves were established in the first edict of this type recorded in the *BH*. After a series of natural anomalies, especially solar eclipses, Emperor Wen (180–157 BCE) was prompted to query his scholar-officials in 178 BCE.

[*Move 1*] I have heard that Heaven creates humans and installs the gentleman-leader to provide for and govern them. When the leader is morally corrupt and his governance unfair, Heaven sets off disasters as warnings. [*Move 2*] The last day of November saw a solar eclipse; I was chided by Heaven. What great disaster has the second eclipse portended? [*Move 3*] While keeping the royal family temple intact, I have humbly arisen above the commoners and the fiefs. The duty of bringing the state peace and order has fallen on me. Two or three government officials have worked for me like my hands. Unable to manage or provide for my subjects on earth and with the brightness of the sun, moon, and stars abating, I am truly morally corrupted. [*Move 4*] Upon receiving this order, review my mistakes and identify my weaknesses; speak to me without reserve. Recommend morally and culturally superior ones who could speak about my mistakes candidly and courageously, to help me rectify them. (Ban 2007, 28–29)

What these rhetorical moves construe is an industrious and humble ethos: The emperor is devoted to his subjects, and he seeks the assistance of the learned and the capable for fulfilling his moral obligation. Unlike the authoritative voice in edicts on other subject matters, the emperor confessed his weakness and incapacity, inviting a discussion on his legitimacy as a ruler.

What is significant about this first recorded edict concerning omens is that it endorsed a particular political philosophy and set in motion a genre network. Future edicts on omens would be built on a similar philosophy. The first three moves of the edict promote a particular epistemology as the basis for political discourse: there is a connection between Heaven and government, and it is worth exploring. The fourth move calls for assistance from officials. They were to identify talents from every commandery and kingdom based on their cultural and moral qualities and send them to the capital city.[2] Next, I will elaborate on this epistemology, which was endorsed by Confucius and Dong Zhongshu (董仲舒; 179–104 BCE), one of the culturally and morally cultivated who attended a court exam administered by Emperor Wu (141–87 BCE) and answered the emperor's queries on the relationship between Heaven and the *dao*, or the Way, of government. In his response essays, called *dui* (對), Dong expanded Confucius's thoughts on history, rites, and spirits.

Dao, Heaven, Rites, and Historical Knowledge

Confucian thinking is centrally concerned about seeking *dao*, or the way of benevolent governance. In metaphysical speculations from ancient China, the universe did not start from a clear distinction of different worlds, but rather from a chaotic mass. What most attracted the ancient Chinese was not something that would transcend this chaotic state, but the innermost essence of the chaos that remained hidden and mysterious. The answer to everything about this world that lay at the heart of the chaos is called *dao* (道). Among ancient Chinese thinkers, Confucius was particularly keen in seeking out the *dao* of government in order to cease the turmoil of the Zhou dynasty. For him, *dao* offers not only the answer to how the natural world operates but, more importantly, the key to the moral-spiritual order and the prosperity of human society. In Confucius's view, an ideal ruler or gentleman is characterized by his authoritative conduct or benevolence called *ren* (仁). Pursuing the way of benevolent governing throughout his adult life, therefore, Confucius once said, "If

Reading the Heavenly Mandate 57

at dawn you learn of and tread the [W]ay, you can face death at dusk" (*Analects* 1998, 91). *Dao* thus constitutes the proper realm of Confucian epistemology.

In seeking the *dao* of humane governance, Confucius was most concerned about human society and refrained from entering the realm of the Spirits and Heaven. For him, the desirable knowledge or wisdom for an individual is the mastery of attributes of being good, or, in practical terms, seventeen kinds of established rites in the early Zhou dynasty. Being good involves concern about human affairs rather than about any supernatural or metaphysical matters. A true gentleman shows respect to the Spirits but maintains a distance from them (*Analects* 1998, 108). He takes as his sole responsibility seeking to exemplify the desirable attributes of being good to the multitude. Heaven is the dispenser of life and death, wealth and rank; therefore, a gentleman must learn to know the will of Heaven and submit to it patiently (154, 229). However, Confucius is unwilling to discourse on "the ways of Heaven" with his students (98, 126), probably due to his conviction that they were not ready for this subject. He once confessed that he came to understand Heaven's will quite late himself (76).

Confucius saw rites (*li* 禮) as an indicator of *dao* in a society. Rites were a sophisticated complex of social codes that signify what was valued most in Zhou society. They embody the total spectrum of social norms, customs, and mores, covering increasingly complicated relationships and institutions. The appropriate acts prescribed by the rites not only overlook ceremonial occasions, but also govern daily human interactions. Confucius praised the rites of the past, critiqued their practice in the present, and envisioned an ideal society of rites for the future. For example, when consulted about statesmanship, Confucius referred to ritualistic features of previous dynasties as ideal practices: "Introduce the calendar of the Xia dynasty, ride on the large yet plain chariot of the Yin, wear the ceremonial cap of the Zhou, and as for music, play the *shao* and *wu*. Abolish the 'music' from the state of Zheng" (*Analects* 1998, 187). State calendars, the chariot, the ceremonial cap, and music are all key features of state rites. In Confucius's view, certain ritualistic features in the antiquity perfectly embodied *dao*. Sound historical knowledge, thus, allows one to identify rites that were practiced in alignment with *dao*, and to employ them for state-making.

Due to the pivotal role that historical knowledge plays in practicing *dao*, Confucius portrayed himself as a cultural transmitter. Allegedly, he edited several ancient texts, which became the Confucian classics. These texts embody the knowledge of ancient Chinese history and tradition that Confucius believed a statesman should master. Thus, when one of his students quoted from the *Book of Songs* to elucidate the hardship of seeking out *dao*, Confucius was delighted. He remarked, "It is only with the likes of you then that I can discuss the *Songs*! On the basis of what has been said, you know that is yet to come" (*Analects* 1998, 75).

Emphasizing human history for ritualizing a gentleman and guiding state-making, Confucius adopted as an archetypical line of reasoning in his teaching. It works in this way: The past informs and guides the present. Something happened in the past because someone did or did not practice rites in the spirit of *dao*. Therefore, we need to practice rituals in accordance with *dao*, and peace and harmony will arrive. In the *Analects*, Confucius commented on historical figures and events numerous times with the intent to encourage his students to emulate the great deeds of certain figures and avoid the weaknesses of other figures.[3]

Confucian thinking on *dao* and human history was later revised by Dong Zhongshu and others. Harboring proclivities for Confucian thought, Emperor Wu of the Western Han invited Confucian literati to discuss state matters with him in 134 BCE through a network of genres: edicts, queries, and exam essays. One of those learned men was Dong Zhongshu, an adept of the *Spring and Autumn Annals* in the Gong-Yang interpretive lineage. In his three renowned responses to Emperor Wu's queries, he expounded political matters grounded in his exegesis of the *Annals*, asserting and expanding Confucius's view of history and state-making.

In developing his exam essays, Dong reinterpreted the *Annals*. Dong repositioned history as an archetypical topos by including Heaven as the most powerful interlocutor of *dao*. He concurred with Confucius that historical knowledge possesses ritualizing power for cultivating a righteous leader. He claimed, for example, that, as the *Documents* recorded previous kings' achievements, they would familiarize a leader with government affairs; he also claimed that since the *Annals* focused on telling apart righteous and wicked behaviors, they would teach a leader how to manage the masses in a morally proper manner (Dong 2016, 85). However, more emphatically than Confucius, Dong conceived human history as directly correlating to the Heavenly Mandate. Before Dong, Heaven was perceived in two vaguely related ways: as the tangible universe or sky filled with celestial bodies and as a metaphysical being which

Reading the Heavenly Mandate 59

could exercise influence over the human world. Different intellectual schools of the Warring States era each developed their own take on the nature of such influence. Drawing on Confucianism, Huang-Lao philosophy, and the Yin-Yang school,[4] Dong developed a theory of Heaven by assigning it multiple roles—a mediator between human and *dao*, a dispenser of *dao*, an arbiter of human affairs, and an interlocutor—in its interaction with the human world.

Dong invoked Heaven as a mediator between the humans and *dao*, asserting that Heaven, earth, and humans share the same origin (*yuan* 元), that is, *dao*. In human society, the king is the son of Heaven, supposedly representing and operating in *dao*. Hence, Dong suggested that the Chinese character for king (*wang* 王) consists of three horizontal stokes signifying Heaven, humans, and earth, with a vertical stroke signifying the king (Dong 2016, 399). On the one hand, the king needs to understand Heaven's will by studying history and the natural world and then enact this will in his human reign. On the other hand, if the king misunderstands Heaven's will and governs his people ruthlessly, Heaven will warn him with natural signs, punish him and his people with natural disasters, or even dethrone him. Thus, human society as led by the king was under the constant gaze of Heaven. The rise and fall of human history was framed by Dong as a result of obtaining or losing the Heavenly Mandate rather than as following or not following the appropriate rituals, as Confucius so emphasized.[5]

Dong invoked the new line of reasoning when answering Emperor Wu's queries during the court exam. On one occasion, the emperor asked Dong to elucidate one of his doubts in studying history: "[Some claim] that the teachings of the Three Kings differed in their origins and each had its failings. [Yet] others say that to endure without changing is the Way. How can these differences be explained?" (Dong 2016, 640). The emperor was most concerned about how to govern the empire in the true spirit of *dao*. While revealing his thoughts on human history, Dong's response equated Heaven as the dispenser of *dao*. Dong replied:

> The great source of the Way emanates from Heaven. Heaven does not change; the Way also does not change. Thus when Yu succeeded Shun and Shun succeeded Yao, these three sages received and safeguarded the same Way. There were no policies [needed] to repair flaws, and so there is no discussion of what they diminished and what they augmented. Looking at the issue from this perspective, for a ruler who succeeds a

Reading the Heavenly Mandate

well-governed age, the Way remains the same. For a ruler who succeeds a chaotic age, the Way changes. (Dong 2016, 640–41)

Like scholar-officials during the Warring State era, Dong draws on the legends of the early tribal leaders Yao, Shun, Yu and the myths of the Xia, Shang, and Zhou dynasties for his own political purpose.[6] He wants to affirm that the Han House followed the same lineage for ruling the Middle Kingdom and that, like previous dynasties, its ruler was chosen by Heaven. Repeatedly made by rulers during the Spring and Autumn and the Warring States periods,[7] the same political argument continued in the context of empire.

The heavy reliance on historical events and classical texts as the backing of Dong's exposition reveals his line of historical reasoning. The rise and fall of human history reflect the Heavenly Mandate and *dao*; therefore, what happened in the past can be a reference for the present and the future. As Dong claims in the passage, "The great source of the Way emanates from Heaven. Heaven does not change; the Way also does not change." In response to Emperor Wu's query, Dong also asked, "[The] empire of antiquity is no different from the empire of today, and the empire of today is no different from the empire of antiquity. Both are empires, but in antiquity the empire was immeasurably well ordered. . . . Measuring the past against the present, how far removed is the present from the past! How is it that we have arrived at such a state of insult and injury?" (Dong 2016, 641–42). In other words, the *dao* of Heaven does not change; therefore, the *dao* of the ancients can be studied and enacted in the present.

Dong positioned Heaven as the most powerful interlocutor in the discourse of *dao*. Confucius's discursive system chiefly involves three parties—the ritualized and learned gentleman, the ruler, and the masses. The gentleman and the ruler sometimes converge. The gentleman counsels the ruler on how to govern the state by conforming to *dao*, and the ruler tries to convince the masses about the legitimacy of his leadership through wise and humane governance and proper ritual performance. Confucius respected Heaven but excluded it as a major discursive participant. Dong ushered in Heaven not only as an overseer and a protector of humans, but also as an emotionally charged arbitrator of human affairs. In foregrounding a transcendent interlocutor with anthropomorphic qualities, Dong's discourse of *dao* departed from that of preimperial Confucians. Assigning Heaven anthropomorphic qualities, Dong shifted Confucian thinking from secularism to the realm of the divine.

Not only affirming Heaven's anthropomorphic qualities, Dong also infused into them Confucian morality. In his response to the emperor's inquiry, he agreed with the emperor that different phenomena are signs of Heaven's emotions and of His omnipotent power in both the natural and human realms. However, Heaven is not senseless; His emotions and ways of exercising power are both rational and ethical. As Dong explained,

> When a state is about to suffer a defeat because [the ruler] has strayed from the proper path. Heaven first sends forth disastrous and harmful [signs] to reprimand and warn him. If the [ruler] does not know to look into himself [in response], then Heaven again sends forth strange and bizarre [signs] to frighten and startle him. If he still does not know [that he should] change, only then will he suffer ruin and defeat. From this, we observe that Heaven's heart is humane and loving toward the people's ruler and that Heaven desires to keep him from chaos. (Dong 2016, 622)

While Dong confirmed these signs as being manifestations of Heaven's rationality, he read Heaven's various intents as originating from a benevolent heart. The Confucian school had long held that humans are born with pure, benevolent hearts. It is through the shared heart, which Dong assigned to Heaven, that humans can understand Heaven's values, emotions, and intents.

To explicate the intents of Heaven, Dong mobilized the concepts of *yin* and *yang*. They were used as classificatory terms up to the late Warring States era when scholars began to construe them as the primary pair of cosmological forces underlying natural processes. This transition is clearly shown in texts recently discovered by archaeologists and identified as belonging to the Huang-Lao School (Peerenboom 1993). Echoing this school, Dong explained Heaven's moral values and His strategic use of power as manifested in nature on the following terms:

> The most important aspect of Heaven's Way is yin and yang. Yang corresponds to beneficence; yin corresponds to punishment. Punishment presides over death; beneficence presides over life. Thus yang always takes up its position at the height of summer, taking engendering, nurturing, nourishing, and maturing as its tasks; yin always takes up its position at the height of winter, accumulating in empty, vacuous, and useless places. From this perspective, we see that Heaven relies on beneficence and does not rely on punishment. Heaven causes yang to emerge, circulate,

and operate above the ground to preside over the achievements of the year. Heaven causes yin to retire and prostrate itself below the ground, seasonally emerging to assist yang. If yang does not obtain yin's assistance, it cannot complete the year on its own. Ultimately, however, it is yang that is noted for completing the year. Such is Heaven's intent. (Dong 2016, 625; cf. Peerenboom 1993, 45–46)

Through the dialectics of *yin* and *yang*, Dong underscored Heaven's rationality, or the cosmic norms. The *dao* of Heaven governs the change of seasons. By observing how summer and winter alternate, as Dong suggested, one could understand Heaven's moral propensity and His preferred way of governing the world; He places virtue (*yang*) before punishment (*yin*) in order to nourish life. Heaven's intentions account for the assertion that Heaven loves, nurtures, and benefits all living things. Thus, as Sarah Queen states, "[Dong] read the location of yin and yang during a particular season, or the direction toward which they moved, as cosmological proof of Heaven's preference for virtue over punishment" (1996, 211). Through a Confucian reading of the natural signs, Dong ascribed Heaven a particular anthropomorphic quality, turning Heaven into a Confucian deity.

As Heaven shares a benevolent heart with humans, Dong believed that the two parties were able to communicate with each other. First of all, as an erudite of the *Spring and Autumn Annals*, Dong had been initiated into such an ontological frame early in his intellectual life. Chronicles like the *Annals* consist of notices that state ritual functionaries probably announced day by day, month by month, and year by year. As ancient historians carefully documented such state affairs as court divination, ceremony, and sacrifice, Queen posits, "the religious dimension of the *Spring and Autumn* exemplifies the ancient Chinese belief that communication between the human realm and that of Heaven was not only possible but essential to Chinese civilization" (1996, 117). With training in the *Annals*, Dong was familiar with the ritualistic means that previous kings had employed to communicate with Heaven. When he expounded his view of history to the emperor, for example, he quoted an event recorded in the *Annals* to show human-Heaven communications—when King Shun (舜, about twenty-first century BCE) was conferred his reign, he changed the first month of the calendar and the color of court dress to acknowledge the Heavenly Mandate (Dong 2016, 640). Therefore, Dong was concerned with the state rituals being performed appropriately because, first, they were institutionalized means of communication with Heaven, and second, appropriate performance of state rituals indicates an understanding of the Heavenly Mandate and acknowledges hierarchical relations between Heaven and His human subjects.

According to *Luxuriant Gems of the Spring and Autumn*, a collection of Dong's essays, Dong sought to institute two state rites to reflect the relationship between Heaven and humans. First, he suggested that the emperor offer sacrifice to Heaven once a year at the suburban altar and offer sacrifice four times a year at the ancestral temple and that the sacrifices at the ancestral temple follow the four seasons and the suburban sacrifice the beginning of the new year. Such a regimented schedule, according to Dong, is derived from the hierarchical relationship between Heaven and other minor deities. Heaven is the ruler of hundreds of Spirits, including the Spirits of deceased human ancestors. Heaven rules over His human subjects, dead or alive. Second, Dong suggested that upon being conferred the Heavenly Mandate, the emperor change state regulations (*gaizhi* 改制), as King Shun had done two thousand years before. The change of state regulations conveys to the supreme deity that His mandate has been received and will be enacted in the human realm.

To sustain such communication channels as the state rites, Dong argued at the end of his court exam essay that more exegetes of the Confucian classics be trained. Misled by other schools of thought, Dong suggests, previous rulers changed state regulations constantly, which confused the masses and failed to serve Heaven properly. Therefore, Dong believed that only by subscribing to the Confucian exegesis of Heaven and human history would the Han court avoid ritual transgressions (Dong 2016, 644). Thanks to Dong's eloquence, Emperor Wu took some of his suggestions and implemented a series of reforms, one of which established the imperial academy to promote Confucian thoughts and to recruit scholars to study the *dao* of Heaven and earth. The state sponsorship for the study of the "six arts" (the six classics) and other texts of the Confucian school fortified the network of circulation for these classical genres, which would be sources for arguments made to strengthen or to undermine the sovereign's legitimacy.

Counseling the Son of Heaven

Once the court exam was established to select scholars, it mobilized people, texts, and dialects across the empire.[8] As the edict of Emperor Wen reveals, the emperor ordered the executive offices in each kingdom and every commandery to recommend culturally and morally superior individuals. The order put officials to work. And for months, selected literati would travel thousands of *li* to congregate in the capital city. In the court exam in which Dong Zhongshu participated, he met with hundreds of literati like himself, one of them being Gongsun Hong (公孫弘), who later became a chancellor. Dong and Gongsun came from Zhao (趙) and Zichuan (菑川), respectively, two kingdoms a thousand *li* apart, and they found that many of the literati spoke distinct dialects.[9] When Gongsun ran the imperial academy, he petitioned Emperor Wu to expand enrollment. With the emperor's approval, an erudite (*boshi* 博士) of each classic was allowed to take on fifty students. By the end of Emperor Cheng's reign (33 BCE–7 CE), the enrollment number in the academy surpassed three thousand students (Ban 2007, 875–76). As the number of students increased, each of the classics developed several lineages, not only diversifying the exegeses of the text but also leading to debates and tensions between the lineages.

The court exam helped to solidify the meaning of the Heavenly Mandate. As explained earlier, Dong's discursive system involves four interlocutors—Heaven, the ruler, the scholar-officials, and the masses. The discourse is premised on the assumptions that Heaven is the most powerful deity and that the ruler is His hand-picked earthly son, and that history serves as a guide to reading Heaven and carrying out His mandate. Installed in the minds of the scholar-officials through the exam system, these assumptions formed the backbone of the numerous exam essays as well as officials' commentaries on natural anomalies and disasters archived in the dynastic histories of the Han.

While the exam essay was dialogical in form, with the emperor's queries interlaced with the scholar's responses, the commentary was monologic.[10] In their response to the emperor's queries on state-making, particularly after natural anomalies and disasters, the scholar-officials tended to follow a recognizable textual pattern. They start off with an elaborate opening, in which they reiterate the premises about history and the Heavenly Mandate. They recount historical anecdotes or cite the Confucian classics. Additionally, they may praise what the emperor has achieved in his reign or thank him for being willing to listen to an "unworthy" scholar-official. In this elaborate opening, the intention is unambiguous. The scholar-official hopes to establish the premises for their reasoning to come, to demonstrate that he understands the emperor's concern, which is the legitimacy of his reign in the eyes of Heaven.

Reading the Heavenly Mandate

Stating these premises, the scholar-officials submitted to the assertion that the Han ruler was the legitimate successor of the great ancient kings who reigned the Middle Kingdom.

In the commentaries submitted to the emperor, the scholar-officials made a variety of suggestions, nudging the emperor to take action. These suggestions are wide-ranging, including recruiting talents, reviewing the performance of government officials, adjusting laws and regulations, reducing capital punishment and other penalties, weakening the political power of eunuchs and the emperor's maternal family, and reigning in the emperor's indulgence with his concubines. In these suggestions, historical anecdotes are often evoked as examples to illustrate the consequences of following or not following the *dao*, and the classics are drawn as authoritative sources. The scholar-officials' calls for action tend to appear at the end of the commentaries.

While most commentaries were written in a soft tone, carefully leading the emperor toward the writer's points, there were exceptions. In these exceptions, the officials perceived crises with the government and felt compelled to evoke the legitimacy question. They called the ruler for self-examination and cultivation. For instance, in his four commentaries that are archived in the *BH*, Gu Yong (穀永) of the Western Han sounded exceptionally critical. In one of them composed in 15 CE, he offered his interpretation of a series of natural anomalies, including the appearance of a black dragon (snake). Gu opens the commentary by following a seemingly familiar pattern. He first underscores the need for the emperor to seek critical voices when the state faces a life-or-death situation, and he thanks him for being willing to listen. Then he draws on historical anecdotes and the Confucian classics to establish the premises of his criticisms to come, premises that he assumes the emperor would agree with. When articulating these premises, he identifies the crises the state faced and suggests their causes.

> Han follows the calendar of Xia, and Xia's state color is black. Thus, the black dragon is suggestive of the Han. Representing yang, a dragon grows from weak to strong. Thus, its appearance is a sign of Heavenly blessing. However, has any of the royal family members foreseen any celebration for the birth of heirs or spotted those who are plotting riots by taking advantage of the life-and-death situations the state is facing? Aren't there those who, cruel and vicious, coveted the throne like the former kings of Guangling and Changyi? Being unintelligent, I cannot make a wise

judgment on these matters. A black dragon appeared, the sky fell dark, and a solar eclipse occurred in September last year. A comet came and was followed by a solar eclipse in February this year. Four grand anomalies came within six months and two within the same month. This never happened even at the end of the reign of Yao, Shun, and Yu or during the tumultuous Spring and Autumn period. I have heard that the state built by Yao, Shun, and Yu collapsed due to the ruler's indulgence in drinking with women and the wicked. The *Documents* says, "Resorting to Dayi's counsel, the King of Shang seeks self-destruction rather than being punished by Heaven." "The King befriended criminals as confidants and employed them." The *Book of Songs* says, "The fires burning fiercely, who can put them off? The majestic capital of Zhou, Lady Bo Si destroyed it." The *Book of Changes* says, "He wets his head when drunk, thus losing the trust of others." Qin collapsed within sixteen years of its second emperor's reign because the rulers squandered resources before and after they died. Your Highness has suffered from all these lapses. Please allow me to elaborate each of them. (Ban 2007, 841)

The motive of this commentary would have become readily clear to the emperor. Gu capitalized on the occurrence of anomalies to criticize the ruler's governance. He first used two rhetorical questions to identify the state crises. He then draws on three classics and historical precedents concerning the state established by Yao, Shun, and Yu and the Qin dynasty to suggest causes for the crises. The emperor's shortcomings are thus identified: dependence on women's counsel, indulgence in drinking with the wicked, and squandering wealth. In what follows, Gu elaborates each of these issues and offers scathing criticisms.

Although criticizing the emperor's ruling was commonly seen in the commentaries on natural anomalies, Gu's candidness was almost unmatched among his peers. Like most officials composing such texts, he concluded his remonstration with a set expression: "I said what I am not supposed to say in my counsel, so I should be put to death ten thousand times." This is a consequence, however, that most scholar-officials would try to avert by being less candid and less critical. Gu's commentary, as the *BH* reveals, was composed at the invitation of the emperor's mother and uncles. They worried about the emperor on the matters that Gu commented on. As anticipated, the emperor was infuriated and demoted Gu, sending him back to his birthplace (Ban

2007, 842–43). Gu was not executed thanks to the strings that the emperor's maternal family pulled.

Gu's case reveals that commentaries could be easily used for a partisan agenda. The partisan nature of the commentaries on natural anomalies, or of the theories of the Heavenly Mandate, was critically commented on by several scholar-officials toward the end of the Western Han, including Zhang Yu (張禹), one of Gu's contemporaries. During Emperor Cheng's reign (33–7 BCE), court officials were discontented with the regency of a general, who was in connection with the emperor's maternal family. In their commentaries submitted to the emperor, they attributed the frequent natural anomalies to the general's control of the imperial court. Overwhelmed by these accusations, the emperor showed these commentaries to Zhang, seeking his advice on the natural anomalies. Afraid of the emperor's maternal family, Zhang disparaged those accusations as heresy.

> Within the two hundred and forty-two years the *Spring and Autumn* covers, more than thirty solar eclipses and five earthquakes were recorded. Dukes fought against each other, and foreign peoples invaded the Middle Kingdom. Natural anomalies and disasters are difficult to predict. Therefore, Confucius rarely commented on the Heavenly Mandate nor on ghosts and spirits. His students like Zhigong rarely commented on the Heavenly Mandate either, so how could the less-learned scholars now? Your Highness can adjust your governance and share Heavenly blessings with your subjects. This is the right thing to do. The newly minted scholars misled people with their wanton interpretation of *dao*. You should neither trust nor use them but make judgments based on the classics. (Ban 2007, 807)

After hearing Zhang's comments, the emperor ceased to worry about the maternal family's regency. Refuting the accusations made by other officials, Zhang won the favor of the regents. Zhang's case offers insights into the commentaries on natural anomalies in the Han. First, the commentaries not only served as a tool for deliberating on the ways to secure peace and order, but also a tool for brokering power in the imperial court. Second, while theories were developed by Confucian scholars to interpret the Heavenly Mandate in association with anomalies and disasters, some scholar-officials harbored deep doubts about these theories.

Expanding the Theory of Heaven-Human Relations

Doubts raised by Zhang and others were a natural response to the fact that commentaries on natural anomalies, or theories on reading the Heavenly Mandate, multiplied in the Han dynasty. These commentaries further perpetuated the ancient view of the world as transcendental, transactional, and translingual. In these epistemological endeavors, genre networks also expanded. First, texts of various intellectual schools were referenced and thus gained authority; second, exam essays and commentaries transmuted into other genres.

Theories are hypotheses about the reality built with arguments. Dong Zhongshu, who specialized in the *Spring and Autumn Annals*, drew historical anecdotes to develop his theory about Heaven as the ultimate arbiter of human affairs. Drawing on the *Annals*, the Yin-Yang school, and the theory of five phases (*wuxing* 五行), Dong and Liu Xiang, another Western Han scholar specialized in the *Annals*, invented systematic accounts for natural anomalies.[11] The five phases refer to five agents or processes called Wood (*mu* 木), Fire (*huo* 火), Earth (*tu* 土), Metal (*jing* 金), and Water (*shui* 水). They constitute a fivefold conceptual scheme that many traditional Chinese fields used to explain a wide array of phenomena, from cosmic cycles to the interaction between internal organs, and from the succession of political regimes to the properties of medicinal drugs. After the court exam, Dong Zhongshu submitted to the throne commentaries on disasters and anomalies, collected in the *Records of Disasters and Anomalies* (*Zaiyi zhiji* 災異之記). His commentaries were then selectively recorded in the *Treatise on Five Phases* (*Wuxing zhi* 五行志) in *BH* (Ban 2007, 216–78), together with Liu Xiang's the *Tradition of Hongfan Five Phases* (*Hongfan wuxing chuan* 洪範五行傳) and portent studies by Jing Fang (京房). In their treatises, Dong and Liu reviewed historical events and connected them to natural anomalies and disasters. They viewed these social and natural phenomena as having resulted from their interactions with one another based on the five phases theory.

Scholar-officials trained in other Confucian classics exploited these texts for their theories and arguments. After the *Annals*, the *Book of Changes* was the next most popular source for interpreting natural anomalies, especially in the Eastern Han. Some scholar-officials relied on the eight diagrams, the focus of the text, for divination. Each of the diagrams is supposed to represent an element of the universe: heaven, earth, wind, thunder, water, fire, mountain, and river. Each of the eight diagrams could be paired together to generate a total of sixty-four possible combinations. These combinations were used by the scholar-officials to predict natural and societal changes. In addition to the *Book of Changes*, scholars were also interested in astrology and mathematics. The movements of stars and the formation of constellations were used to explain or predict changes in the human realm.

The expanding theoretical apparatus was also joined by Buddhism. The religion entered the Central Plains, or the middle and lower reaches of the Yellow River, through the western territory in the beginning of the Eastern Han. When it spread among the learned in the early years, it was viewed as similar to the Huang-Lao school, advocating a laissez-faire approach toward life and politics. Its proposal of Nirvana and reincarnation appealed to both the emperor and his subjects. This new proposal was an argument for action: Life is suffering; suffering is caused by craving and aversion; suffering can be overcome and happiness (Nirvana) can be attained if one gives up useless craving and learns to live each day at a time (not dwelling in the past nor the imagined future). The path to achieve Nirvana is living a moral life, focusing the mind on being fully aware of one's thoughts and actions. The Buddhist moral code includes such precepts as: not taking the life of anything living, not taking anything that is not freely given, abstaining from sexual misconduct and sensual indulgence, refraining from untrue speech, and avoiding intoxication, that is, losing mindfulness (Ch'en 1964, 4–11).

To join the state-sponsored theoretical apparatus, the Buddhists resorted to traditional Chinese concepts and ideas to introduce their ontology, epistemology, and practice (Ren Jiyu 1985, 188–230). Responding to doubts raised by Confucians and the Daoists, they used *taisu* (太素) and *taishi* (太始) to explain the evolution of the universe. They suggested that the ultimate purpose of life is seeking the *dao*, specifically nonaction and living a simple life (*wuwei danbo* 無為淡泊) as Laozi had advocated. In doing so, they modified the original Buddhist goal of overcoming suffering and attaining Nirvana by means of giving up human desires. Some of the Buddhist moral code was introduced as noncontradictory to the Confucian code. For instance, abandoning family to become a monk was justified as not being against the spirit of filial piety, which was a hallmark of the Confucian code. Drawing on traditional ideas of spirits and ghosts, the Buddhists introduced the brand-new notion of reincarnation. Their audiences, including the emperors, were intrigued by the notion that, after death, they could return to another life if they had done good deeds in this life. Introduced to the elites on terms that were accessible and could satisfy their personal desires, Buddhism gradually won their favor.

In the Eastern Han, scholar-officials Su Jing (蘇竟), Yang Hou (楊厚), Lang Yi (郎顗), and Xiang Kai (襄楷) were known for being skilled in drawing on the expanding theoretical apparatus. In two commentaries submitted to Emperor Shun in 133 CE, for instance, Lang Yi proposed eleven reforms. He drew on the Confucian classics, most heavily on the *Book of Changes*. In two commentaries submitted to Emperor Heng in 166 CE, Xiang Kai developed lines of reasoning based on astrology, mathematics, the Huang-Lao school, and Buddhism. In one of the commentaries, for instance, he first draws on astrology and mathematics to argue that a large number of lawsuits have been processed unjustly and need to be corrected (Fan 2007, 319). In building his argument, Xiang presents the movements of three celestial bodies, Venus, Mars, and Jupiter, as his primary evidence for reading the Heavenly will. What provides the premise for his line of reasoning was the *santong* (三統) calendar popularized in the Eastern Han. The calendar enabled one to calculate dates, seasons, and years based on the movements of sun, moon, Mercury, Venus, Mars, Jupiter, and Saturn. Using his calendrical knowledge, Xiang calculated the movement of Mars and asserted that it should have appeared in the sky. However, the movements of the stars were also used for divination by the school of Huang-Lao. Its followers personified each of the five stars with certain moral propensities, and they viewed the stars' appearance or movement as signifying particular natural or societal tendencies. Xiang's reasoning is built exactly on these assumptions: Venus and Mars stand for warnings for battles, plotting, or unjust lawsuits, while Jupiter signs of law-abiding and Heavenly blessings.

In building his proposals for the emperor, next Xiang drew on the Huang-Lao school and Buddhism for criticizing the emperor's sensual indulgence. He fuses the two schools of thought in ideals, argument, and language. He consolidates their ideals into the single notion of *dao* and introduces it as the premise of his reasoning up front. In actuality, while the Huang-Lao school promotes quietism and favors nonaction, Buddhism detests killings and abhors indulgence in sensual desires. As his reasoning unfolds, Xiang draws heavily on Buddhist thinking to condemn the emperor for excessive use of his legal authority and his sensual indulgence, behaviors that are abhorred by Heaven. In developing this line of reasoning, he borrows a Buddhist claim. When Buddhism was first introduced into the Middle Kingdom, its believers devised a strategy to recruit nonbelievers. Couching Buddhist teaching on the thoughts of the Huang-Lao school, they claimed Buddhism was developed by Laozi. Marginalized in the Eastern Han society due to the dominance of Confucianism, the followers of the Huang-Lao school did not openly reject this claim but found the Buddhists a palatable ally. This claim was appropriated by Xiang when he nodded to the legend that Laozi went westward and became the Buddha. The conflation of the two schools of thought also manifests in the language that Xiang used. He borrowed terms typically used in the Huang-Lao school when he introduced the Buddhist teaching. For instance, he says, "Guarding his natural self (*shouyi* 守一) like this, Buddha found the true *dao* (道)" (Fan 2007, 320). Both *shouyi* and *dao* were originally Daoist terms. *Shouyi* refers to the idea that one guards one's natural self and lives a quiet life. In contrast, in Buddhist discourse it means that one focuses on Buddhist teaching in one's meditation.

Political Participation, Self-Cultivation, and Government

While the genre events examined thus far took place in the court, the genre networks reached the peripheries of the empire. In addition to shoring up an expanding theoretical apparatus to account for Heaven-human relations, the networks led to lasting policy impact.

These genre networks enabled the establishment of Confucian academies across the empire and widened political participation. In the capital city and in the kingdoms, the princes were instructed by erudites of the classics. Several emperors, such as Zhao, Xuan, and Yuan, became scholars of the classics themselves and active promoters of Confucian education.[12] In the reign of Emperor Ping (1–6 CE) in the Western Han, state-sponsored academies were established in commanderies and kingdoms; a master of the *Book of Piety* was installed in village schools and a master of the classics in county schools (Ban 2007, 91). To staff these academies, the government sought masters of astrology, calendars, technologies, medicine, the Confucian classics, the *Analects*, and the *Book of Piety* throughout the empire; several thousand literati were identified by local officials as being qualified and were dispatched to the capital city (Ban 2007, 92). The propagation of the academies helped to produce a large cadre of literati; many of them went on to serve in government offices.

Discourses on the natural anomalies and disasters also prompted self-examination and cultivation in the governing body. In almost every edict that was issued ensuing a natural anomaly or disaster, the emperor would express his fear of Heavenly warnings. Consequently, an emperor sought to examine his governance by requesting that officials submit confidential memorials to point out his negligence. Further, he required that officials throughout the empire review their administrative work and correct any unfairly tried cases; sometimes he sent supervisory envoys to evaluate local officials (Fan 2007, 13). He promoted Confucian moral values by requesting officials to identify and award paragons of virtue in counties and villages.

These genre networks sometimes led to the lessening of the commoners' legal and agricultural burdens. To appease Heavenly "rage" and to demonstrate his benevolence, the emperor would issue executive orders to assist those affected by natural disasters. In response to a severe earthquake that took place in 46 CE, for instance, Emperor Guangwu issued an edict offering a series of relief measures: the affected commandery be waived of agricultural taxes; individuals convicted of the death penalty before the quake have their penalty reduced by one grade; other convicts be unbounded; those who were killed by the quake be buried with government funds; those who still owned taxes but whose houses were damaged be tax exempt; and those who were buried in collapsed walls and houses be retrieved with government funds (Fan 2007, 20). In the epigraph of this chapter, Emperor Guangwu is cited as admitting his negligence and expressing his repentance. His expressions of fear and sorrow turned into policies, which enabled the commoners to experience the imperial power and hailed them into being imperial subjects.

As a historiographic emphasis, archiving genre networks centering on natural anomalies and disasters served both administrative and epistemic functions. The dynastic historians typically placed edicts in the biographies of rulers, and exam essays and commentaries in the biographies of officials. This could be a bibliographic strategy used by court historians to archive the words and deeds of the ruler and his officials. Working in the office of the minister of ceremony and the imperial libraries, their duty involved sorting, labeling, and shelving documents. For Sima Qian and Ban Gu, who invented and fortified this historiographic approach, archiving the genre networks on natural anomalies allowed them to continue promulgating a spirit of the *Spring and Autumn Annals*. That is, political events and natural anomalies were not only connected but could provide crucial knowledge for government.

The epistemology espoused by these genre networks helped to forestall bloodshed in otherwise dangerous power transitions. There were two peaceful transitions in the Han dynasty: Wang Mang (王莽) usurped power at the end of the Western Han and Cao Pi (曹丕) at the end of the Eastern Han. In both transitions, the incumbent and the successor encouraged officials to construct arguments drawing on prophetic texts, auspicious omens, and new interpretations of the classics. Their arguments suggested that the Heavenly Mandate for the Liu clan had expired and been transferred to the Wang or the Cao clan. These arguments were made, again, through genre networks, which led to elaborate ceremonies of abdication and accession.[13]

Conclusion

Dao was foundational in ancient Chinese epistemology. Literati, represented by the hundred schools of thought in the Spring and Autumn and the Warring States periods, had long debated its meanings and ways to practice it properly in the human realm (Graham 1989). *Dao* was also the concern of the emperors because of its promise to provide answers to the legitimacy question. As the son of Heaven, they felt the urge to understand Heaven and the need to grasp the Heaven-approved *dao* to govern their subjects. From the very beginning of the Han dynasty, the emperors recruited the assistance of Confucian scholars to decipher the will of Heaven. Dong Zhongshu offered his theory of reading the Heavenly Mandate, which effectively transposed Confucianism from the secular to the divine. In his theory, Heaven gains human attributes and becomes a deity. Confucian scholars that came after him continued to expand the theoretical apparatus, solidifying a metaphysical order of the empire.

While previous scholarship has examined ancient Chinese discourse of *dao* taking place in a manuscript culture, this chapter highlights state-sponsored genre networks in engineering this discourse for imperial government. Recruiting Confucian scholars to read the Heavenly Mandate gave rise to edicts, queries, exam essays, and commentaries on natural anomalies and disasters. Together, these texts worked to form genre networks involving the emperor, the scholar-officials, Heaven, and the masses. Puzzled by natural anomalies and disasters allegedly orchestrated by Heaven, the emperor would voice his concerns in cabinet meetings and then through edicts. The scholar-officials answered his concerns by offering their readings of Heaven as well as of the masses. These texts joined a network of human and nonhuman actors to stabilize or destabilize the empire. They also directed scholars who aspired for civil service to Confucian academies for education and propagated them to the state capital. In their exam essays and commentaries, they directed the emperor's attention to areas of his weaknesses, ultimately leading to enlarged political participation, an improved governing body, and humane treatment of the commoners.

CHAPTER 3

Regulating the Inner Court

The *yin* overpowered the *yang*, causing solar eclipses. Is this not a sign that the inferior has offended the superior, the wife bullied the husband, or a base person superseded a noble person? 夫以陰而侵陽, 虧其正體, 是非下陵上, 妻乘夫, 賤逾貴之變與?

—Emperor Cheng

In addition to self-examination, the legitimacy question forced the Han rulers to regulate their own house, recognizing that this was inseparable from the ruling of the state. A series of discourses were recorded in the dynastic histories, especially since Emperor Cheng's reign (33–7 BCE), with an unequivocal emphasis on regulating the inner court, or the harem. In memorials submitted to the sovereign, for instance, officials such as Gu Yong and Liu Xiang identified various social and natural woes and attributed them to the unruly court ladies. They urged the emperor to refrain from indulgence with concubines and to regulate the inner court. Emperor Cheng responded by issuing an edict to the empress, trying to rein in the harem's extravagant spending and encouraging court ladies to pursue proper womanly conduct. The empress protested and defended her governance in a memorial (Ban 2007, 993–94).

In these men's efforts to control the elite women, they made double moves in correlative thinking—framing gender relations with the *yin-yang* theory and connecting natural anomalies, disasters, and social woes to the allegedly unruly conduct of women in the royal family—to establish a gender hierarchy. In discussing gender identities, they inherited a *yin-yang* theory from Dong Zhongshu. According to Robin R. Wang (2005), Dong remolded and impoverished the theory in two ways, with far-reaching impact on gender relations in imperial China. First, while earlier the theory had placed emphasis on the harmony of *yin* and *yang* as vital energies or attributes of matters in constant interaction, Dong placed *yin* and *yang* in an imposed unity, thus requiring an order of the two. Second, Dong interpreted human nature in terms of *yin* and *yang* by identifying *yang* with human nature and benevolence and *yin* with emotion and greed. This *yin-yang* division helped to reconcile earlier debates concerning the good and bad aspects of human nature. However, by establishing *yang* as masculine and *yin* as feminine, the division also ended up serving as the justification for disparaging womanly character and virtues and the need for male domination. This reformulated *yin-yang* theory would shadow and be fortified by genre networks dealing with gender relations starting from Emperor Cheng's reign.

The instances of blaming women for natural anomalies and disasters were spurred by two peculiar events. First, solar eclipses occurred frequently during Emperor Cheng's reign. In Liu Xiang's study of astrological records, on average, an eclipse occurred every three years and one month during Emperor Jing's reign (157–141 BCE) but every two and half years during Emperor Cheng's reign (Ban 2007, 405). Second, Emperor Cheng lost several heirs due to natural or human causes, an issue that deeply concerned the royal family. These rather unusual events prompted court officials to speculate what these events insinuated. Some, such as Liu Xiang, took the opportunity to criticize the regency of General Wang, the brother of the empress dowager, suggesting that astrological aberrations and natural disasters were heavenly warnings about the ruler's improper use of officials. Others, such as Gu Yong, who were afraid of General Wang, attributed the natural anomalies to the unruly conduct of the court ladies. Responding to the empress's protest, Emperor Cheng issued a second edict, in which he adopted Gu's interpretative frame. In the beginning of his response, cited in the epigraph of this chapter, the emperor made two rhetorical moves: he framed gender relations in *yin-yang*, and he inferred that solar eclipses were caused by the unruly court ladies.

This chapter will trace the discourses, as performed in genre networks, on regulating the inner court in the Han. The inner court refers to the living quarters designated for the imperial consorts and their support staff; by extension, it signifies the domestic sphere traditionally relegated to elite women. While the narrative of progress of civilization and religion growing out of European imperialism has erased women's voices (Binkley 2009, 80), as a decolonial move, this chapter seeks to demonstrate that women's voices were also marginalized if not completely erased by men in early Chinese imperialism. I will first examine the efforts of elite men in the late Western Han, including Emperor Cheng's second edict responding to the empress's protest and Liu Xiang's compilation of women's biographies. Drawing on the classics, these men endeavored to establish legal and moral codes for the court ladies. Next, the elite women's voices will be considered, focusing on the edicts issued by two empress dowagers of the Eastern Han, who ruled the state on behalf of junior emperors. These edicts reveal their own philosophy and approach to regulating the inner court, particularly the emperor's maternal family. Finally, I will examine the genre events in which Ban Zhao, one of the court ladies, participated to understand further what role an elite woman outside the immediate royal family could play in the Han rulership. Although the dynastic histories portrayed these eminent women from a Confucian male perspective, their genre activities demonstrate their variegated ways of negotiating patriarchy and gaining political power. The following are the key discourses concerning the inner court to be examined in this chapter (see table 3.1).

Men's Efforts in Limiting the Powers of the Imperial Consorts

Emperor Cheng's edicts on the inner court, with their legal authority, came at the end of a genre chain which spanned across physical and political spaces. In 30 BCE, after a solar eclipse and an earthquake, the emperor issued an edict calling for culturally and morally cultivated scholars to advise him on these natural anomalies (Ban 2007, 77–78). In the ensuing court exam, Gu Yong proposed in his essay that natural anomalies were signs of the untamed ladies in the inner court. As the emperor indulged in the concubines, Gu observed, the ladies were emboldened to trespass the code of womanly conduct and vied for the sovereign's favor. Once they gained favor, they demanded more, leading to interference with government beyond the inner court (Ban 2007, 837–38). In several commentaries Gu submitted later, he continued to associate natural anomalies with the "moral degradation" of the court ladies. Influenced by Gu and others, the emperor issued an edict addressing Empress Xu, the head of the harem, demanding that she reduce spending and respect the ritual practice prescribed to court ladies. Dispatched from the emperor's palace, the edict arrived at the hands of *Dachangqiu* (大長秋), the chief of staff in the empress's

TABLE 3.1 *Key Discourses Concerning the Inner Court*

Author	Discourse
Gu Yong 穀永	A court exam essay on regulating the imperial consorts (29 BCE)
Emperor Cheng 成帝	Two edicts warning Empress Xu on her governance of the harem
Empress Xu 許皇后	A memorial protesting to Emperor Cheng and defending her governance of the harem
Liu Xiang 劉向	*Biographies of Eminent Women* (20 BCE)
Empress Dowager Ma 馬皇太后	Four edicts on according her brothers noble titles (77–81 CE)
Empress Dowager Deng 鄧皇太后	An edict requesting officials to guard against her family members meddling in government matters (106 CE) An edict addressing her brothers on the importance of a classical education for the ruling class (119 CE)
Ban Zhao 班昭	Rhapsody "A Bird from the Far West" A memorial on her brother's retirement (101 CE) "Treatise on Astrology" (102 CE) "Lessons for Women" (106 CE) A memorial on Empress Dowager Deng's brothers' retirement

palace, before reaching the target reader. The empress protested, arguing in a memorial called *shu* (疏) that her spending was measured. In the end, the emperor issued another edict to explicate his reprimand, legally establishing the code of conduct for the court ladies. This genre chain, thus, enjoined two discrete physical and political spaces occupied by both male and female actors.

In the second edict, the emperor first reasserted both his supreme power on earth and the correlative thinking connecting natural anomalies with the inner court. The emperor opens his edict, as quoted in the epigraph, by adopting the theory of the Heavenly Mandate developed earlier by Confucian scholars and reintroducing it to a specific domain of government: the inner court. He enumerates a series of natural anomalies: the aberrant movements of the stars and constellations, the collapse of levies on the Yellow River, the incineration of bird nests in the Mount Tai area, and high winds causing severe damage to royal ancestral temples. As the other domains of government were peaceful, the emperor concludes, these natural anomalies must have implicated the unruly harem.

Next, drawing on the classics, such as the *Documents*, the *Odes*, and the *Analects*, the emperor introduced a series of premises for reforming the inner court. For example, when early rulers responded to natural anomalies with government reforms, the anomalies would disappear. Only when abiding by the laws and regulations would the womanly virtues prevail. And laws and regulations from the previous emperors form the core foundation of government for the present. The emperor then concludes by underscoring the need to abide by the rules established for the inner court and for pursuing womanly virtues. In light of the classics the emperor referenced, the rules established for women refer to the three types of obedience (三從) and four womanly virtues (四德) that are stipulated in conduct books, such as the *Record of Rites* (禮記) and the *Rites of Zhou* (周禮). In terms of the three types of obedience, a woman needs to obey her father before marriage, her husband during a marriage, and her son after her husband passes away. According to the four womanly virtues, a woman needs to strengthen her moral character, speak properly, behave appropriately, and manage the household well. In the edict, the empress was instructed to show obedience to the emperor and his mother, and to establish herself as a model among the concubines by performing the four womanly virtues. As the two edicts were the only ones recorded in the *BH* on regulating the inner court, it can be inferred that they were among the essential legal documents on this matter.[1]

The genre chain that led to the two edicts reveals a rising literacy level among elite women. Among the accounts of the empresses, Empress Xu was the first one who was noted as being intelligent and versed in the classics (Ban 2007, 993). The memorial defending her governance of the harem was the first written text by a woman archived in the *BH*. Her defense was cogent, with every one of her points supported with evidence. There was a notable stylistic difference, though, between her text and those of the men: she did not include any citations from the classics, a feature observable in texts by other empresses and empress dowagers archived in Han histories. This stylistic feature signifies a distance that she managed to maintain between two political positions that characterized court politics in her time: the Machiavellian cunning of some court ladies and the Confucian conformism of others.[2] After the state had championed the study of classics, the rise of the literacy level among a small group of elite women did not come as a surprise. Literacy enabled them to wrestle with the powerful and mark their gendered and, in the case of Empress Xu, political voice.

Women's improved literacy levels also encouraged men to invent new ways to regulate the inner court. Liu Xiang, who was also interested in interpreting natural anomalies, agreed with Gu Yong that the court ladies must be tamed according to the established moral and ritual code. When working in the royal libraries, around 20 BCE, he compiled several dozen stories of women for the sovereign and the court ladies. Inspired by the biographic genre invented by Sima Qian in history writing, he titled his book *Biographies of Eminent Women* (*Lienü zhuan* 列女傳).[3] Two key features of this text clearly made it a supplement to Emperor Cheng's edicts that worked toward regulating the inner court. First, the book divided the biographies into seven categories based on Confucian moral values. In biographies belonging to six of the seven categories, the women described therein represent praiseworthy values: the maternal models (*muyi* 母儀), the worthy and enlightened (*xianming* 賢明), the sympathetic and wise (*renzhi* 仁智), the chaste and compliant (*zhenshun* 貞順), the principled and righteous (*jieyi* 節義), and the accomplished rhetoricians (*biantong* 辯通). One category, the depraved and favored (*niebi* 孽嬖), is filled with biographies illustrative of damning values. Second, the text includes a verse from the *Odes* at the end of each biography, which echoes with the story in theme or in values according to the dominant Confucian exegesis of the *Odes* at that time. The unifying theme of these biographies can thus be understood with reference to what Anne Behnke Kinney terms "dynastics," an ideology for reinforcing habits of deference to a family-based hierarchy, such as in the family, political unit, state, and dynasty, for its ongoing continuity and prestige (2014, xxiv).

While the *Biographies of Eminent Women* was created for taming court ladies, it also introduced a model for writing women into history with developed characters and voices. For instance, the *BH* contains one stand-alone biography for an empress in addition to a number of biographies of empresses clustered under "Memoires of Maternal Families" (外戚傳). In the *BLH*, there were both "Annals of the Empresses" (皇后紀) and "Biographies of Eminent Women" (列女傳). As these biographies were written by men, the female characters and their voices were selected and mediated to represent imperial, Confucian, and male perspectives. Still, thanks to these biographies, we now have access to and can turn to women's voices.

Regulating the Inner Court

Empress Dowagers' Voices in Governing the Inner Court

In the Eastern Han, six empress dowagers served as regent because the sovereign was a minor. Two of them, Empress Dowagers Ma (39–79 CE) and Deng (81–121 CE), received elaborate accounts in the *BLH*. They did so because they each were in power for more than two decades and made tremendous efforts in ruling the state. But more importantly, in the view of the author of the *BLH*, Fan Ye, they served as the paragons of virtue for other court ladies and reined in the political influence of the emperor's maternal family—a success hardly achieved by the emperors themselves. Emperor Cheng, for example, afraid of the maternal family, only issued edicts to regulate the harem. As regents, these empress dowagers shuttled between the inner court and the emperor's palace, where they received officials' briefings and issued imperial edicts, a genre traditionally belonging to the emperor. Their efforts in regulating the inner court were dramatized by chains of carefully cited oral and written discourses. By contrast, their achievements in executive and judicial work in the outer court were narrated sparsely without the corroboration of any original documents.

Empress Dowager Ma was portrayed as an intelligent and literate woman interested in government. Born into a noble family, she demonstrated her ability in managing the domestic economy "like an adult" when she was ten. She "was able to recite the *Book of Changes*, enjoyed reading the *Spring and Autumn Annals*, and was especially familiar with the *Rites of Zhou* and Dong Zhongshu's *Luxuriant Gems of the Spring and Autumn*" (Fan 2007, 118). When serving in Emperor Ming's palace, she was often invited to deliberate on executive, judicial, and military matters. "When generals submitted reports or the ministers disagreed over complicated matters, the emperor forwarded these matters to the empress to test her ability. Her analysis and interpretation were always logical and clear, and the matters were judicated fairly" (Fan 2007, 119). After the emperor died, she continued to discuss state matters with the new emperor.

The empress dowager's rule of the inner court, particularly of her own family, was administered through a series of imperial edicts, in which she argued against according her brothers noble titles. The argument started when the young emperor wanted to bestow his uncles titles upon his ascension to the throne in 76 CE. The empress dowager rejected the idea. The

82   *Regulating the Inner Court*

following summer saw a severe drought; some officials suggested that it was a heavenly reprimand because the uncles were not titled. The empress dowager issued the first edict defending her decision. Her defense starts by exposing the problematic reasoning among the officials and the danger of bestowing titles to the maternal uncles. "Those who proposed according honor titles only coveted favor from me. Emperor Cheng once accorded five marquis titles to the Wang family, but yellow fog formed without the much-needed auspicious rain. Or upon gaining favor from Emperor Wu, his uncles Tian Fen and Dou Ying became ruthless, causing the demise of their families. Their story has become a well-known lesson. Therefore, cautious with his maternal uncles, the former emperor did not place them in vital government positions" (Fan 2007, 119). The empress dowager drew on historical precedents to challenge the officials' interpretation of the drought, hence undermining their correlative logic. Further, as her historical thinking went, according titles might not be auspicious to the maternal family in the end. She not only explained restricting her bothers' access to political power, but in the second part of the edict, the empress dowager also explained the ways she encouraged her family to refrain from excess desires and spending: she dressed herself and her servants coarsely to serve as a model for the inner court, and curtailed appropriations for her parents' house. While countering the officials with her rationalism, she stressed her embodied rhetoric among court ladies and mothers.

In the next two edicts, speaking to the emperor, the empress dowager portrays herself as a mother who is more concerned about the welfare of the state than that of her family. After she issued the initial edict, the emperor still persisted. She declined the offer with her second edict. Four years later, the matter was brought up again, and she issued her third edict. In these commands, she underscores the deep connections between the inner court, the maternal family, and the state. In her second edict, for instance, she rejects the emperor's offer by first pointing out that the maternal family has already enjoyed privileges without making a significant contribution to the state. Then, speaking as the first mother of the state, she educates the young sovereign about filial piety in rulership:

> The utmost filial act is ensuring the safety of the family. Our people have suffered multiple natural disasters, and the grain price has gone up several folds, a crisis that has deeply worried me. Bestowing honor titles

Regulating the Inner Court   83

amidst the crisis works against the heart of a caring mother. I have an upright and impetuous temperament. When *qi* gathers in my heart it must be scattered. Only after the *yin* and the *yang* forces are rebalanced and our borders regain peace, can you go back to practice filial piety as a son. (Fan 2007, 120)

In this statement, the empress dowager underscores her identity as the head of the state, who is deeply concerned about the people suffering from natural disasters. In the meantime, she took the opportunity to educate the emperor about filial piety, a key Confucian value. She highlighted for the emperor his multiple identities and asserted that the identity of son of Heaven ought to come before all others. As ruler of the state, he should place the welfare of his people ahead of that of the royal family.

Like Empress Dowager Ma, Deng was portrayed as a well-educated court lady who closely followed established rules for the harem. She started reading when she was six years old and was conversant with the *Odes* and the *Analects* when she was twelve. When her brothers read aloud from the classics, she always consulted them on difficult questions (Fan 2007, 122). After she was chosen as one of the emperor's concubines, she observed the palace codes closely, treating the emperor and the empress with humility and all other people with respect. Recognized by many as a woman of great virtue, after the empress was demoted, she was named as her successor. After the emperor died, she became the regent. During her reign, she participated in the judgment of hundreds of legal cases and issued numerous edicts.

However, each of the few edicts quoted at length in the *BLH* deals with the inner court and royal families. For example, as she was deeply involved in judging legal cases, the empress dowager was wary of her family members meddling in government matters. In 106 CE, she issued an edict requesting commandery governors and law enforcement officials to guard against those individuals.

Every time I reviewed records of my family visitors in the former emperor's reign, I saw that leveraging their connections with the court, some spoke frivolously and intervened in government procedures, acts causing great pains in the people. The law enforcers should be held accountable because they were lax and did not administer punishments according to the law. Although General Deng Lu was respectful of the law, he has grown a large family with many in-laws. Cunning and treacherous, many of the family relatives have broken the law. You must examine their cases carefully and refrain from leniency. (Fan 2007, 124)

Issuing the warning as an edict, the empress dowager acknowledged family members meddling with government affairs as a serious issue. In humiliating her own family in public, she not only tried to prevent family members from committing further wrongs, but also, more importantly, upheld the supreme power of laws and regulations in governing the family and the state.

In addition to laws and regulations, Empress Dowager Deng emphasized self-cultivation and education in governing the inner court. After she entered the harem, she studied classics, math, and astronomy with Ban Zhao, a learned court lady. She called upon several dozen scholars to collate the classics stored in the royal libraries and to correct errors in them. She asked court officials to study the classics and to teach them to the court servants (Fan 2007, 124). She gathered in the capital city more than seventy children from the royal families and provided them with instruction on the classics. In an edict issued to her brothers in 119 CE, she explains the need to promote the classics among the ruling class, echoing arguments made by Confucian scholars on the political significance of these ancient texts: "Influenced by the pernicious effects of poor government in the past, people became frivolous and treacherous and studies on the five classics declined. Without proper guidance, society will fall into further decadence. Therefore, I want to promote the sagely way to rectify these social woes" (Fan 2007, 125).

With their sensitivity as both rulers and mothers, the two empress dowagers recontextualized Confucian values in their rulership. They employed edicts to elaborate their thinking on the relationship between family and state and established new rules for governing them. In repeatedly refusing to bestow honor titles to her brothers, Ma encouraged members of the inner court to examine their assumptions and deportment against the established moral code; and she educated the new emperor about what filial piety meant for a son when ruling a state. In criticizing her family members for meddling in government matters, Deng toed a fine line between family and state, and underscored the supreme power of laws and regulations in governing both. Well-educated in the classics, both women viewed education through the classics as key to cultivating the ruling class. Thus, in their unique ways, the two women contributed to empire building by strengthening the Confucian value system.

Regulating the Inner Court   85

In developing memoires of the emperors' maternal families and of the empresses, a new genre at the time, the dynastic historians intended to offer the future ruling class moral lessons. The author of the *BH*, for instance, concluded the "Memoires of Maternal Families" by lamenting the demise or dislocation of most of the maternal families in the end (Ban 2007, 1005). Archiving the discourses that led to Emperor Cheng's two edicts thus helped to highlight the need for establishing regulations for the harem to avoid such tragedies. Similarly, in discussing the character of Empress Dowager Deng and archiving her edicts, the author of the *BLH* criticized her for usurping power from the young emperor, an act he viewed as unintelligent. In the meantime, with ambivalence, he acknowledged the fact that the empress dowager conducted her ruling tirelessly for the benefit of her people (Fan 2007, 126). Despite such ambivalence, these imperial, male perspectives nevertheless brought to light another court lady, Ban Zhao, in the "Biographies of Eminent Women" in the *BLH*. She contributed to the imperial governance as an erudite, an official, and a mother.

Ban Zhao on the Heavenly Mandate and Government

Ban Zhao (班昭 45 CE–117) came from a wealthy and educated family with many ties to the royal family. Her great-aunt, Ban Jieyü, was one of Emperor Cheng's concubines. One of her great-uncles, Ban Yu, collaborated with Liu Xiang in editing and cataloging books in the royal libraries. Her father, Ban Biao, served as an adviser and military officer under the person who later became Emperor Guangwu. Her brother Ban Gu was assigned by Emperor He to compile the *BH*. When Ban Gu died in 102 CE, the sovereign asked her to complete the work. Ban also tutored Empress Deng and other court ladies. After Emperor He died in 105 CE, Empress Deng became regent and Ban was constantly at her side to provide counsel for fifteen years. Ban's well-known conduct book, *Lessons for Women*, was either written or published in 106 CE, which was the beginning of her counsel for the regent.

Like how the two empress dowagers were treated in the dynastic history, only Ban's writings dealing with the domestic sphere were archived by Fan Ye. However, Ban had a strong presence in traditionally male domains, or the outer court, as demonstrated by the genres she practiced. Among her surviving pieces, the "Treatise on Astrology" (*Tianwen zhi* 天文志), as part of the *BH*, represents her history writing. In addition, Ban ventured into other political genres: *fu* 賦 (rhapsody), *song* 頌 (commemorative writing), *ming* 銘 (inscription), *lei* 誄 (eulogy), *wen* 問 (query), *zhu* 注 (annotation), *aici* 哀辭 (elegy), *shu* 書 (letter or argument), *lun* 論 (commentary), *shangshu* 上疏 (memorial), and *yiling* 遺令 (will or final instruction) (Fan 2007, 821). Among them, *ming* and *shangshu* were always used on political occasions, from which women were supposed to absent themselves. *Ming* is usually composed to praise the achievements of the state or of individuals in ceremonies. *Shangshu* refers to memorials submitted to the ruler. Other genres, commonly used by educated men, often deal with political matters as well. Writing in these genres demonstrated Ban's involvement in the outer court, an involvement that Fan did not value. To restore Ban's voice, thus, we must examine her genre activities in both the inner and the outer court.

Composing the astrological treatise allowed Ban Zhao to join the discourse on the Heavenly Mandate. She addresses the Mandate, omens, and auguries through her reworking of Sima Qian's "Treatise on the Heavens" in the *GSR*. According to traditional Chinese astrology, there were twenty-eight constellations in the sky, matching twelve ancient Chinese states on earth. By observing the movement of stars in a constellation, an astrologist could prophesize political events about to happen in a state. In his astrological treatise, Sima first introduces the constellations, planets, and stars and what their movements portended on earth. Next, he briefly discusses some astrological observations made in the past and presumably correlated political events until the early Han dynasty. Two centuries later, Ban extensively revised Sima's text in several major aspects, speaking subversively in an imbalanced gender power structure.

First, instead of delving directly into the constellations, Ban offers an overview of astrology, introducing widely accepted beliefs on astrology and government. She writes in a somber, restrained, and factual tone, presenting the astrological and ontological beliefs of the Han period as a given. By contrast, Sima extensively comments on the relationship between astrological observations and the ruling of a state in the end of his text. He openly admonishes the emperor to govern with benevolence. The two authors' messages and their language can be compared. Sima concludes his treatise as follows:

> The ruler should cultivate benevolence after a solar eclipse, reassess his retributive practice after a lunar eclipse, and seek harmony inside and outside the state when stars show anomalies. When celestial objects move anomalously, one will practice divination. When a ruler is great

Regulating the Inner Court   87

and virtuous, the state will prevail; when he is weak and mean, the state will go into extinction. A ruler should foremost cultivate his benevolence and then improve his governance. After perceiving his errors, he should make amendments. Or worse, only after natural disasters will he appeal to Heaven for mercy. In the worst case, he totally ignores the problems. (Sima 2006, 162)

In this passage, Sima assumes a moral high ground by taking on a pedantic, uncompromising tone. Placing the ruler in the center of his admonition, he warns the ruler by listing a series of possible celestial anomalies that the latter should heed. His gesture resembles that of Confucius and Dong Zhongshu, who both harbor a deep trust in the antiquity and the natural signs for their ability to teach the ruler about the Heavenly Mandate, humility, and benevolent ruling. In contrast, Ban presents the astrological values as the given, rather than using them to warn state leaders: "These natural occurrences all originate from *yin* and *yang*. They are rooted on earth but prompted by Heaven. When corrupted ruling happens here, signs will arise over there just like an object creates its shadow or a sound its echo. Therefore, an enlightened ruler will understand the message when he sees a sign. He will rectify his governance and reflect upon his errors. Thereafter disasters will dissipate and blessings descend. These are signs of Heavenly approval" (Ban 2007, 198). Ban's message was a political truism in her day. As part of a larger historical treatise, her text was purported to enlighten and admonish rulers and officials, as Sima's text did. But her gender role and her knowledge of the risks involved in history writing might have prevented her from assuming the imposing, critical tone that Sima adopted.

Second, Ban quoted astrological classics extensively to triangulate records of a star's movement or its interpretation. In contrast, while Sima acknowledged that he had read extensively on astrology, he did not quote from those classics explicitly (Sima 2006, 162). For example, Ban discussed the movement of Jupiter in the year of *yin* (寅) or *shetige* (攝提格) as follows:

When god Taisui is in the yin position, it is the year of *shetige*. In January, Jupiter rises early in the morning from the east. *Shishi* (石氏) records that it appears together with *Duo* and *Qianniu* constellations, a phenomenon the text calls *Jiande*. We can observe the tip of the Dipper to tell whether Jupiter has appeared early or late in a constellation. The former suggests flooding and the latter drought. *Ganshi* (甘氏) records

Jupiter's coappearance with *Jianxing* and *Shuinü* constellations, while *Taichu li* (太初曆) records its coappearance with *Yingshi* and *Dongbi* constellations. (Ban 2007, 204)

To introduce the movements of Jupiter, Ban drew records from three sources. These records capture different movements of Jupiter because, as Ban explains, "the stars' movements happened first, and these texts simply recorded the movements later" (Ban 2007, 204). Rather than questioning any of these sources, Ban values the diverse information they could furnish. Drawing evidence from different sources suggests that Ban holds factuality as a scholarly value. It could also be her strategy to divert any blame or charges that might come from the ruler and his officials.

Third, Ban constructed a lineage of astrological divinations. In contrast, Sima treated this section with extreme brevity. When narrating a specific divination, Ban mapped its trajectory schematically—the time, the anomalous movement of stars or clouds, the divination, and related political or natural events that happened thereafter. In the forty-six divinations that Ban compiled for the Western Han period, she sounded factual by refraining from making any personal comments. In contrast, Sima openly critiqued divinatory methods used before the Han as conflicting and unreliable (Sima 2006, 161–62), which could explain why he had treated this section briefly. Considering Ban's preference for triangulation and factuality, it is reasonable to infer that she wanted to remain detached when compiling the divinations. She understood that overt expression of personal opinion could incur retribution.

Ban's scholarly detachment, however, enabled her to be critical of men who associated solar eclipses with the inner court. As discussed earlier, during Emperor Cheng's reign, male officials often connected solar eclipses, disasters, and other natural anomalies with the unruliness of the court ladies. In a list of astrological divinations produced during Emperor Cheng's period, Ban did not include any related to solar eclipses. In contrast, in the "Treatise on Five Phases" (五行志) in the *BH*, her brother Ban Gu archived the associations made by officials between other sorts of natural anomalies and the court ladies. For Ban Zhao, an astrological divination was only archived when its message matched what actually happened later. Ban's reticence shows that in her view, the men's correlative thinking linking the solar eclipses with the inner court was unwarranted.

Regulating the Inner Court

Meanwhile, Ban Zhao also discoursed on the Heavenly Mandate and government through poems and memorials. In a rhapsody titled "The Bird from the Far West" (*Daque fu* 大雀賦), Ban tries to make sense of and include the Other in the Confucian state. She conceives the empire as extending its limbs through the force of music and ritual rather than military power. When her brother Ban Chao, the governor-general of the Han colony of East Turkestan, presented a large bird to Emperor He as a gift, the emporer asked her to compose verses suitable to the occasion. In the first stanza of her poem, Ban compares the bird to a phoenix, an augury in traditional Chinese mythology, as a way to affirm the emperor's benevolence. The phoenix is also a sign of the Heavenly Mandate, confirming the ruler's legitimacy. In the second stanza, Ban portrays the bird vicariously as judicious Heaven seeking the virtuous ruler on earth: "In his breast he cherishes virtue, he seeks the righteous one; / Soaring ten thousand *li* he has come, traveling (eastward). / Alighting at the imperial court, he halts, resting; / He delights in the Spirit of Harmony, so at leisure here he roams" (Swann 2001, 100). By describing the bird roaming over the court, Ban exalts the emperor, preparing him for an admonition to come.

The bird not only signifies Heavenly approval; through it, Ban also suggests the proper way to rule the empire, which had substantially expanded its territory in her time. The bird, representing the augury sent by Heaven, is seeking virtue, righteousness, and harmony on earth: "He delights in the Spirit of Harmony, so at leisure here he roams." Like the bird, when those desirable attributes—virtue, righteousness, and harmony—are achieved by the emperor, regional leaders would delight in the spirit of harmony and submit to his leadership. Ban writes in the last stanza: "(All ranks at court,) high and low, dwell in mutual love; / They listen to the harmony of music in its refined praise. / (Themselves) from east and west, from south and north; All think of submitting, and coming to serve and live" (Swann 2001, 100). Besides underscoring the moral force of a benevolent emperor, the stanza highlights the mesmerizing power of music and ritual in bringing regional rulers and politicians from afar. The emphasis on moral power, music, and ritual rather than military power to build an empire finds echoes among officials and the literati in court debates, such as those dealing with foreign relations and the state monopoly on the salt and iron industries (see chapter 4). Through the rhapsody, Ban reiterated the same moralist, humanistic approach to empire building.

90   *Regulating the Inner Court*

If the rhapsody marked Ban's indirect participation in the outer court, her two extant memorials marked her direct involvement in it. On one occasion she pleaded to the emperor to allow her aging brother Chao to return to the capital from the western frontier. On another occasion, she petitioned Empress Dowager Deng to allow the empress's four brothers to retire. One of the brothers was a general, who was assigned to fight against the Xiongnu troops in the northwestern frontier. On both occassions, Ban's petitions were granted, posing direct influence on personnel deployment in the Han government.

Different from the strategies she used in the astrological treatise and the rhapsody, Ban resorted to family values to bolster her petitions. In her astrological treatise and rhapsody, she appeals to humanity (*ren* 仁), virtue (*de* 德), music (*yue* 樂), and ritual (*li* 禮), concepts commonly used by men. She continues to appeal to them in her memorials but adds a familial dimension. In the memorial to the emperor, she speaks about kindred relations from a female's perspective:

> He [Ban Chao] has been separated from those of the same bone and flesh (so that they) no longer recognize each other. . . . (Ban) Chao has sent a letter in which while yet alive he bids farewell to your handmaiden. He fears that the two of us will never see each other again. Your handmaiden is really distressed about Chao. He gave his vigorous years in loyal service in the sandy desert, and now exhausted by old age for him to die in the distant wilds would be heartbreaking. (Swann 2001, 74–76)

In the quote, Ban appeals to the close ties of family members, who share the same "bone and flesh." In addition to the advocacy of respect and love for elder brothers (*ti* 悌), a key Confucian value, her personal feelings on the occasion could be deeply felt. In her memorial to Empress Deng, Ban similarly frames the petition on the basis of a family value, specifically, filial piety (*xiao* 孝): "At this time (Your Majesty's brothers), the Four Uncles, maintaining their loyalty and filial piety, seek to retire (from office) . . ." (Swann 2001, 77). The four brothers seek to retire because they want to take care of their ill-stricken mother.

The invocation of family values in the memorials adds a unique dimension to the discourse of state government. In court debates, antiwar officials and literati tended to advocate the use of rhetoric, ritual, and music to pacify the neighboring states. Ban's memorials lend support to the antiwar rhetoric by emphasizing the priority of the family. In her reasoning, family relations are

Regulating the Inner Court

part of the interests of the state, and the latter could be accommodated by the former. In the plea for her brother, Ban quotes a verse from the *Odes* to suggest a solution to the state-family conflict: "The people are indeed heavily burdened, / But perhaps a little relief may be secured for them. / Let us cherish the Middle Kingdom / To secure the repose of the Four Quarters of the Empire" (Swann 2001, 75). For Ban, reconciliation is possible: by giving the soldiers relief time to spend with their families, peace would descend in the empire.

In addition, Ban's feminine voice added a unique dimension to her petitions. In general, her petitions follow the basic rule in persuading a ruler: "affect-fortify," or holding his inmost self (*nei jian* 内揵), as articulated in *The Master of the Ghost Valley* which explains that one deals with matters by thoroughly assessing the situation and building a strong bond with the ruler. He achieves his goals by discussing the Way, virtue, benevolence, fraternity, ritual, and music as plans and schemes (Wu and Swearingen 2016, 51). Ban abides by the rule by both appealing to Confucian values and citing the classics. Memorials archived in both the *BH* and the *BLH* show that the rule of holding the ruler's inmost self was followed regardless of the writer's gender. However, compared to her male counterparts who expressed themselves through gender-neutral phrases, Ban establishes and maintains her hold by effusively emphasizing her gendered position, including as "Your handmaiden," in her own words. She does this in an extremely humble fashion. For example, she opens her petition to Empress Deng as follows:

> Below the steps of the Throne, (the unworthy writer) prostrates herself before the Great Empress, the beauty of whose overflowing virtue fills up the measure of the imperial rule of Yao and Shun. (Your Majesty) opens the gates to the four quarters of the empire, takes knowledge of all events in the four directions, and chooses (to follow) unintelligent words of irresponsible persons who offer deliberations of straw and stubble. Your handmaiden Zhao is both stupid and old, (but she is fortunate) to happen to live in this prosperous and brilliant age, and dares not but reveal her inmost self, if only to render (the minutest service—a proportion of) one to ten thousand. (Swann 2001, 76)

Ban reveals her vulnerable position first, describing herself as "unworthy," "irresponsible," "stupid," and "old," and her words as "unintelligent." She concludes her petition by repeating some of these self-deprecating expressions. As Swann rightly points out, most of Ban's humble expressions are part of the convention for petitions (Swann 2001, 79). However, such lavish self-deprecation is not commonly seen in memorials by males, who tend to use such expressions sparsely. What Ban has achieved from her style is a tight hold of the ruler's inmost self. Praising the empress's rule, she reminds her that, as a royal hand-maiden, she speaks for the interests of both the royal family and the state.

Thus, it becomes clear that Ban was skilled in shuttling between discourse domains. In her astrological treatise, she participated in the discourse of the Heavenly Mandate while resorting to facts and detachment as primary rhetorical values. In her rhapsody about the large bird and her two memorials, she moved strategically between the discourse of the state and the discourse of family. In the rhapsody, she evoked values such as benevolence, virtue, ritual, and music as the foundation of a Confucian state. In the memorials, she juxtaposed these values with family values to form the premises of her petitions, a strategy also found in the imperial commands of Empress Dowagers Ma and Deng.

When the above texts are examined together, they reveal that Ban was deeply invested in the state. In "The Great Learning," Confucius claims that "their persons being cultivated, their families were regulated. Their families being regulated, their states were rightly governed. Their states being rightly governed, the whole kingdom was made tranquil and happy" (Confucius 1971, 358–59). Similar to Confucius, Ban was concerned about how the elites could cultivate themselves, regulate their families, and assist the ruler to bring about a tranquil empire. This neo-Confucian rhetoric was further developed in her *Lessons for Women*.

Lessons for Women as a Discourse on Family and State

Lessons for Women was archived in *BLH*. Fan Ye chose to do so probably because it was one of the earliest writings by a woman stipulating the order of the domestic sphere. Appealing to both the male and the female, Ban Zhao discusses how a woman should handle matters within her marital family and manage the relationship with her husband and in-laws. This feminine articulation amounted to the cultural height of the *Record of Rites*, allegedly composed by Confucius and his disciples and stipulating proper human behaviors on political, diplomatic, and familial occasions. Before Ban's *Lessons*, the *Record* was the primary conduct manual for both elite men and women. Used side by side with the *Record*, the wide circulation of the *Lessons* in later dynasties underscores its significance in the discourse of the domestic sphere. While seemingly conforming to elite men's expectations of women, Ban was subversive. She argued for women's education, took the instruction of women from the hands of men, and conceptualized a rhetorically savvy woman.

Ban does not simply repeat the *Record of Rites'* take on women's mannerisms but rationalizes it through Han Confucianism. She repeatedly borrows canonical concepts to frame her admonitions for her daughters, who were the immediate audience. For example, she evokes *yin-yang* to explain the complementary relationship between wife and husband, hence their different but interconnected responsibilities to the family. Probably influenced by Dong Zhongshu, she likens the husband to the omnipotent and omnipresent Heaven (*tian* 天), whom the wife should trust, embrace, and not part from. Ban further suggests that by practicing four womanly qualifications (*de* 德), a woman realizes the humanity (*ren* 仁) advocated by Confucians. Additionally, by showing esteem to the husband through exchanging respectful words and refusing to quarrel, the wife nurtures love (*en* 恩) and a proper relationship (*yi* 義) with him. In addition to canonical concepts, Ban appeals directly to the *Record of Rites*, the *Odes*, and the *Changes* to corroborate her points.

Building on Han Confucianism, Ban argued for women's equal access to education. She first appeals to the *Record of Rites* and the *Odes* to highlight the fundamental husband-wife relationship in human society. She suggests that both parties need to be worthy (*xian* 賢) so that the husband can control his wife and the wife can serve her husband. However, men of Ban's day failed to honor their responsibility for supporting the intellectual and cultural cultivation of their wives, which would make the wives worthy of their role in the family: "I find that nowadays gentlemen-scholars only know that wives ought to be moderated by their husbands, and the authority and dignity of a husband ought to be properly established. For this reason, they instruct their sons and teach them canonical classics. They hardly realize that husbands ought to be served [by their wives], and ritual propriety and righteousness ought to exist" (Pang-White 2018, 47–48). Therefore, Ban concludes, girls should receive an education so that they could serve their future husbands and maintain the proper husband-wife relationship and rites. By not allowing women to be educated, men have ignored the most essential human relationship. Ban's argument illustrates her rationalism and rhetorical acumen. She establishes the premises of her reasoning by appealing to Confucian values and men's practical interests. Ban's argument for women's education has been read by

94   *Regulating the Inner Court*

Hui Wu as a series of moves to regender the *yin-yang* concept against Dong Zhongshu's unequal *yin-yang* gender positions. In making her argument, Wu suggests, "Ban reshaped Dong's sexually unequal yin-yang theory into an interdependent and interactive notion of equity to endow the female with positive traits and characters" (2020, 191).

The *Lessons* was part of Ban's engagement with the discourse of the state. As Confucius admonishes in "The Great Learning," one has to regulate his family as a precondition for properly governing the state and bringing about a tranquil and happy kingdom. The wellbeing of a state is inseparable from that of the family. In the *Lessons*, Ban emphasizes a couple's complementary responsibilities in regulating a family: "If a husband cannot moderate his wife, his authority and dignity are abolished and lost. If a wife cannot serve her husband, her principle of righteousness has fallen. Although the cases are two, their use is one" (Pang-White 2018, 47). The purpose of these two cases rests at regulating the family. As Ban was deeply engaged in the discourse of the Confucian state, the *Lessons* can be viewed as her deliberation of the topic in yet another context—specifically, the moment her daughters were about to marry. This reading might seem hegemonic, as it is underdeveloped in the *Lessons*. What we gain from such a reading, nevertheless, is an awareness of the interconnected discursive domains in which Ban has ventured as "a historian, or a moralist, or a writer of varied literary talent" and rhetorical adroitness (Swann 2001, xvii). She should not be viewed simply as a mother prescribing her daughters conduct rules, but also as a Confucian moralist with an imperial vision.

While continuing the instructional tradition for women, Ban placed it in women's hands. According to Lisa Raphals (1998), Confucian literati in the Eastern Han gradually shifted their attention from cosmological concerns to human relationships and the family. They were concerned about providing appropriate guides for ritual and conduct for the population at large. Raphals suggests that the *Lessons* aligns itself with other ritual texts for the instruction of the general public, departing from ritual texts before the Western Han such as the *Record of Rites*, which adheres to a ritual system designed for the emperor and the nobility. Despite a departure from the Western Han conduct texts, I suggest that Ban's *Lessons* bears direct influence from Liu Xiang's *Biographies of Eminent Women*, a text composed for the admonition of the royal family. Liu groups the stories of one hundred and five women in seven books based on womanly virtues and vices. Similarly, Ban divides her *Lessons* into

Regulating the Inner Court   95

seven chapters largely based on womanly virtues (such as humility, respect and caution, womanly qualifications, whole-hearted devotion, and implicit obedience). Through the *Lessons*, Ban joins men in teaching about womanly conduct, moving toward a grand rhetoric of the Confucian state.

In joining men to educate women, Ban utilizes rhetorical strategies that she acquired in her discourse with men. Although conversing with her daughters in the *Lessons*, she speaks formally——more like a scholar than a mother. This is significant because scholarship and motherhood were incompatible notions in Ban's time. For example, much like in her astrological treatise, she widely uses divisions and categories to organize her arguments. She refers to three things that were done by the ancients after a girl's birth (placing the baby below the bed, giving her a potsherd to play with, and announcing her birth to the ancestors through an offering) to suggest the three womanly duties in a family (humbling herself before others, practicing labor and being industrious, and continuing the observance of worship in the home). She talks about four womanly qualifications: womanly virtues, womanly words, womanly bearing, and womanly work. When explaining the husband-wife relationship, she evokes *yin* and *yang*. Furthermore, as in her other formal writings, she quotes widely from texts on related subjects such as the *Record of Rites*, the *Changes* (*Yi* 易), the *Book of Conducts* (*Yili* 儀禮), and the *Rules for Women* (*Nüxian* 女憲). By applying categories, divisions, and citations, Ban positions herself as a scholar. Yet, she also positions herself as a mother who is concerned about her uninitiated daughters. In the preface, she explains her life experience and the motivation for composing the text from a first-person perspective (*biren* 鄙人) and addresses her daughters in second person (*ru* 汝). Thus, the *Lessons* becomes a rhetorical hybrid by blending two seemingly incompatible identities.

While exemplifying her rhetorical dexterity, Ban drew from multiple intellectual schools to conceptualize a rhetorical woman. Yu-Shih Chen (1996) argues that Ban advocates Confucian virtues such as humanity, proper relationship, love, and ritual in her *Lessons* not as personal characteristics to be internalized but as survival skills for women to master in order to avert the dangers of living with her husband and her marital family. Tracing Ban's involvement in perilous court politics, Chen suggests that she was influenced more by Daoist and Militarist schools than orthodox Confucianism. Such an influence is demonstrable in her use of some terms in the *Lessons*: *ro* 弱 (weakness, meekness), *rou* 柔 (submissive, supple, yielding), *bei* 卑 (base, low), *qü* 曲

(bend, bow down), and *daoshu* 道數 (the way of preserving life and a mastery of the calculable pros and cons in the interrelationships among people and things). The Daoists and the Militarists advocated understanding the natural way and preserving oneself by feigning weakness and submissiveness (Combs 2000). Chen's argument is supported by Hui Wu, whose analysis reveals that Ban taught and performed an embodied *yin-yang* rhetoric that resonates with the teaching of *Guiguzi* (2020). Through the strategy of self-degradation and teaching of female humility, Ban demonstrated how women could deploy *yin* to acquire *yang*, a very Daoist lesson.

Conclusion

Through networks of genres—edicts, memorials, and history writing—the Han monarchy and officials evoked natural anomalies and *yin-yang* as tropes to address issues of the harem. On the one hand, these discourses were partisan, inspired by the interests of different cliques. Using correlative thinking to advance their agendas, they often challenged each other's conclusions, as in the case of Empress Dowager Ma refusing to bestow honor titles upon her brothers. On the other hand, these discourses led to epistemological and legal establishments essential for ruling the state. Owing to the collaborative work of the government bureaus, court historians were able to record a series of divinations in response to omens, natural anomalies, and disasters. This knowledge then allowed court officials such as Gu Yong and Liu Xiang to develop arguments around natural anomalies and draw political inferences, and it allowed the sovereign such as Emperor Cheng to establish regulations for the harem.

Court historians played a unique role in establishing the gender hierarchy of the empire. They did so by choosing which genre networks to archive and to what extent. They not only recorded those orchestrated by the elite men but also those by elite women that dealt with regulating the domestic sphere. However, their archival work was partial. Despite their voices being partially represented, these women were subversive in joining men in the epistemological and legal endeavors. They traversed between the inner court and the outer court, shuttled between discourse domains, took the instruction for women into their own hands, and modeled a rhetorically savvy woman in their writings. In doing so, they complicated Han Confucianism and underscored the contributing roles of women in the Confucian state.

CHAPTER 4

Weighing the Ways of Government

Ever since the House of Han established its government, it blended the Despotic and the Kingly Way. 漢家自有制度，本以霸王道雜之。—Emperor Xuan

Inheriting a tumultuous state from the Qin, the rulers of the Han were perplexed by the question of how to govern this vast and multiethnic land. The powerful but short-lived Qin left the rulers and their ministers a contrasting case, a mirror, enticing them to examine their daily dealings. They kept searching for answers as to why the Qin failed by parsing out the similitudes and differences between the two houses. They reasoned with one another about ways the Han might prevail in genres such as edicts, memorials, and court discussions.

Taking a position on the way of government, however, was risky. For example, after two court officials were executed by Emperor Xuan, who reigned between 74–49 BCE, crown prince Liu Shi remonstrated his father at a banquet for his excessive use of stringent laws. With a predilection for Confucianism, he then proposed that the court recruit the service of more Confucian literati. Agitated, the emperor retorted that the Han had long blended the Despotic and the Kingly Way, and that it would be foolish if he had solely resorted to moral regulations of the former Zhou dynasty. Further, he ridiculed Confucian literati for being unadaptable to their times, for favoring the antiquity and despising the present, and for confusing theory with reality (Ban 2007, 69). After this clash, the emperor considered abandoning the prince as the heir apparent. This short interchange not only marks the rifts in the Han court on the way of government but also suggests trajectories of arguments

98 *Weighing the Ways of Government*

taking place before the clash, arguments made for or against the Kingly Way (*wangdao* 王道), the Despotic Way (*badao* 霸道), or the moral regulations of the former Zhou dynasty. Arguments for or against these orientations, in fact, threaded the Han dynasty.

This chapter will examine court discussions on the way of government before this father-son clash. As a decolonial move, it explores how these discussions worked to establish ethnic and epistemic hierarchies crucial for imperial control. I will first trace the concepts of the Kingly Way and the Despotic Way in early China. With philosophical roots in Confucianism and Legalism, they often stood as polarized orientations to government, each drawing on its adherents during the preimperial era. After an introduction to these orientations, arguments for or against them across several court consultation meetings in the Western Han will be examined, focusing on one that was arguably the most expansive in topical coverage. Involving more than sixty debaters for several months, this meeting was held in 81 BCE, six years after the death of Emperor Wu, on whether a series of wartime economic measures launched in his reign should be abandoned or modified. In these court consultations, debaters drew on different intellectual schools to substantiate their arguments, which dealt with labor, ethnic, and epistemic hierarchies. In constantly shifting grounds, the Kingly Way and the Despotic Way both served as heuristics to accommodate diverse voices and interests in the imperial government.

By focusing on court discussions (*yi* 議, *chaoyi* 朝議, or *tingyi* 廷議), I want to argue for an expansive understanding of them.[1] Scholars past and present tend to focus on the written speeches presented by officials because of their interest in written genres.[2] In addition to delivering written speeches, officials spoke extemporaneously. The case of court discussion exemplifies how, while a genre network may consist of multiple genre events, a genre event such as the court discussion could involve a heavy traffic of texts and genres; and that the court discussion is not only written but also oral, embodied, performative, and ritualistic. Therefore, I will end the chapter by considering court discussion as an embodied practice. The following are the key court discussions to be examined in this chapter (see table 4.1).

The Kingly Way and the Despotic Way

The Kingly Way and the Despotic Way were, foremost, descriptive terms, referring to orientations to government as practiced in the Spring and Autumn

Weighing the Ways of Government

TABLE 4.1 *Key Court Discussions in the Western Han*

Participants	Topic
Emperor Wen and his cabinet	Changing penalty rules inherited from the Qin dynasty (167 BCE)
Gongsun Hong (公孫弘) and Wuqiu Shouwang (吾丘壽王)	Allowing commoners to carry bows and arrows (sometime between 128 and 123 BC)
Liu Hui (劉恢) and Han Anguo (韓安國)	Reverting foreign policy with the Xiongnu from interethnic marriage to military aggression (135–134 BCE)
San Hongyang (桑弘羊), Tian Qianqiu (田千秋), their staffers, and Confucian literati	Abandoning the state monopoly on salt, iron, and liquor industries (81 BCE)

period. The founders of the Zhou dynasty, King Wen and King Wu, as well as the latter's brother Duke Zhou, were historically portrayed by the literati as practitioners of the Kingly Way. They demonstrated benevolence to their people by maintaining high moral standards, using lenient laws and regulations, and guarding the unity of the state. Several generations later, the central government grew weak and the dukes became stronger. They fought against each other for land and political power. Those who won the fight and ascended as the hegemon were called *ba* (霸). Their approach to strengthening their fiefdom and developing political, military, and economic power was called the Despotic Way. Some of the hegemons were willing to show respect to the King of Zhou and restrained from excessive use of laws and military force. Once, Zhi Gong, one of Confucius's disciples, asked his master to evaluate Guan Zhong, an adviser to Duke Huan of the state of Qi. Confucius praised Guan for his benevolence: "When Guanzhong served as chancellor for Duke Huan, he enabled the duke to become leader of the various feudal lords, uniting and bringing order to the empire. Even today the people still benefit from his largesse" (*Analects* 1998, 176). Confucius refrained from censuring Guan for assisting a hegemon because Guan brought unification to the Kingdom of Zhou and peace to the people.[3] On practical terms the Kingly Way and the Despotic Way were not considered opposite but with overlapping characteristics and were used to describe the government of the kings of Zhou and the hegemons.

The Kingly Way and the Despotic Way went through an abstraction process and metamorphosed as standards for evaluating government in the Warring States era. This was an era in which the central government was almost negligible and the dukes constantly fought for the leadership position. Their battles and shifting borders inflicted great pains to their people. A follower of Confucius, Mencius traveled among some of these states and offered their rulers remonstrance. He used the two concepts extensively to educate them about benevolent governing (*renzheng* 仁政). When queried about his attitudes toward politics in his time, Mencius differentiated the two orientations as general, absolute standards for moral judgment:

> One who, supported by force, pretends to being humane is a hegemon, and a hegemon has to have a large state. One who out of Virtue practice humaneness is a true king, and a true king does not need anything large. Tang did it with only seventy *li*, and King Wen did it with a hundred. When one uses force to make people submit, they do not submit in their hearts but only because their strength is insufficient. When one uses Virtue to make people submit, they are pleased to the depths of their hearts and they sincerely submit. (*Mencius* 2009, 33)

In Mencius's definition of the Kingly Way and the Despotic Way, he presented them as contrasting political strategies for achieving lofty ideals. The Kingly Way was defined by the use of suasive power of moral force (virtue) in managing the people. A king or a despot no longer referred to a particular individual, but an abstracted persona exercising a certain governance style, using military, legal, or moral force. With his definition, on a different occasion, Mencius went so far as to charge that all leaders after King Wu were not kings because they heavily relied on military or legal force in their rise to the leadership position.

When evaluating the leaders of the preimperial period, however, most literati were not as strict as Mencius in applying these terms. Some leaders and their advisers were considered kingly while others despotic. Taking Duke Huan of Qi and his adviser Guan Zhong as an example again, Confucius and Sima Qian both found in them kingly attributes. Sima praised the duke for preventing merchants from monopolizing the market by leveraging the fluctuating prices of goods and for developing forestry and aquatic industries.[4] These economic measures benefited the people of Qi, bringing them peace and prosperity. In contrast, Duke Xiao of Qin and his adviser Shang Yang were

Weighing the Ways of Government

viewed as less kingly by Jia Yi and Sima Qian in their commentaries.[5] For instance, Sima criticized Shang for his degraded moral quality: "Once employed [by Duke Xiao], he mutilated Nobel Scion Ch'ien, deceived Wei's commander Ang, and failed to follow Chao Liang's advice. This alone is enough to reveal the Lord of Shang's lack of mercy" (Ssu-ma 1994b, 95). In these accounts, the Kingly Way refers to a host of attributes in government that are conducive to the unity, stability, prosperity, and humanity of the state.

In assessing government, literati and politicians since the Warring States period often cited Guan Zhong (725–645 BCE) and Shang Yang (390–338 BCE) as contrasting figures, the former as a practitioner of the Kingly Way and the latter of the Despotic Way. They were credited for the political strategies that they put forward to the dukes and that eventually transformed their respective states. Their strategies were cited by later generations as precedents to construct, support, or attack a government policy. Therefore, it is necessary to sum up their political strategies here.

When approached by Duke Huan inquiring about the way to become a hegemon, Guan Zhong recommended a series of measures for strengthening the state of Qi (*Guoyu* 2014, 124–43). First, he proposed that the state promote professionalism among literati, farmers, handicraft artisans, and merchants. They should live in separate quarters and cultivate expertise in their fields, not coveting other trades. Second, Guan urged that old laws be amended to ensure that the people are treated with benevolence, welfare, and respect. Third, he recommended that military preparation be integrated into community building. Families could be grouped to form a chain of command. They conduct community rituals and military exercises together, thus forming close-knit, combat-ready groups. Fourth, he suggested that talents be recruited through the recommendation of country leaders and officials and through interviews with the duke. In addition, recruiters could be dispatched to other states for scouting talents. Fifth, he insisted that good terms with neighboring states be established by repatriating their land and through diplomacy and gifts. Several years after these measures were implemented, the state of Qi became a military and economic power. In historical accounts, Guan was thus portrayed as being adroit at marshaling economic and military power for uniting the central states and bringing peace to their people.

To strengthen the state of Qin, Shang Yang proposed a different suite of measures to Duke Xiao.[6] First, he proposed that agriculture and military preparation be promoted as the most important tasks of the state because they could support its military efforts. Shang argued that the state should devalue the work of literati, handicraft artisans, and merchants and channel them to agricultural work. Second, he insisted that stringent laws be established as the standards for government.[7] Shang contends that once laws are established, they should not be interpreted by the ruler and his family at will but by those trained as judges. The laws were to be written in plain language accessible to ordinary people. To build their trust in the laws, Shang promulgated that violators would be punished regardless of their ties with the ruler. He practiced what he preached; for example, he punished the prince's teacher and other government officials for violations. With these new reforms in place, in a few years, Qin rose as a strong state and, through intrigues, annexed parts of the state of Wei. The Confucian literati tended to depict Shang as a representative of the Despotic Way because of the stringent legal system he introduced and his allegedly inhumane approach to the people.

Debating the Way of Government in the Western Han

The Kingly Way and the Despotic Way were recorded in dynastic histories as polarized orientations in several high-profile court discussions in the Western Han. Portrayed as having practiced the Despotic Way, the Qin dynasty served as a warning case for the Han officials in their policy deliberations. Emperor Wen, for instance, used the case of the Qin to argue for his laissez-faire approach at cabinet meetings. In 178 BCE, he argued against the practice inherited from the Qin of penalizing three families related to the one charged or found guilty of a crime (Ban 2007, 154). In 167 BCE, a woman named Chunyu Tiying (淳於緹縈) approached the imperial palace gate and presented a letter. She petitioned the emperor to exonerate her father and argued for changing the law of bodily mutilations. Her letter triggered a court consultation on the legal practice of bodily mutilations. The emperor first issued an edict, ordering that this practice be replaced by a more humane one. He argued: "Punishing criminals by dismemberment and engraving their skin would make them permanently disabled. How painful and inhumane this punishment is! How could we claim to be the parents of the commoners?" (Ban 2007, 152).[8] His cabinet discussed the order, and the Chancellor and the Imperial Counselor submitted a memorial providing suggestions on ways to replace the old practice, which were then approved by the monarch.

Weighing the Ways of Government   103

Because Emperor Wen saw the Qin as a despotic institution that practiced ruthless penalty rules that the Han must depart from, it was more often evoked as a trope in court discussions. The Qin was evoked, for instance, in a well-known court debate dealing with the question of whether commoners should be allowed to carry bows and arrows, a debate taking place sometime between 128–123 BCE. Chancellor Gongsun Hong proposed that they should not be allowed because bandits so armed would more easily win over government troops than if they were armed with short-ranged weapons. Court counselor Wuqiu Shouwang (吾丘壽王) argued against Gongsun's proposal for two reasons: First, the increasing number of bandits had nothing to do with bows and arrows; instead, it resulted from incompetent governance in the commanderies. Second, bowing was a long-established rite shared by the ruler and his subjects. Banning bows and arrows was equivalent to abandoning the rite. In accusing the governors of failed governance, Wuqiu positioned the Qin as a comparable case.

> When the Qin annexed other central states, it abandoned the Kingly Way and installed an autocratic regime; it burned Confucian books and emphasized laws and orders; it gave up benevolence and care and overused penalties and killings; it conquered famed cities and executed great leaders; and it crushed armored soldiers and blunted their weapons. The masses were forced to rebel with their farming tools. More and more people committed crimes; bandits were seen everywhere. Prisoners crowded the roads, and bandits occupied mountains. Thus, the Qin collapsed. A sage king would focus on the use of moral force rather than restrictions and preventive measures. (Ban 2007, 637–38)

In accounting for the collapse of the Qin, Wuqiu first employs several parallelisms to bring the Despotic Way of governance into sharp relief. Pointing out that crushing armored soldiers and blunting their weapons did not prevent the fall of the Qin, he proves his point that people carrying bows and arrows were not the real issue. Instead, as he concludes, the issue was whether the Kingly Way had been practiced. Here, Wuqiu elevates the contention from a specific policy measure to a broad governance orientation, shifting the focus from control over the commoners to a demand for self-examination of the governing body.

Debating the way of government was part of the mechanism supporting military expansion in the Han. In the first five generations, the Han court took measures to avert military conflicts with neighboring ethnic groups. In the north, annual tributes and interethnic marriages were arranged. In the south, local rulers were recognized as legitimate leaders of their people. In Emperor Wu's reign (141–87 BCE), as the state economy and military power significantly grew, he adopted active military expansionism. This policy shift was mediated through heated court debates. The most renowned ones took place in 135 BCE and 134 BCE and were on strategies for containing Xiongnu, a northern ethnic group, dramatized in the wrangling between General Wang Hui (王恢) and Imperial Counselor Han Anguo (韓安國; Ban 2007, 532–33). In those debates, Wang proposed that the government replace interethnic marriage with aggressive military actions. Han argued against the proposal because interethnic marriage had brought peace to the people for generations. Their debates marked a watershed in the Han policy toward the neighboring ethnic groups, and their arguments were later rehearsed in court debates dealing with relations with the Other, such as the debate on wartime economic measures held in 81 BCE and that on the status of the Zhuya commandery in the southernmost part of the empire held in 48 BCE.

Often viewed as a clash between the Confucian and the Legalist approaches to dealing with the Other, the Wang-Han debate could also be parsed as a wrangling between the Kingly Way and the Despotic Way. Their debates resembled the one in which Shang Yang persuaded Duke Xiao to adopt agriculture- and military-centered reforms more than two centuries before.[9] The pragmatists, such as Shang Yang and Wang Hui, argued for the need to adapt state laws and policies to the changing situation. The conservatives, such as Gan Long, Du Zhi, and Han Anguo, praised the ways of governance established by former rulers and emphasized the importance of adhering to them. As Shang was recognized as a legalist and a practitioner of the Despotic Way by the Han scholars, Wang could also be viewed as a champion of the Despotic Way. It is worth noting that despite their contention, both Wang and Han shared similar moral premises, such as benevolence and humanity in government, premises found in addresses across a variety of topics archived in the dynastic history (Loewe 2006; Olberding 2012).[10]

With a predilection for wars, the emperor accepted Wang's proposal, officiating the Despotic Way in state-making. At the policy level, the Han court completely abandoned the age-old practice of interethnic marriage and reverted to military aggression. On the ground, first, multidirectional communication channels were strengthened between the Han court, remote

Weighing the Ways of Government

agricultural-military posts, and ethnic groups through couriers, horses, and postal stations. Second, tens of thousands of troops and a large number of support personnel were mobilized. Third, large-scale wars were waged for decades, which led to a government monopoly in salt, iron, and liquor industries; the widening and deepening of taxation; the recruitment of soldiers for the battlefield; and the heart-wrenching separation of family members. Generals would be promoted or killed in the wars. Wang, the winner of the debate, for instance, was executed by Emperor Wu after the military campaign failed.

Emperor Wu's expansionism was hardly challenged by his officials until after his death. When the young Emperor Zhao ascended to the throne, General Huo Guan (霍光) became the regent. Working with Emperor Wu during his last years, Huo perceived the dire consequences of the wars: tens of thousands of Han soldiers were killed in the battlefield, the resulting labor force shortage led to reduced agricultural production and a shrinking state coffer, and deep taxation heightened the tensions between the commoners and the government. Therefore, Huo hoped to assess and revamp relevant government policies. To conduct the assessment, Emperor Zhao gathered his officials and more than sixty literati for consultation in 81 BCE. The consultation turned into a debate lasting for several months, dealing not only with economic issues, but also with topics such as agriculture, border defense, diplomacy, legality, and Confucianism. Records of the debate tend to represent it as a division between court officials and literati, or between the Legalists and the Confucians. The debate could be profitably read as a struggle for redefining and reinterpreting the Kingly Way and the Despotic Way at the pinnacle of the Han.[11]

The debate was later reconstructed under the title *Yantielun* (鹽鐵論 *Discourses on Salt and Iron*) by Huan Kuan (桓寬), a scholar-official who served in Emperor Xuan's court. Huan consulted both historical records and living debaters.[12] The text delineates the debate in fifty-nine episodes, and in each episode, the debaters focus on a specific issue. Similar to the structure of the debates between Wang and Han, each debater takes turns in presenting their arguments. One elaborates his position on an issue before surrendering the floor to his opponent. After his opponent responds to and rebuts his arguments, he regains his turn to elaborate his position or to make new arguments. After a few turns, the debaters move on to another issue. As Huan consulted the surviving debaters and probably experienced court debates of a similar kind, the debate format that he describes in *Yantielun* is likely to be reliable, though the content of the debates is subject to question.

To gain insights into court discussion as a genre, particularly on its regularities, logic, strategy, and reason in relation to government, I will perform content and rhetorical analysis of the text. I will pay particular attention to key concepts used by the debaters, their knowledge base, and debating as embodied practice. In terms of the key concepts, the analysis will focus on those which assumed prominence in the debate, such as rectifying names, ritual, *yin-yang*, and nonaction. It is important to understand how these concepts were used in the context of the empire to advance the debaters' arguments. The analysis will suggest that, while centered on the Confucian tradition, political debates in the middle of the Western Han were open to thoughts and concepts of other schools. This inclusive attitude was a proactive response to the multiethnic society that the Han had increasingly become. Among those concepts, the Kingly Way and the Despotic Way served as the heuristic for deliberating policy orientations in constantly shifting grounds.

The Discourse of the Officials

Well before the consultation began, a rift ran deep between the officials and the literati. The officials—including Imperial Counselor San Hongyang (represented as the Dafu 大夫), those working in his office (as the Yushi 禦史), Chancellor Tian Qianqiu (represented as the Chengxian 丞相), and those working in his office (as the Chengxianshi 丞相史)—were historically labeled as Legalists (Liang, 1974).[13] Although the government did not endorse Legalism, as enforcers of state power, officials were favorably disposed toward Legalist thoughts and practices. Distrustful of the discursive power of individuals, Legalists resorted to the state law, or institutionalized virtue, to regulate the people. Because most officials had worked with Emperor Wu, they continued to entertain an imperialist vision for the Han. The literati fell into the Confucian camp, represented by two figures Xianliang (賢良 virtue) and Wenxue (文學 culture) in *Yantielun*.[14] The literati were summoned to the capital Chang'an by an edict, after a selection process at the commandery level. Coming from many different parts of the country, they represented the voices of the people, particularly those of the landlords and merchants whose interests had been infringed upon by the state monopoly.

The first exchange between the two groups draws a sketch of the entire debate. Wenxue opens the debate by accusing the state of taking fortune away from the people by monopolizing salt, iron, and liquor, and by operating retail

Weighing the Ways of Government 107

businesses. Such a practice, he contends, draws people away from their natural kindness and simplicity; it cultivates greed and selfishness. When officials gained windfall fortunes through state-operated industries, the people became envious and they slighted agriculture. Without sufficient agricultural products, people would suffer from hunger and starvation; therefore, Wenxue proposes that the state relinquish its monopoly and prioritize agriculture over handicraft industry and commercial activities. Such a forceful opening shows Wenxue's directness despite the imbalanced power relation he faced.

Defensive, the Dafu claims that the Xiongnu people have been rebellious, and that they regularly harass and rob the Han people living in the borderlands. Concerned about his people, Emperor Wu had ordered the construction of fortresses and message stations along the borders; he sent troops to station and to cultivate new farmland along the borders. Because these defensive moves were costly, the emperor had sanctioned state monopoly over various industries to collect funds for the state treasury. The Dafu argues that once the monopoly ended, the state coffers would dry up, the troops would not be able to afford new military equipment, and the soldiers would suffer from both hunger and cold weather. Thus, the monopoly should continue. In this rebuttal, the Dafu invokes the authority of the deceased emperor to defend government policies.

The opening exchange offers one a first glimpse of the debaters' intellectual training. Both groups borrowed arguments from the Legalist rhetorical arsenal. The literati's argument for accentuating agriculture by weakening the handicraft industry and commercial activities is, oddly, reminiscent of the one made by Shang Yang to Duke Xiao. However, they differed in their aims. While Shang intended to build a strong economic and social basis for cultivating military power in the Qin, the literati hoped to bring peace and relief to the people. On the other hand, the Dafu's argument echoes Guan Zhong's insights that a state must seek a balanced development of agriculture, handicraft industry, and business—a balance that would lead to the strengthening of the state militarily, economically, and politically. Shang Yang and Guan Zhong are cited multiple times by both parties in the rest of the debate, a practice which confirms the wide circulation of the Legalist thoughts in the Han.

The Dafu's proclivity for the Legalist school became clear in the ensuing exchanges. When defending the current economic and military policies, the Dafu repeatedly cited the achievements of Shang Yang, respectfully calling him "the Marquis of Shang" ("商君"). In applauding the Marquis, the minister

108 *Weighing the Ways of Government*

implicitly expressed his admiration for the Despotic Way practiced by the Qin. In contrast, the literati called the Marquis by the neutral name "Shang Yang." The Dafu recounted Shang's deeds with admiration:

> He established a civil code and punished violators severely. He reformed politics and education, so evil and dishonesty had nowhere to hide. He found countless ways to fill up the state coffer and taxed those who developed woods and lakes. The country became rich and the people healthy. Farmers had sufficient equipment and harvested more than what they needed. Therefore, the Qin was able to conquer its rivals and expand its territory; it was able to support its troops without taxing its own people. (*Yantielun* 1992, 93)

With Shang Yang's measures, the state of Qin finally annexed the other six central states. Comparing the current policies to those of Shang, the Dafu argued that they similarly benefited the state and did no harm to the people. By making the comparison, and by favorably citing Shang Yang's example thirteen times in the entire debate, the Dafu identified himself as a contemporary Shang Yang—a reformer and a loyalist to Legalism.

The officials further revealed their Legalist leanings when explicating the suasive power of the civil code. The Dafu argued that when strict law and order are established, they deter the people from behaving recklessly or dishonestly. He then cited the *Spring and Autumn Annals*, a Confucian classic, to argue for the need to punish offenders based on their intentions. "We judge robbery-inflicted injuries as the same crime as homicide because we want to castigate the offender's evil intentions. Likewise, the *Spring and Autumn Annals* condemned the state of Lu despite it attacking the state of Qi indirectly by using the state of Chu's troops. So there are good reasons why a light offense should be severely punished or why a minor crime should be judged the same way as a major crime is judged" (*Yantielun* 1992, 566). When making the same argument, his staffer, the Yushi, cited another renowned Legalist, Han Fei, for understanding the nuanced rhetorical power of the civil code: "Master Han was angry that rulers did not understand the power of either the common law or their unique social position in governing their officials. [. . .] Confused by the words of Confucian literati, these rulers even became doubtful of the strategies proposed by their advisors" (*Yantielun* 1992, 567). By citing Legalist sources, the officials showed that they clearly harbored a deep trust in the Legalist approach to governing a state, that is, "to establish unity and stability through the singularities of a common law or order (*fa*), strategic method (*shu*), and position/power of the ruler (*shi*)" (Lyon 2008, 56).

To demarcate their positions, the officials attacked Confucianism, or, more exactly, the Confucian literati, whenever they could. Disparaging the entire school would corrupt the literati's ethos and logos. The officials first recounted the political and cultural activities of Confucian adherents in the past, and then accused them of having never brought peace to the state or glory to the ruler (*Yantielun* 1992, 149). As the logic went, the literati's proposal to end the monopoly would certainly not benefit the state either. Next, the officials questioned the usefulness of Confucian training for governing the state, and they ridiculed the personal traits of the literati, arguing that they were not virtuous, wise, honest, or brave (*Yantielun* 1992, 285). Further, the officials chided the literati for habitually using vague and bookish language in the debate: "You are talking gibberish. Your suggestions need to be practical. Don't use big, outdated words to confuse us" (*Yantielun* 1992, 507). Questioning the literati's training and criticizing their language indirectly cast doubt on the soundness of the literati's arguments. Criticizing Confucianism and its adherents relentlessly underscored a clear divide between the two groups in terms of their political philosophy.

While questioning Confucianism relentlessly, the officials mobilized resources to the likings of the school nevertheless. Seemingly following the instructions of the *Master of Ghost Valley*, they first adopted the same moral terms as the literati. For example, when discussing strategies to deal with the Xiongnu, the Dafu portrayed these people as violating basic human values such as *xian* (賢 virtue), *ren* (仁 humanity), and *yi* (義 justice or righteousness). Therefore, the government should take military actions against these "inhuman," "unjust" beings without showing any mercy (*Yantielun* 1992, 444). By portraying the Xiongnu as possessing of attributes disdained by the Confucians, the Dafu tried to justify the state's foreign policies. However, Xianliang refuted the Dafu's argument by exposing his ethnocentrism: as the Xiongnu had cultivated a lifestyle different from the Han's, they should not be judged by the Han values such as justice and ritual. Further, the officials strengthened their arguments by citing from the Confucian classics, such as the *Spring and Autumn Annals* and the *Analects*. Because the officials appealed to the same moral terms as the Confucian literati and cited from various schools, their discourse was an intellectual hybrid. Nonetheless, this pro-Legalist hybrid was subsumed to the authority of the law and used to support imperial control and dominance rather than to promote peace among ethnic groups.

Understanding the officials' discourse as a pro-Legalist hybrid underscores the complexity of the intellectual culture in the Han. Although Confucianism was endorsed by the state and the Confucian classics were studied in the imperial academy, the other schools were not banned. The following analysis will continue to show that the debaters were well versed in several major schools: Legalism, Confucianism, Daoism, and the Yin-Yang school. They shared a loose canon consisting of texts drawn from each of these schools. Because some officials, like Imperial Counselor San Hongyang, were not recruited through court exams but through connections with the royal clan (*Yantielun* 1992, 219), their training was not confined to the Confucian classics.[15]

The Discourse of the Literati

Arguing for the Kingly Way, Confucian literati mobilized a cluster of concepts. While using Confucius's concepts strategically, like the pro-Legalist officials, they unapologetically borrowed concepts from other schools to build their rhetorical arsenal. Their discourse suggests that flexibility and hybridity characterized Confucianism in the Han.

Rectification of Names

Rectification of names (*zhengming* 正名) is a key concept in Confucius's discourse of language and society. In the *Analects*, Confucius emphasizes correcting the language to ensure a truthful representation of reality. Xing Lu (1998) argues that such a perspective implies that a clear demarcation of individual social status and kinship identities will lead to social stability and harmony (160–62). In the context where Confucius employs the concept, he specifically addresses the relation between correct language and effective government. When conversing with his student Zilu, who aspires to enter civil service, the Master instructs: "When names are not used properly, language will not be used effectively . . . , matters will not be taken care of . . . , the observance of ritual propriety and the playing of music will not flourish . . . , the application of laws and punishments will not be on the mark . . . , the people will not know what to do with themselves" (*Analects* 1998, 162). For Confucius, correct language regulates not only the relationnship between

Weighing the Ways of Government

individuals, but also that between the ruler and his subjects; both are vital to social harmony and stability.

The literati widely used this concept to advance their arguments, attaching new significance to it. On one occasion, for instance, they quoted Confucius verbatim to clarify the appropriate way to enter officialdom. The Yushi suggested that, as aspirants to officialdom, the literati should not always cling to fundamental Confucian values. Instead, they should be flexible and adaptable like the renowned ancient advisors Yi Yi and Baili Xi. In order to approach their rulers, Yi Yi cooked meat for King Tang and Baili Xi fed oxen for King Mo of Qin. The Dafu commented on these two advisors: "They compromised their values (*gouhe* 苟合) in the beginning. Once they had gained the ruler's trust, they actualized their aspirations by assisting the ruler to become a great king" (*Yantielun* 1992, 150). In response, Wenxue accused the Dafu of misrepresenting Yi Yi and Baili Xi. He argued that the two advisors approached the rulers successfully because they had long developed their administrative wisdom, which highly appealed to the rulers. Then Wenxue said, "The Master says, 'When names are not used properly, language will not be used effectively; when language is not used effectively, matters will not be taken care of.' How could they have helped the rulers to become great kings by compromising their own values?" (*Yantielun* 1992, 150). By quoting Confucius's rectification of names, Wenxue not only debunked the Dafu's interpretation of the two historic figures but, more importantly, refused to compromise his values in pursuit of officialdom.

Often the literati slyly used the concept to criticize the pro-Legalist perspective on government and to gain a moral high ground. Although both groups shared certain moral terms, they interpreted them differently in context. Employing the concept, the literati not only defended the Confucian interpretation of these values, but also demonstrated their moral superiority, thus strengthening their ethos. For example, when the Dafu argued that mutilation and law could stop violence and assist the ruler in governing his subjects, Wenxue sneered at such a Legalist position by invoking the Qin as representing the Despotic Way, echoing Wuqiu Shouwang's argumentative strategy: "The Emperor of Qin Junior was misled by Zhao Gao's approach, believing in severe mutilating punishments and law. Mutilated people were seen everywhere and the number of executed people increased day by day. Those who killed the most were considered loyal (*zhong* 忠) and those who severely harmed people were considered capable (*neng* 能)" (*Yantielun* 1992, 595). In response, the Dafu argued that times had changed. Officials could not use an approach developed in an era of natural simplicity and kindness to govern the cunning people of the present age. Wenxue refuted this argument, stressing the cultivation of a humane and kind character among the people rather than depending on mutilating punishments and laws to manage them: "When one does not tackle the major cause but the minor cause of an issue, he would be called stupid (*yu* 愚) in the past but is called wise (*zhi* 智) now. When one flogs violators gravely with a stick to stop chaos or scratches off words on the bamboo slips with a knife, he would be considered unjust (*zei* 賊) before but is called virtuous (*xian* 賢) now" (*Yantielun* 1992, 604). Wenxue believed that in those instances, terms such as *loyal, capable, wise,* and *virtuous* were used erratically to embellish pro-Legalist acts. To rectify these terms meant to prioritize humanity and justice over severe laws and mutilation, or the Kingly Way over the Despotic Way.

The Suasive Potential of Ritual

Confucius valued the suasive potential of rites and encouraged his students to study rites of the Western Zhou dynasty. Rites are a complex of social codes that signify what society values most. They embody the total spectrum of social norms, customs, and mores, covering increasingly complicated relationships and institutions. The appropriate acts prescribed by the rites not only regulate ceremonial occasions, but also govern daily human interactions. By performing or participating in the rituals, one would become identified with the community values and be persuaded of them automatically (You 2006). Confucius sees the performance of rites as a social barometer of the Way of government. When he talks about ritual, he hopes to use it as a means to restore peace and integrity to the disintegrated Zhou society.

When evoking the suasive potential of ritual, the literati believed that it would work with people beyond the empire. It was a means to befriend, if not to conquer, the enemies. When dealing with neighboring states, particularly with the Xiongnu, the Dafu-led officials believed that only strong military actions would contain them. In contrast, the literati insisted on treating the other states with humanity and ritual. Wenxue argued, "The *Book of Songs* says that 'When one presents me with peaches as a gift, I will return him with pears.' I've never heard that one who treats others with kindness will be rewarded with evil. Thus a gentleman, instead of offending them, should respect others following the ritual. People all over the world are brothers. If we can examine ourselves reflectively and candidly, what do we need to worry about?" (*Yantielun* 1992, 513). As Confucius once admonished his disciples, to be a gentleman and an ideal ruler, one has to cultivate himself and his own people first through culture and morality. Wenxue concurred with Confucius on the universal validity of ethical norms, believing that the suasive power of ritual performance, constitutive of culture and morality, would positively affect any human being. Wenxue's argument thus continued the thought shared among the preimperial thinkers: aliens were not biologically, but instead culturally, inferior to the Han people, and thus they were transformable.[16]

The officials and the literati were fundamentally divided in their convictions about non-Han people. As the above quotation reveals, the literati demonstrated a familial, empathetic view toward the Other by calling them brothers. Therefore, they were confident that the power of ritual could transcend and transform ethnic differences. In contrast, the Dafu harbored a more ethnocentric and chauvinist view by portraying the Xiongnu as irrational animals. For example, in response to Wenxue's proposal of treating Xiongnu with respect following the ritual, the Dafu contended that it would not work: "During the Spring and Autumn period, the six warring states formed an alliance by the rulers exchanging their hats and belts. However, they reneged on the agreement. How can you expect a country of animals to follow through a truce? . . . Xiongnu made peace agreements with us many times through interethnic marriages. However, they often broke the agreement first" (*Yantielun* 1992, 513–14). In other places, the Dafu used animalization as a strategy to cast doubts on the Xiongnu people's ethos and to refuse any engaged dialogue with them. He described the Xiongnu people specifically as "termites" ("蠹"), "greedy wolves" ("貪狼"), and "fierce tigers" ("猛虎") that needed to be contained with force (*Yantielun* 1992, 507–8).

Thanks to their trust in the suasive potential of rituals, the literati envisioned a world united under an enlightened ruler. In their both ethnocentric and imperialistic view, the ruler led the world not through military force but through his virtuous government, which manifested partly through the ritual symbols. Wenxue elaborated on the workings of virtue and ritual:

> The ruler stands in his court but he listens to the rest of the world. As his benevolence affects people afar, even distant nations that enjoy distinct customs send delegates to his court. Regardless of phoenixes in the woods

or unicorns by the lake, everything in the world will be blessed by his virtue. The ruler does not work on everything himself but his humanity travels in all directions. Fan Li came from ethnic Yue and You Yu grew up as an ethnic Hu, but they all advised the great king willingly. Government stipulations may not work, but nobody in the world is insusceptible to the workings of virtue and ritual. (*Yantielun* 1992, 514)

On the one hand, Wenxue shared Confucius's conviction that a ruler's benevolence and justice would affect his subjects like a gentle wind blowing over the grass. As the Han gradually annexed tribe states in the eastern, southern, and southwestern regions, this political conviction became even more pivotal in pacifying and uniting these new peoples. On the other hand, Wenxue actively used Confucius's notion of rites as a counterstrategy to the officials' military and antirhetorical strategy. If ethnic minorities Fan Li and You Yu were persuaded by, or identified with, the ruler's benevolence, the Xiongnu might respond positively to the emperor's benevolence, which would thus be conducive to the Han's territorial ambition. The literati's trust in humanity and human fraternity undergirded their ritualistic-rhetorical approach to empire building.

While the literati trusted the power of ritual in dealing with ethnic relations, the dynastic historians were less optimistic. In the memoirs of the Xiongnu and the South Yue, they noted these groups' appropriations of and resistances to the Han ritual practice. For instance, they depicted how Xiongnu leaders subversively engaged the Han imperial power in a series of epistles. According to Sima Qian, the Xiongnu people did not have written words of their own and had to use spoken words to regulate their behaviors ("毋文書, 以言語為約束"; Ssu-ma 2011, 241). However, they learned Chinese writing from the Han emissaries and wrote to the Han court to make requests and negotiate peace treaties. In those communications, often the Xiongnu leader assumed a dominating posture by subverting the Han rituals. For example, while the Han emperor used wood strips measured as one Han foot and one inch long for an epistle, the Xiongnu leader used strips measured one Han foot and two inches long. Further, the leader started his letter with a greeting similar to that of the Han emperor but explicitly emphasized the leader's Heaven-endowed power ("天地所生日月所置"; Ssu-ma 2011, 274). As the epistolary conventions were developed as part of the court ritual of the Han, the Xiongnu leader's writing suggests his attempt to outwit the Han imperial power in rhetoric. In addition to these negotiations with the Han ritual, the court historians also narrated direct, oral engagements between the Xiongnu leaders and the Han diplomats, in which the Xiongnu leaders defended the ritual practice of their own. Narrating these cross-cultural encounters, the court historians harbored a more nuanced understanding of the power of ritual in foreign relations.

Yin-Yang and Nonaction

Yin-yang entered political discourse in the Warring States period and prominently in the Han because of Dong Zhongshu. Dong evoked *yin-yang* to explain the way of Heaven in his court exam essays, responding to Emperor Wu's inquiries. By the time the debate on salt and iron took place, *yin-yang*, being a central tenet of Dong's theory about communication between the anthropomorphic Heaven and humans, had become part of the standard intellectual training. On one occasion, when the Dafu asked the literati to explain the correspondence between natural signs and happenings within the empire, Wenxue answered the call by evoking *yin-yang* and by attributing the concept to Dong (*Yantielun* 1992, 556).

In debate, both sides used *yin-yang* to advance their arguments. On one occasion, for instance, the literati used the concept to criticize the ills of Han society. Wenxue made an analogy: a good doctor would be able to cure a patient by adjusting the *yin* and *yang* forces in the sickened body. When the veins and airways were unblocked, the evil air would leave the body. However, in the present Han "body," the rich became richer while the poor poorer. The officials established severe laws and enforced mutilating punishments to stop violence and evil; however, violence and evil grew more rampant. Therefore, the officials proved to be unqualified social "doctors" who had failed their jobs miserably (*Yantielun* 1992, 179). This analogy reveals the epistemological power of the concept of *yin-yang* in the Han society. The concept had become the common vocabulary of Chinese medicine: doctors used *yin* and *yang* to explain how the body works and to argue for the method of treatment of a certain disease. In addition, the concept had become a heuristic for the literati to interpret and to argue about the evolution of human society. Like Dong Zhongshu, Wenxue connected the workings of Han society to the workings of the universe in general.

Whereas Wenxue resorted to *yin-yang* to criticize the malfunctioning of the officials, the Dafu used the same concept to respond to Wenxue's criticism.

He explained that everything happens according to the way of Heaven, and one should not only blame the officials: "Floods and droughts are caused by Heaven; hunger and good harvests reflect the change of *yin* and *yang*. People will suffer from drought when Lord Taishui (太歲) is in the *yang* position, or suffer from floods when it is in the *yin* position. Hunger occurs every six years while bad harvest comes once every twelve years" (*Yantielun* 1992, 428). The Dafu turned *yin-yang* to his own service. However, while Confucians believed that a balance of *yin-yang* could be acquired through human knowledge and effort, the Dafu harbored a more deterministic conception of *yin-yang*.

Besides borrowing from the Yin-Yang school, the literati also embraced Daoist notions, particularly the concept of nonaction (*wuwei* 無為), in envisioning the Kingly Way. The Daoists, headed by Laozi, emphasized speaking, acting, and governing according to *dao*, or the Way, which was the most efficient and effective way to persuade and to govern (Combs 2000). In governing the populace, Daoists advocated for the least intrusive approach, called nonaction. The literati repeatedly appealed to this approach. For example, Wenxue praised earlier Han emperors for taking a Daoist laissez-faire approach to state-making in order to contrast with and attack the monopoly policy (*Yantielun* 1992, 479). On another occasion, the literati criticized a severe legal practice by mixing Laozi's nonaction with Confucius's rectification of names. According to the civil code of the Western Han, when one family committed a crime, the neighboring four or nine families would also be punished. Wenxue argued against such a practice: "Laozi says, 'The ruler has no desires and the people return to the good and simple life. The ruler does nothing and people become rich.' When the ruler and his officials, or the father and his son, submitted to their socially designated roles, why do we need to group five families together (to prevent crimes) or what does the government need to worry about?" (*Yantielun* 1992, 585).

Like the discourse of the pro-Legalist officials, the literati's discourse was a cultural and rhetorical hybrid. Concerned about uniting the warring states, Confucius developed a system of thoughts on governing the state. While continuing to use Confucius's favorite concepts, such as rectification of names and ritual, the literati borrowed concepts from other schools. Responding to the exigencies of their times, such as the rise of Confucianism as the state orthodox and the Han metamorphosing into an increasingly multiethnic society, the literati retooled old concepts to construct new meanings.

Court Debates as Embodied Practice

Not a mere collision of ideas, court debates were embodied practice with material consequences. Through genre networks, the debates mobilized bodies, dialects, and customs from afar and placed them in physical proximity. Huan Kuan emphasized the embodied acts of the debaters by repeatedly describing the officials' bodily expressions when being cornered by the literati. For instance, he portrayed the moment of their defeat at the end of the debate: "Disappointed and ashamed, the Dafu laxed his limbs without speaking further. Meanwhile, sitting in a line, his subservient staff members were stunned, with their mouths widely open and tongues long raised. Downcast, they seemed to be carrying a heavy heart after being chided" ("大夫憮然內慚, 四據而不言。當此之時, 順風承意之士如編, 口張而不歙, 舌舉而不下, 暗然而懷重負而見責"; *Yantielun* 1992, 605). Further, through the words of the debaters, Huan spelled out the high stakes of the loss, including death, as well as other possibilities that court debates could entail for the speaking bodies.

It was conspicuous that the ruler was silent, if not absent, in the court debate. The Han ruler often presided over court debates. The debates dealt with not only issues of government policy but also scholastic matters. Confucian literati often debated exegetical issues and sometimes had to involve the emperor to judicate the dispute. As the debate on salt and iron shows, both parties constantly cited from the classics. Exegetical questions, therefore, overshadowed political decisions. For instance, the emperor presided over a well-known debate in *Shiquge* (石渠閣), one of the imperial libraries, in 53 BCE, where the classicists tried to resolve disputes surrounding all major Confucian canons (Xu Tianlin 1963b, 231–33). In the debate on salt and iron, General Huo Guan, the regent, presided over the event on behalf of the young emperor. While he was absent from, or not being mentioned in, the *Yantielun*, he was present. He was leaning toward reducing military action and altering the state monopoly on salt, iron, and liquor industries, a position that emboldened the literati to argue against the officials.

Thus, court debates came with high stakes for the speaking bodies. In the debate on salt and iron, Confucian official-orators faced various challenges. For one thing, striving to become a competent official-orator meant risking one's life. In the debate, the officials and the literati cited numerous examples of competent official-orators whose candid criticisms led to praiseworthy political outcomes. However, in the history of the Han, official-orators such as Wang Hui often lost their lives in pursuit of honorary titles such as "loyal official" and "honest advisor." A second challenge was that intellectual training might only produce eloquent officials. However, government positions required both communicative and administrative skills. On many occasions, the Dafu criticized the literati for being out of touch with real-life issues with the understanding that they aspired to join officialdom. He once questioned their competence to govern: "You cherish the past but criticize the present. You talked a lot about the past, which in fact doesn't matter much to the present issues. Probably you don't understand what it truly means to be an official-advisor. Or did you exaggerate your ability with flowery words? Why is it so hard to meet virtuous gentlemen?" (*Yantielun* 1992, 130). Successful court examinees often proved to be incompetent administrators in Chinese imperial history for lack of experience or understanding of present issues, as the Dafu suggested (Elman 2000).

Despite obstacles to becoming ideal official-orators, the literati finally proved themselves, according to *Yantielun*. They demonstrated their oratorical success in two major accounts. First, they achieved part of their political goal: the state abolished its monopoly over iron and liquor in certain regions. Their arguments were later invoked by the literati for opposing state monopoly over salt and iron in the reigns of Emperor Yuan (49–33 BCE) and Emperor Zhang (75–88 CE), leading to tangible policy impact.[17] Second, they were accredited and placed into various government ranks (*Yantielun* 1992, 471).[18] The debate functioned as an excruciating exam. The literati passed it by performing the role of ideal official-orators, who would "risk their lives to point out their master's misbehaviors" and "risk displeasing ranking officials by criticizing their wrongdoings" (*Yantielun* 1992, 256).

The literati's efforts to shape imperial government also manifested in the various accounts of the salt and iron debate that they constructed thereafter. Before Huan Kuan's treatise, there were competing accounts of this event. Discontented with these accounts, Huan went so far as to interview some living debaters to construct his treatise. Based on *Yantielun*, his intent was twofold. First, regretting that the literati's proposals had fallen on deaf ears, he wanted to render his own support of the Kingly Way, specifically for the use of moral power in dealing with ethnic relations and prioritization of agricultural production over commerce. Second, he wanted to recognize several literati who were eloquent defenders of the Kingly Way, who otherwise would fall into oblivion (*Yantielun* 1992, 613–14). Huan's intent was approved by Ban Gu when the latter recounted in his dynastic history of the genre network surrounding this historical debate (Ban 2007, 668). Like Sima Qian, both Huan and Ban believed in the power of such narratives for educating the ruling class and shaping policy decisions in the future, a belief that undoubtedly will leave in perpetual question Huan's accuracy in representing the debate.

Conclusion

Court debates on the way of government would continue in the rest of the Han dynasty and beyond. While the Daoist, laissez-fair approach featured in the early Han government, a mixture of the Despotic Way and the Kingly Way marked the rest of the dynasty. The two orientations would stand as polarized but also complementary. It was through that polarization that diverse views and interests were accommodated inside the imperial government, crucial for accounting for the increased cultural and ethnic diversity. In fact, the latest evocation of the topoi in policy deliberation happened in the Chinese Communist government in the 1950s and 1970s. When being criticized for taking a dangerously leftist approach in state-making, Mao Zedong defended himself by evoking the story of Emperor Xuan childing prince Liu Shi, suggesting the need for both the Despotic Way and the Kingly Way (Wang Ruoshui; Liang Xiao).

As a genre, court discussion was supported by genre networks. On the one hand, the Confucian classics as well as those from other schools furnished the consultants with rhetorical concepts, historical precedents, and sagely opinions for constructing arguments. These texts first converged in the training of the *shi*, and then were cited in arguments unfolding in the court consultations. On the other hand, a consultation meeting enacts a traffic of genres. It could involve an edict to summon the meeting, memorials submitted by officials to express their opinions, in-person court discussions, and an edict that conveyed the emperor's judication of the matter in question. The edict would then lead to other genre activities in local contexts intended to implement the executive order.

CHAPTER 5

Defending Imperial Integrity

I have not heard from you for a long while. Report to me your situation solely in the spirit of the *Spring and Autumn Annals*; do not use Su Qin's Vertical-Horizontal tactics. 間者, 闊焉久不聞問, 具有春秋對, 毋以蘇秦縱橫。—Emperor Wu

The reign of Emperor Wu (141–87 BCE) was a watershed for argumentative practice in Han politics. After he championed Confucianism as the state orthodox, scholars of other schools were forced to disarm and join an enlarged and reformed Confucian circle. In political discourse, the ramifications were tangible. For instance, in the 81 BCE court debate on state monopoly of salt and iron, both parties demonstrated a keen knowledge of Confucian concepts and beliefs. In fact, Emperor Wu explicitly demanded a shift in argumentative style in court deliberations. He once did so when writing to his confidant Yan Zhu (嚴助). A renowned court debater, Yan had been deeply involved in the decisions regarding diplomacy and military relations with the Yue peoples in the south. Years later when he served as the governor of Kuaiji, a commandery neighboring the Yue states and more than two thousand *li* away from the capital city, the emperor requested that he submit a report explaining his long reticence. As quoted in the epigraph, the emperor asked that he does so in the spirit of the *Spring and Autumn Annals* rather than using Vertical-Horizontal school tactics (Ban 2007, 636).

When narrating the life of Yan Zhu, dynastic historian Ban Gu did not explain why the emperor mandated a report in the spirit of the *Annals*. Yan might have been known for his use of Vertical-Horizontal school tactics in court debates, or the tactics might have been widely deployed in discussions

Defending Imperial Integrity

on diplomatic and military relations. Nevertheless, the emperor favored a different style, a style aligned with the spirit of the Confucian classic. However one interprets the emperor's predilection, the two styles stood as mightily different to him, and he took a position against the Vertical-Horizontal school like Confucius's follower Mencius did two centuries before.[1] The emperor's demand begs an exploration of the political and ideological underpinnings of the styles to further unveil deliberative practices in the court.

This chapter focuses on the discourse styles employed in court discussions on politico-military organization and ethnic relations in the Western Han. In particular, it examines genre networks—involving what were later called "dissenting opinions" (*boyi* 駁議) addressed to the emperor or regional rulers and the "sovereign answers" (*bao* 報) —dealing with defending the integrity of the Han empire. As dissenting opinion and sovereign answer were formalized as bureaucratic genres in the Eastern Han, this chapter highlights the formative years of these genres.[2] First, I will survey the argumentative style of the Vertical-Horizontal school and that which is associated with the *Annals*. Next, dissenting opinions submitted by two literati to the king of Wu, dissuading him from revolting against the central government, will be examined to understand how the Vertical-Horizontal school shaped politico-military organization in the early Han. Finally, dissenting opinions submitted to Emperor Wu and Emperor Yuan that deal with the Yue peoples will be analyzed to demonstrate the rhetorical power of Confucian classics in constructing ethnic relations in the mid–Western Han. Moving from the revolt of the seven kingdoms to the issues of the Yue peoples, we observe the rising prominence of the Confucian classics in the genre networks dealing with imperial integrity. Tactics favored by other intellectual schools were constantly utilized but increasingly couched in Confucian ideology. At the same time, the temporal-spatiality of the court debates was enlarged by the postal system, connecting government personnel thousands of *li* apart and enjoining oral and written genres. The following is a list of key discourses on imperial integrity to be examined in this chapter (see table 5.1).

The Vertical-Horizontal Tactics

Su Qin (蘇秦) is the leading figure of the Vertical-Horizontal school. During the Warring States period, the fighting among the central states created a space for eloquent literati to broker political power. These literati fell into

TABLE 5.1 *Key Discourses on the Integrity of the Han*

Author	Discourses
Zou Yang 鄒陽	A dissenting opinion submitted to the king of Wu dissuading him from revolting against the central government (154 BCE)
Mei Cheng 枚乘	Two dissenting opinions submitted to the king of Wu dissuading him from revolting against the central government (154 BCE)
Liu An 劉安	A dissenting opinion submitted to Emperor Wu opposing a military campaign against Min-Yue (135 BCE)
Yan Zhu 嚴助	An oral explication of Emperor Wu's answer to Liu An's dissenting opinion (135 BCE)
Jia Juanzhi 賈捐之	A dissenting opinion submitted to Emperor Yuan opposing a military campaign against South Yue (48 BCE)

different intellectual schools, including the well-known Confucian, Legalist, and Vertical-Horizontal schools. While cross-pollination was the norm, these schools each maintained a distinct political philosophy and developed recognizable discursive strategies. Su Qin was one of the literati who practiced Vertical-Horizontal tactics; therefore, as dynastic historian Sima Qian acknowledges, his name often stood for both the school and the other individuals who practiced similar tactics in the Han dynasty. Understanding Vertical-Horizontal tactics requires an examination of the stories of Su Qin and Zhang Yi (張儀), another representative figure of the school, that Sima narrated. Both Su Qin and Zhang Yi were allegedly students of the Master of the Ghost Valley, therefore, the Master's teaching, as contained in the *Guiguzi*, could be visited to offer additional insights into the school's preferred tactics.

Su Qin and Zhang Yi found the utility of their talents in navigating the contending political powers. Among the warring states, the strong always wanted to annex the land of the weak, so that it could assume commanding power. The weak, in contrast, actively sought to build alliances with others to deter invasion and annexation. Among the strong states, Qin was located in the west, Chu in the south, Zhao in the north, Qi in the east, and Wei in the center. In Su Qin's years, Yan and Han were the weak states caught between strong ones (see figure 5.1). Su Qin was invited by Yan to help forge an alliance

Defending Imperial Integrity

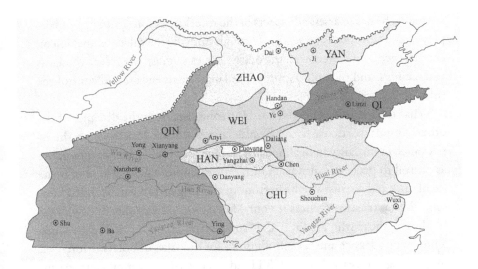

FIGURE 5.1 The Middle Kingdom during the late Warring States period. The map is created by the author.

with other eastern states to counter Qin, the then rising western power. To create such an alliance required an effort to build vertical relations. To break the vertical alliance, Qin hired Zhang Yi to build horizontal relations with the eastern states. Engaged in either forging or destroying these relations, Su Qin and Zhang Yi were called the Vertical-Horizontalists. The wrangling of these states created opportunities for those versed in argumentation to promote their political visions and to make a living.

The Vertical-Horizontal school developed a theory of suasion contained in the *Guiguzi* (Wu and Swearingen 2016). As introduced earlier, the text views speech as constitutive of natural dynamics and as the joint work of *yin* and *yang* forces.[3] Not only are discourses subject to the two forces, so are the interlocutors and their stylistic choices. Therefore, a sagely orator applies the *yin-yang* approach to understand the matrix of human desires and behaviors and uses this understanding to guide his practice in political oratory. In speech making, the *yin-yang* approach is concretized through two everyday motions, opening (*bai* 捭) and closing (*he* 闔). In preparing to speak, the orator needs to weigh (*chuai* 揣) the natural and human resources available to a state and probe the ruler's thoughts and feelings. In engaging the ruler discursively, the orator probes him secretively with patience (*mo* 摩). In choosing suasive strategies, he has to assess all aspects of the ruler's situation (*quan* 權) and deploy tactics kairotically (*mou* 謀). Through studying the ruler's temperament, competence, and preferences, the orator comes to grasp the ruler's thoughts and feelings, and to deploy appropriate language to engage and control the ruler (*fei qian* 飛鉗).

What distinguishes the Vertical-Horizontalists from the disciples of the other schools, particularly the Confucians, was their insistence on the irrelevance of morality in dealing with state relations. They viewed morality as central to personal cultivation only. For example, when accused of being vacillating and untrustworthy in front of the king of Yan, Su defended himself: "My untrustworthiness is your Majesty's good fortune. Your servant has heard 'those who are loyal and trustworthy are so for their own sakes. Those who advance and take profit do so for the sakes of others.' Moreover, in speaking before the King of Ch'I I did not even deceive him. Your servant abandoned his aged mother in East Chou; naturally by doing so I put away action for my own sake and engaged in advancing and taking profit" (Ssu-ma 1994b, 110). Then Su goes on to spell out the dire consequences to the state if he had been a filial son, an honest official, or a trustworthy man. Given a choice, he would rather be trustworthy to the state of Yan than to any individuals. Su's argument for the irrelevance of morality to state interests echoes two thoughts preached by the *Guiguzi*. First, a sagely orator does not need to pledge allegiance to a ruler. He could desert the ruler when the latter was unwise or ruthless (*wu he* 忤合). Second, when a ruler was found to be unfit for the state, the regime could be changed (*di xi* 抵巇). Both ideas corroborated Su's insistence that state interest should outweigh and overwrite the morality of the power broker. Unsurprisingly, Su's position was disapproved of by Sima Qian, as he characterized both Su Qin and Zhang Yi as posing a serious danger to the (Confucian moral) state (Ssu-ma 1994b, 142).

Vertical-Horizontal tactics have been loosely termed "the long and short art" (*chang duan shu* 長短術) based on the metaphor of a measuring stick, or, derogatorily, as "Weighing and Adapting" (*quanbian* 權變) by Sima Qian based on the metaphor of a sliding weight. A measuring stick or a sliding weight is used to arrive at some measurements, which then provide a basis for comparison, calculation, and decision. Likewise, one makes an argument by weighing the pros and cons of a proposed action. In the words of James I. Crump, the long and short art "refers to [the] strong tendency on the part of the persuader (as he is seen in the *Intrigues of the Warring States*) to frame

Defending Imperial Integrity

his persuasions in 'doubles': thesis and antithesis, arguments *for* a certain action and *against* its opposite and other classes of doubles such as paradoxes and dilemma" (Crump 1996, 44, emphasis in original). When Su Qin tried to persuade the eastern states to form a vertical alliance against Qin, for example, he underscored the disadvantages of them pursuing any relationship with Qin: a state will be humiliated if it bows to Qin; once Qin receives some land as a gesture of friendship from a state, it will demand more. In contrast, if an alliance is formed, small states will be secure and strong ones will have the potential to command other states. Traveling from one state to another, Su enumerated the benefits an individual state would reap upon joining the alliance. In the end, he succeeded in uniting the eastern states, which deterred Qin from invading them for fifteen years. Su's story and "the long and short art" generalized by Crump together exemplify the strategies of "weighing" (*chuai* 揣) and "assessing" (*quan* 權) suggested by *Guiguzi*.

To achieve their persuasive goals, the Vertical-Horizontalists relied on detailed calculation in their arguments. Often, they laid plain the scenarios that might occur if an action was taken or not taken. Through these scenarios, they created either fear or excitement to induce the desired actions from the audience, often the king of a state. For example, when Zhang Yi persuaded Wei to join a horizontal relation with Qin, he first created fear through a chain of scenarios: Qin will threaten Han and use it as a steppingstone to invade a small state also called Wei. Once it seizes the small Wei, it will cut off the connections between the big Wei and Zhao and dismantle the eastern alliance, thus endangering Wei. Next, Zhang Yi created excitement and hope in the king through another chain of scenarios on the condition that Wei joins a relationship with Qin. In these political consultations, the Vertical-Horizontalists became both military strategists and verbal artists. Fully cognizant of the kings' ambitions and concerns, they manipulated their feelings and emotions through calculated reasoning and verbal strategies.

The Vertical-Horizontalists were able to play a key role in the warring states' politics because the contending powers fought against each other on a level playing field. The central government of Zhou was negligible. A state had to protect itself by staying wary of its neighbors, who could be friends one day and foes the next. Intending or pretending to maximize a state's gains, the Vertical-Horizontalists favored the use of a series of calculations to induce strong emotional responses in their audiences without bringing in moral values to bear in state relations.

The *Spring and Autumn* Style

The *Spring and Autumn* style not only refers to certain ways of language use, but also ways of reasoning in alignment with Han Confucianism. The annals were allegedly edited by Confucius based on what he experienced or heard of. The document records events that happened between 722 BCE and 481 BCE in a succinct language. The Confucians studied the records closely, believing that the Master must have encoded in the language his political and moral teaching. In the beginning of the Han dynasty, five major exegetical lineages emerged from the annals;[4] by the time of Emperor Wu, they were inducted into the royal academy by means of endowed erudite positions. Their exegeses provided the foundation for making political decisions. Through the Han exegesis, this historical treatise was shown to have demonstrated a political philosophy distinct from that of the Vertical-Horizontalists. Here, we can focus on the exegetical work of Dong Zhongshu, the most eminent erudite of the annals.

For Dong, benevolence and fraternity were foundational values not only in cultivating individuals but also in governing a state. Concurring with Confucius in the *Analects*, he posits that benevolence means to love the people, not just people in one's proximity but everyone under heaven. Fraternity is to be critical of oneself but generous and kind to others. In dealing with state matters, a benevolent ruler tries to bring peace and comfort to the people and to prevent human casualties. Dong differentiates between the Kingly Way and the Despotic Way in terms of loving the people: "[The] love of the king extends to the four tribes; the love of the hegemon extends to the lords of the land" (Dong 2016, 314). To promote fraternity, the ruler should refrain from criticizing others or attacking them militarily. Dong claims that in the annals, Confucius taught the proper way to handle state matters through his particular ways of recording events.

Nevertheless, Confucius holds an ethnocentric and hierarchical view of people. Dong posits that Confucius, from a ruler's perspective, placed people into three categories based on the ruler's personal attachment. For example, the ruler of Lu will feel more attached to his own people than the people of other central states. He feels the least attached to peoples beyond the central states, often termed Yi (夷 people living in the south) and Di (狄 people living in the northwest). The widely held assumption about these peoples, which continued into the Han dynasty, was that they were less cultured, thus, less

Defending Imperial Integrity   127

susceptible to the influence of music and ritual. Despite the low opinion of these peoples, according to Dong, Confucius reminds his audience that they could sometimes act just as benevolently as people of the civilized central states. Likewise, people of a central state could act in an uncivilized fashion as the Yi and Di peoples normally did. Therefore, while, like his contemporaries, Confucius demarcates the people under heaven based on state boundaries, the most meaningful way of demarcation for him comes from the moral conduct of the ruler and the people.

Confucius condemns wars in the annals unequivocally. Wars always lead to human casualties, a result that violates his cardinal rule of benevolence in government. According to Dong, however, Confucius distinguishes between unjust and just wars based on the context: "Compared with a deceitful assault, a prearranged battle is considered righteous. Compared with [the alternative of] not fighting, a prearranged battle is not righteous" (Dong 2016, 95). At one point in the *Analects*, Confucius admonishes his audience that when the Way prevails under heaven, all orders concerning ritual, music, and punitive expeditions are issued by the Son of Heaven (*Analects* 1998, 196). The state ministers should not wage wars against each other, even if they do so in the name of the Son of Heaven. If the state minister is deemed as lacking benevolence and fraternity, a war could be waged against him, although it should be avoided if at all possible. Thus, even if Confucius views a few wars in the *Annals* as just, he would rather that war be avoided.

As an important guide to political thinking in the Han, the annals provide scholar-officials with both Confucian insights and references for arguments. They took on the exegesis as the foundational values and quoted events from the annals. For example, when Emperor Wu asked Yan Zhu to report his work as a governor in light of the *Annals*, the latter responded by quoting an event from the *Annals*.

> According to the *Spring and Autumn*, [because his brother was her mother's favorite choice for the throne] King Xiang left the royal city and lived in Zheng, and therefore could no longer serve his mother on a daily basis. I, your humble servant, should have served your Majesty like a son serving his father. [I failed to do so, therefore,] I should be punished. However, your Majesty was kind enough to have not done so. I beg to be allowed to return to the capital city to work in the accounting department for three years. (Ban 2007, 636)

128 *Defending Imperial Integrity*

Yan's response implies that he left the capital city because he lost the sovereign's favor. Using a historical event recorded in the annals, he compares himself to King Xiang, who was forced to leave the capital city and therefore could not serve his mother anymore. By quoting from the annals, Yan declares that he had always been loyal to the emperor, which is an attribute valued by Confucius. Thus, the annals provided both parties with an ideological frame and a textual reference for the exchange. Yan's apology was accepted, and he returned to the capital city.

Stemming the Centrifugal Tides

Emperor Wu did not favor Vertical-Horizontal tactics because he was wary of the politics of the early Han, politics that encouraged the growth of a Vertical-Horizontal school spirit among the scholar-officials. After the Qin dynasty was overthrown by revolting regional forces in 207 BCE, Liu Bang, the first emperor of the Han, redistributed power by assigning his generals, and later his sons, fiefs (called kingdoms) in the east. It was a strategy to stabilize and bring peace to the country swiftly. A map of the early Han thus resembles that of the late Warring States era. The central government controlled the territory of former Qin and part of Wei, Han, Chu, and Zhao, but relegated the eastern and coastal territories to the rule of the kings and princes.

However, rewarding land to officials and princes ended up nurturing centrifugal forces. In Sima Qian's moral universe, the kings and ministers revolved around the emperor like spokes upholding a hub. When all parties worked in a concerted effort, the spinning of the wheel would create centripetal forces that pull these parties toward the center. In reality, as some kingdoms grew stronger, they challenged the throne by disobeying advice or regulations issued by the central government, even with the threat of overthrowing it. Officials in the Han court repeatedly raised this concern to the emperor and suggested ways to weaken the kingdoms. For example, Jia Yi proposed to Emperor Wen, and Chao Cuo (晁錯) proposed to Emperor Jing, that when a king dies, his kingdom be broken into parts to be shared among his surviving sons. By creating small kingdoms, the central government could dismantle alliances formed among dissenting kingdoms, undermining any serious political challenges from below. Those centripetal initiatives were partially adopted by the emperors. Limiting the power of the kingdoms then gave rise to a struggle between centripetal and centrifugal forces. The struggle created a Warring-States-like

Defending Imperial Integrity   129

situation where all parties sought talented individuals for political advice and strategies. Literati sought patronage among the kings. Led by the king of Wu, the eastern kingdoms secretly plotted a rebellion against the central government.

In narrating the revolt, historian Ban Gu featured a genre network involving the discourses produced in the central government and in the kingdoms. For the latter, he foregrounded those of the two advisors of the king of Wu, Zou Yang (鄒陽) and Mei Cheng (枚乘). Zou and Mei tried to dissuade the king from revolt, but they failed. Ban portrayed them in a positive light because they guarded the imperial authority and contributed to the imperial integrity.[5] Still, their efforts retained the spirit of the Vertical-Horizontal school.

Both Zou and Mei petitioned the king with tactics drawn from the "long and short art." Both focus on the devastating consequences of rebellion against the central government. Zou approaches the dissuasion from several angles: first, he establishes rapport with the king by saying that many other kings were discontented with the emperor; second, he points out that the political power of Wu is unmatched with that of the central government; and finally, he reminds the king that, instigated by their political advisors, a few kings had plotted rebellions before but all failed and faced severe punishment from the emperor. By pointing out the power differential and failed revolts, Zou invited the king to imagine the consequence of his revolt—persuasion strategies similar to those employed by Zhang Yi when speaking to the king of Wei. In contrast, Mei does not explicitly touch on the issue of revolt but emphasizes the importance of weighing the pros and cons of any action. He starts his petition by appealing to ancient sage kings as models of careful planning and then uses a string of analogies and similes to show the dangers of a reckless action.

To gain a better understanding of the "long and short art" practiced in the early Han, we can consider two passages from Zou's and Mei's memorials, which both aim to create fear in the audience through comparison and contrast. In the passage below, Zou reminds the king of an enormous power differential between the kingdom of Wu and the central government through an analogy and historical references.

I have heard that a hundred hawks together could not overcome a giant eagle. Before the state of Zhao was partitioned, a large number of warriors in grand armor could gather in front of the Zhao court overnight. However, they could not prevent the king from being imprisoned [by the

130   *Defending Imperial Integrity*

Empress]. The king of Huainan made friends with peripatetic knights
and his court was filled with followers willing to die for him. But they
could not prevent him from being transferred westward [and dying on
the road]. When actions were not carefully planned, obviously even
great warriors like Zhuan Zhu and Meng Ben could not protect their
kings. Thus, I beg your Highness to reconsider your action carefully.
(Ban 2007, 517)

As commonly practiced in Han arguments, Zou starts this passage with an
analogy. Comparing the kingdoms to hawks and the central government to
a giant eagle, he emphasizes the significant power differential between them.
Next, he uses two recent failed revolts to demonstrate the dire consequences
of ignoring this power differential. Finally, he reiterates the importance of
careful calculation by referencing two renowned warriors during the Warring
States era, suggesting the ruthlessness of abusing military power.[6]

To perform comparison and contrast, Mei relies on analogies and similes,
as illustrated in the following passage.

When something that weighs a ton is hung on a string high in the air
and over an abyss, even a stupid person would worry that the string will
break. When a horse is already alert, drumming will only scare it. When
a string is about to break, someone with poor judgment even tries to
hang a heavy object on it! The string will break in the air and the object
will fall into the abyss. Facing a critical situation, one cannot afford to
be indecisive. When a ruler listens to his faithful officials, a hundred
difficulties will work out his way. However, insistence on a wrong cause
is as dangerous as piling up eggs or as difficult as ascending to the sky.
Changing his cause is as easy as turning his palms and as secure as Mount
Tai. Now, if he desires longevity, endless enjoyment, or the splendor like
that of an emperor, it is as easy as turning his palms. However, despite
a secure life like Mount Tai, he pursues a cause as dangerous as piling
up eggs and travels on a path as difficult as ascending to the sky, actions
which have truly puzzled me. (Ban 2007, 521–22)

Mei uses two analogies ("something that weighs a ton is hung on a string" and
"an alert horse will be scared by drumming") to warn the king of the danger
that he is already in. Then using a series of similes ("piling up eggs," "ascending
to the sky," "turning palms," and "Mount Tai"), Mei lays out the right and

Defending Imperial Integrity

wrong courses of action that the king could take. Analogies create vague and multiple meanings. Mei chooses to use them, being aware of the danger in talking about the plotting openly. In contrast, the similes are derived from everyday life experience, which will help the king perceive the ramifications of his choices unequivocally.

Zou's and Mei's petitions were ignored by the king. Therefore, they left the king and traveled westward. They sought patronage from another king, as the Vertical-Horizontalists would have done in the Warring States era.

When the revolt began in 154 BCE, Mei tried to dissuade the king of Wu with another memorial, adopting a different set of argumentative strategies. By then the king had formed an alliance with six other eastern kings, and the Wu troops were marching westward toward the capital city. Mei tries to create both fear and pride in his audience. He used strategies of *quan* (權) and *mou* (謀) as preached in the *Guiguzi*; he assessed all aspects of the ruler's situation and used persuasive tactics kairotically. When underscoring the central government's advantages over Wu, Mei appeals to historical precedents. During the Warring States period, the state of Qin crushed the alliance of the six eastern states, annexing them in the end. Now that the Han is more resourceful than the Qin, it has a better chance to repeat history by crushing the alliance of the rebelling kingdoms. Mei then praises the king, saying that he has gained splendor in his challenge to the emperor. In addition, his kingdom is already rich, abundant, beautiful, and secure, key features of an ideal state. Finally, Mei creates fear in his audience again: the Wu troops will be defeated by the royal army unless the king retreats swiftly.

Let's consider the passage in which Mei aims at inciting pleasure, pride, and excitement in the king. Mei praises what the king has already achieved and possessed, thus suggesting that there is no need to contend with the Han court.

> Even as a fief, your Highness is richer than his Majesty; although hidden in the southeast, Wu has a greater reputation than the Middle Kingdom. The Han has twenty-four commanderies and seventeen fiefs. When their tributes are sent to the capital, the wagons run one after the other for a thousand *li*. But among them, the jewels and rarities are not as valuable as those produced in Dongshan. When grains are sent to the capital, the roads are jammed by carts and rivers filled by boats. But the grains are not as good as those grown in Hailing. In the emperor's Shanglin Garden, there are palaces, rare treasures, and zoos. But his garden is not

132   *Defending Imperial Integrity*

as impressive as the Changzhou Garden. Enjoying his time in Qutai Palace, the emperor has a bird's view of the wide roads. But it is not as enjoyable as appreciating the tidal waves in Wu. The Han builds high and fortified city walls and the Great Walls, but they are not as secure as the Yangtze and Huai Rivers that circle Wu. Owing to these strengths, I am truly happy for your Highness. (Ban 2007, 522–23)

Mei starts this passage by praising the king for the wealth and the reputation of his kingdom. Then, he elaborates this point by constructing five contrasts between the Han and Wu. In these contrasts, he uses doublets, a triplet, and a quadruplet to describe the situation of the central government, and then uses five *buru* ("不如"), meaning "but not as . . . as," to vary the rhythm and to emphasize Wu's strengths. Effusive with descriptive and rhythmic terms, these consecutive contrasts could easily evoke pleasure, pride, and excitement in the king under normal circumstances.

After the praise, Mei uses a threat and sympathy to generate fear in the king. He first predicts the military moves that the emperor might take to attack Wu. Then he describes the current situation as extremely unfavorable to the king: Wu's alliance with the other dissenting kingdoms has crumbled and its troops are besieged by the royal army.

If your Highness withdrew your troops swiftly, the chance of being punished would be cut in half. Once his Majesty discovers your interest in the throne, infuriated he will order the royal navy to sail down the Yangtze River to attack your capital. He will order the king of Lu to block your grain transport routes in East Sea. He will order the king of Liang to repair their chariots, train their soldiers in archery, and store food. Liang will guard Xingyang, the gateway to the royal capital, and starve the Wu troops. Your Highness will not be able to return to your capital. The three kings of Huainan have kept their promises made to his Majesty and refused to rebel. The king of Qi committed suicide to cover up his rebellion. The four kings in Shandong could not send troops to assist you. The king of Zhao was detained in Handan. Clearly, the crime of revolt has nowhere to hide. Already a thousand *li* away from home, your Highness is being besieged by the royal troops within a ten-*li* perimeter. Generals Zhang Yi and Han Anguo are stationed in the north and Han Tuo in the east and west. The Wu troops cannot conquer Liang's city walls nor can they take a good rest. I feel sad for them. I beg your Highness to reconsider your actions. (Ban 2007, 523)

What Mei demonstrates in this passage is the wisdom of a military strategist. Like a general, he spreads out a mental map in front of the king. Then he points out the moves that the imperial troops might make: They will attack the king's capital and cut off his grain transport routes. The kingdom of Liang, ruled by the emperor's brother, will block the king's move west and the imperial army will round up his troops. Other kings in the alliance will not be able to rescue him. Thus, in the end, the king is doomed to fail. Mei's calculations soon proved accurate (see the military moves of the central government and of the king of Wu in figure 5.2); after turning a deaf ear to Mei's petition, the king was killed, and the revolt was crushed.

The wide spectrum of argumentative strategies used in Zou's and Mei's memorials demonstrates the vestige of the Vertical-Horizontal spirit in the early Han. Before the revolt, they opted to engage in explicit or vague discussions of the matter. During the revolt, Mei turned into a military strategist, performing a series of calculations on military actions. In their petitions, both weighed the cons of a rebellion against the emperor. They tried to create in the king pride and excitement for his kingdom and fear of the emperor through a variety of figures of speech. In their arguments, they were pragmatists, aiming to help the king guard the interests of Wu. The Warring-States-like political situation in the early Han encouraged these Vertical-Horizontal practices.

In their arguments, Zou and Mei did not brush away moral values nor accentuate them. In dissuading the king, they implicitly underscore the authority of the central government, a spirit that aligned with the Han exegesis of the *Spring and Autumn Annals*. Nevertheless, they evoked moral values marginally, hardly factoring them into their arguments. For example, Zou evokes virtue and fraternity when explaining why he serves the king: "When a sage king disciplines himself and cultivates his virtue, attracted by his fraternity the peripatetic literati will come to serve him and make a name out of it" ("聖王底節修德, 則遊談之士歸義思名"; Ban 2007, 517). Mei invokes benevolence, fraternity, and the Way when urging the king to reconsider his actions: "When one practices benevolence and good deeds daily, he may not recognize his goodness. But its work will show one day. If one abandons fraternity and acts against the Way, he may not feel his evil. But it will lead to failure one day" ("積德累行, 不知其善, 有時而用; 棄義背理, 不知其惡,

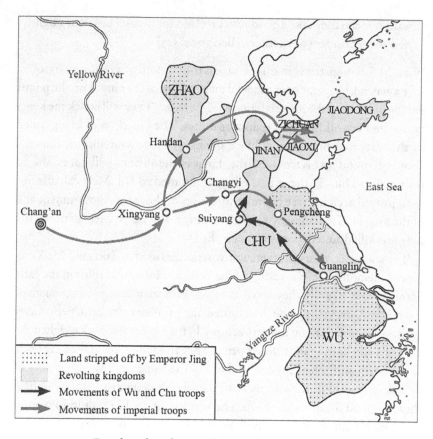

FIGURE 5.2 Revolting kingdoms and their military incursions in 154 BCE. The map is created by the author.

有時而亡"; Ban 2007, 522). In these remarks, the moral values are invoked as shared cultural knowledge, as the background of their arguments, a common practice among different schools of thought in the Warring States era.

While invoking moral values championed by the Confucians did not make Zou and Mei Confucian, they understood that the exegesis served as an epistemic foundation in the imperial court. After the revolt was quelled, kings who were involved desperately sought to evade monarchical punishments. Zou and his peers assisted them by crafting arguments that they could make to the emperor to get themselves exonerated. In these arguments, the exegesis of the *Spring and Autumn Annals* was used to form the backbone of the reasoning

Defending Imperial Integrity   135

(Ban 2007, 520–21). Zou and other peripatetic literati were more interested in helping the kings solve a practical issue than fortifying Confucian morality.

While Zou and Mei continued the Vertical-Horizontal spirit in their moral positioning and suasive strategies, their memorials marked a major genre shift caused by the pervasive postal system. During the Warring States era, the peripatetic *shi* focused on oral deliberation and persuasion. They brokered political power through face-to-face interactions, giving rise to numerous accounts of oral exchange recorded in texts of different intellectual schools. The unification and strengthening of the postal relay system in the Qin and Han dynasties gradually gave prominence to written genres. Compared with oral interactions, written texts could be easily transported, stored, and studied. This convenience encouraged the Han literati to develop a complex taxonomy of texts, which in turn helped to solidify a series of written genres for government (Giele 2006).

Containing the Barbarians

In Emperor Wu's reign, military actions were a frequent topic in foreign policy debates. While court officials continued to adopt Vertical-Horizontal tactics, the exegesis of the Confucian classics gained increasing weight. Through genre networks, the classics helped to evoke an imperial myth in these debates.

The mixed tactics drawn from both schools can be observed in the debates over the Yue peoples. In the late years of the Qin dynasty, the Yue people in the south broke away from the central states and formed three kingdoms— East Yue, Min-Yue, and South Yue. The Han court maintained a respectful distance with the Yue until Emperor Wu came to power. Worried that the borders would be assaulted by neighbors as they had been in the past, the emperor attacked the neighboring states and established new commanderies along the border regions as a shield. His attempts at containing and later annexing the Yue kingdoms manifested an approach to national defense that would be adopted by his successors. Although the Han rulers after Emperor Wu favored this approach, it was always negotiated and often compromised. Historian Ban Gu recorded two prominent genre networks concerning the Yue kingdoms. In the first instance, Min-Yue launched an attack against South Yue in 135 BCE. The Han court debated whether it should send its troops to the latter's rescue. More than a thousand *li* away, Liu An (劉安), the prince of Huainan, participated in the debate by submitting a memorial

136 *Defending Imperial Integrity*

to the emperor. In a second instance, occurring in 48 BCE, court official Jia Juanzi (賈捐之) debated with other officials on how to handle the dissenting Yue people. While illustrating the blending of tactics drawn from the two schools, both genre networks reveal the preponderance of Confucian classics in framing policy debates.

Living by the borders, geographically between the Han capital and the Yue people, Liu An played the role of a cultural translator and a power broker. In the memorial to Emperor Wu, Liu opposed the dispatch of the imperial army for a number of reasons, all based on verifiable factual evidence, and argued for diplomacy. For example, despite the fact that the Yue people constantly fought against each other, the Han court had never bothered to intervene in the past; the Yue people lived by water and were accustomed to battles over the water, an advantage which the Han troops lacked; the Han people had suffered loss in harvest for several consecutive years and they would suffer more if their sons were sent for the expedition; and with enough vigilance, the Han's border guards could prevent the Yue troops from assaulting the southern borders. In the end, Liu suggested that an emissary could achieve the same goal of sending one hundred thousand soldiers. Like Zou Yang and Mei Cheng, while appealing to the audience's interests, Liu intended to create fear in the audience.

Different from Zou and Mei, Liu appealed explicitly to the classics to bolster his antiwar argument. In the second half of his petition, he described the setback of the Qin dynasty in its attempt to conquer the Yue and then attributed its collapse to its perennial wars on the borders. He concludes his historical account by citing both Daoist and Confucian texts.

> This is exactly what Laozi meant by saying "Where the troops go, thistles and thorns grow." Wars are inauspicious: once a danger arises, many more will follow. I fear that unexpected happenings and evils will come after the attacks against the Yue. The *Changes* says, "Gaozong attacked Guifang but took three years to conquer it." Guifang is a minor barbaric tribe; Gaozong is the great king of Yin. It took the king three years to conquer a minor tribe, meaning caution is due when waging a war. (Ban 2007, 634)

The quotes from the *Laozi* and the *Changes* corroborated his historical account of the Qin. In his next point, he suggests that a sage king does not depend on military attacks to govern his people. He again quotes a Confucian classic: "The *Odes* says, 'When the Kingly Way prevails, people of Xufang will submit

Defending Imperial Integrity

themselves,' meaning that the Kingly Way is broad and it embraces people living afar" ("詩雲 "王猶允塞, 徐方既來", 言王道甚大, 而遠方懷之也"; Ban 2007, 634). Quoting from the classics, although a central strategy in his argument, should probably be viewed as a transient choice. Liu is neither a Daoist nor a Confucian. In the book, *Huainanzi*, that he compiled with guest scholars, Liu also extensively quotes Daoist and Confucian classics. His antiwar rhetoric in this petition agrees with the political philosophy revealed in *Huainanzi* (Ames). In both texts, Liu negotiates with Daoist philosophy and Confucian perspectives of government and advocates a less intrusive approach. Cognizant of the emperor's predilection for Confucianism, Liu appeals to the *Changes* and the *Odes* to strengthen his antiwar petition.

If the Han court generally viewed Xiongnu as an ethnic other, Liu did not take such a perspective to the Yue people. This was because of a tributary relation that the Yue states had nominally maintained with the Han court and their historical interactions with the Central States. In Liu's petition, he mentioned that the kingdom of Huainan used to border with the Yue states, and some of his officials used to serve in their governments. These connections gave him insights to the Yue people, including their land, their living habits, their military strengths and strategies, and their attitudes toward the Han. Despite his sympathetic knowledge, Liu maintained an ethnocentrism in his framing of Han-Yue relations. In the outset of the petition, he reiterated the ancient notion of five submissions, which viewed All-under-Heaven (*tianxia* 天下) from the perspective of the ruler of the Middle Kingdom ("故古者封內甸服, 封外侯服, 侯衛賓服, 蠻夷要服, 戎狄荒服, 遠近勢異也"; Ban 2007, 633). This rhetorical move reinforced the imperial myth that the Han was united, with the emperor holding the commanding power.

In response, the emperor, through his confidant Yan Zhu, repudiated Liu by invoking the same myth. Before Liu's memorial reached the royal capital, the decision to attack Min-Yue was made. Shortly after, Min-Yue surrendered to the Han troops. After the expedition, the emperor issued an edict called *bao* (報 sovereign answer) to Liu and sent Yan to deliver it. In the brief edict, the emperor defended his military decision. Yan elaborated on the defense in his ensuing meeting with the king. In one place, Yan justifies the expedition by invoking the imperial myth:

> The Han emperor heads the people under Heaven and controls their lives and deaths. Those in danger look to him for security; those in chaos look

138 *Defending Imperial Integrity*

to him for governance. Cruel and inhuman, the king of Min-Yue killed his brothers and alienated his relatives. Most things he did were unjust. He invaded Bai Yue repeatedly and annexed his neighbors, showing off his strength through brutality. Using schemes, his troops entered the Han territory and burned our naval vessels in Xunyang. He intended to follow the imperial course of Goujian, the former king of Yue, by occupying Kuaiji commandery. Recently, he reportedly led two kingdoms to attack South Yue. Concerned about the long-term security of all people, his Majesty wrote to the Yue rulers stating, "For the peace and security of the world, please continue your predecessors' course to pacify your people. Annexation is prohibited." (Ban 2007, 635)

In perpetuating the myth, Yan also appeals to an ethnocentric and imperialistic notion of Heavenly power. According to the *Analects*, Confucius held that when the Way prevails, all orders for punitive expeditions should be issued by the Son of Heaven. The expeditions are intended to punish local rulers and their people for behaviors that violate the Way. In this particular incident, the king of Yue was portrayed by Yan as inhuman (*buren* 不仁) and unjust (*buyi* 不義), two moral weaknesses condemned by Confucius. The king not only invaded and annexed his neighbors but also coveted Han territory. In Yan's defense, the emperor views himself as the Son of Heaven, who controls the lives and deaths of all people and has the responsibility to regulate relations between peoples inside and outside of Han. In this exchange, Yan not only defends the imperial expedition but also spells out Han's foreign policy for many years to come.

It was under this imperial myth that Emperor Wu later launched a series of attacks against the Yue people. In the above exchange, the emperor accused Min-Yue of being unjust in its attack against South Yue. Ironically, two decades later, his own troops invaded and annexed South Yue by accusing them of disobeying the Han court. After South Yue came under the Han's rule in 110 BCE, numerous revolts arose over the next sixty years. When one occurred in 48 BCE, Emperor Yuan convened his ministers to seek a solution. While most officials argued for a military solution, Jia Juanzhi was adamant in opposing it. Deeply entrenched in the imperial myth molded by Emperor Wu and Yan Zhu, the officials were appalled by his opposition. One chided him: "Zhuya has been a Han commandery for many years. Now its people rebelled and disobeyed the orders of the Han court. You oppose taking military actions, a position which will only encourage the barbarians'

Defending Imperial Integrity 139

disobedience and cancel the former emperors' efforts. Where among the classics could you find support for your argument?" (Ban 2007, 647). In urging Jia to defend himself within the exegetical space of the Confucian classics, the official's rhetorical question suggests that the imperial myth had become foundational in policy debates.

While both took an antiwar stance, Jia differs from Liu An by grounding his argument centrally in Confucian ideas, while the latter did not. In response to the official's challenge, Jia starts his memorial by drawing on stories of sage kings from the Confucian classics, emphasizing the importance of benevolent governance. Implicitly, the lineage of sage kings depicted by Jia confirmed the imperial myth—that is, as the son of Heaven, the emperor would join these sage kings in benevolent rule (Ban 2007, 647). Amid his effusive use of historical anecdotes, Jia's argument was resoundingly clear to his audience. That is, a ruler should only govern those who willingly submit themselves to his moral influences and give up those who do not. As his peers often did, Jia reviews the mythic sagely rule in different periods. Despite their relatively small territories, the sage kings governed their people through moral power instead of wars. Reviewing the sagely rule in one period after another, Jia uses a recognizable pattern to reinforce his point. In narrating the sage kings, Jia quotes the *Analects*, the *Book of Music*, and the *Spring and Autumn Annals* to provide both historical examples and their Confucian interpretations. The Confucian interpretations respect and accentuate the authority of the emperor and call for the submission of dukes and their subjects. Jia's historiography naturally leads to the conclusion that sagely rule does not allow wars and territory expansions. Embedding his interpretation in the citations from the classics was his strategy to speak to power.

Citing classical sources, Jia not only teaches his audience a lesson about the past but also explicates the political situation that the Han faces. In the rest of his memorial, he gradually moves from the Qin to the Han and from Emperor Wu to Emperor Yuan, commenting on the destructive forces of expansionism championed by Emperor Wu and his successors. Focusing on the various issues that plagued the Han in his time, Jia explains:

> Today, the Han territory mostly lies east of Hanguguan. There, the Qi and Chu are the largest areas. Stricken by poverty, the Qi and Chu people had to desert their homes and cities, drifting and sleeping on the road for years. Of human relations, there is nothing more intimate than those with

140 *Defending Imperial Integrity*

one's parents and nothing happier than those with one's spouse. However, people now are so wretched that they have to remarry their wives or sell their sons. Neither laws nor intimate relations can prevent them from doing so, a dire situation that has become a major concern of the state. Now, unable to stand people's complaints, his Majesty wants to crowd them into the seas and let them seek happiness in dark and dangerous places. This is not a viable solution to famine and insecurity. The *Odes* says, "The barbarians in Jingzhou are in motion, plotting wars against the large state." It means that when a sage rises the barbarians will submit themselves to his rule; that when the Middle Kingdom declines, they will revolt against it. Internal disturbance will plague the state, a problem that has worried us since ancient times, not to mention the additional threat posed by barbarians ten thousand *li* away in the south. (Ban 2007, 648)

In this passage, Jia uses specifics to depict a thorny issue in the Han society: perennial poverty in the Qi and Chu areas. Quoting from the *Odes*, Jia emphasizes this eminent issue over others. Without attending to it, the emperor would lose his moral authority; this social disturbance would weaken the Han and potentially lead to assaults from the "barbarians" in the south. A comparable historical precedent drawn from the Confucian classics helped strengthen his argument. Upon hearing from Jia and other court officials, Emperor Yuan gave up the military plan and abandoned the commandery Zhuya in the former South Yue area.

These two renowned court debates over Han-Yue relations reveal that the Confucian classics were prominently used in foreign policy deliberations. All parties appealed to them, using quotes either marginally or centrally in their arguments. Whether against or for wars, one could find support from the classics. The classics not only furnished historical precedents and ideas but also allowed multiple interpretations, thus varied meanings, of these historical events and ideas. Thus, anyone versed in the classics could recruit history to shore up his arguments. Emperor Wu explicitly ordered Yan Zhu to answer to him abiding by the spirit of the *Annals*. Jia Juanzhi was requested by fellow officials to explicate his opposition in light of the classics. These repeated demands indicate that a shift toward arguments centered on Confucian classics was tangible after Emperor Wu. The emperor favored Confucianism because it helped bolster the imperial myth. In turn, Confucian scholars were granted the authority to interpret the classics to the extent that even if they did not hold important official positions, they held the discursive power.

Despite the prominence of Confucian classics, the court officials also drew from other intellectual schools. Their choices were made based on their intellectual lineages and the nature of their arguments. For example, when addressing Han-Xiongnu relations, Zhong Jun (終軍) appealed to the Confucian classics in one of his memorials, calling for the ruler's cultivation of moral authority (Ban 2007, 643–44). In contrast, trained in multiple schools, Zhufu Yan (主父偃) appealed to militarist texts in one of his memorials. He cites from the *Strategies of Sima*: "Obsessed with wars, even a large state will collapse; although the world is peaceful, it is dangerous to neglect military preparation" ("國雖大, 好戰必亡; 天下雖平, 忘戰必危"), and from Sunzi's *Art of War*, "Running a hundred thousand troops costs a thousand *liang* of gold a day" ("興師十萬, 日費千金"). He warns Emperor Wu about the inherent dangers and costs that wars with the Xiongnu can bring to the Han people (Ban 2007, 638–39). By examining the citation practices in the memorials, we can observe the ceaseless circulation of thoughts and perspectives from different intellectual schools. Being the bedrock of the court debates, the Confucian classics were often appropriated for diametrically opposite opinions. In the process, their exegetical space was stretched and renewed.

Conclusion

Despite a unified territory state, the Han was challenged by centrifugal forces. In navigating these forces, Zou Yang, Mei Cheng, and Yan Zhu were known for their skilled use of Vertical-Horizontal tactics. When Emperor Wu rose to power, he promoted an argumentative style grounded in the spirit of the annals because its exegetic tradition upheld a myth that respected the monarchical authority and sought to maintain imperial integrity. Thereafter, while Vertical-Horizontal tactics continued to be employed in court debates on issues of diplomacy and ethnic relations, they were couched within Confucianism. In time, this practice came to influence the discourses of regional lords such as Kui Xiao (隗囂), Dou Rong (竇融), and Gongsun Guo (公孫過) and their supporters in the early Eastern Han when they staged claims for imperial power.[7]

In addition to shifting argumentative styles, the court deliberations examined in this chapter reveal the portability of arguments in the Han. With the word *portability*, I want to underscore the materiality and mobility of the memorials and edicts and, by extension, of the genre networks that they were part of. Written on bamboo slips or silk cloths with care, often these materials had to traverse thousands of *li* before reaching their intended audiences. Writing enabled individuals like Mei Cheng from Liang, Liu An from Huainan, and Yan Zhu from Kuaiji to perform deliberation across a vast land. Traveling across spatiotemporal distances, their texts helped to invent not only the various politico-military relations but also ethnic relations.

Judged by their original intents, Zou Yang, Mei Cheng, and Liu An all failed in their persuasions—their advice was either ignored or rejected. Nevertheless, their memorials were archived in the dynastic history as key addresses in the genre networks on imperial integrity. Ban Gu did so because Zou and Mei "guarded the righteous Way with words" (*yanzheng* 言正; Ban 2007, 525) and Liu was "the most profound and clear" (*shenqie* 深切) on ethnic relations (650). In other words, their petitions lent support to the imperial ideologies and functions. Studied by literati and officials of later generations, their memorials would serve as pedagogical material. In contrast, those who successfully persuaded the king of Wu to revolt against the Han court were dealt with marginally and their petitions were not recorded in the dynastic history. Like the memorials submitted by Zhou, Mei, and Liu, this historiographic practice equally lent support to the imperial myth.

CHAPTER 6

Praising and Criticizing as Entertainment

The grandiose kingly troops fought in the wilderness.
Crushing the fierce and the cruel, they united the realm.
Traversing ten thousand *li*, they reached the end of land and sea.
Consecrating holy mountains, they erected memorials.
Recounting the imperial deeds, they would inspire ten thousand generations.

鑠王師兮征荒裔
剿凶虐兮截海外
夐其邈兮亙地界
封神丘兮建隆嵑
熙帝載兮振萬世

—Ban Gu

In July 2017, a group of Chinese and Mongolian archaeologists discovered the cliff where the renowned "Mt. Yanran Inscription" (燕然山銘) was staged (Gao and An 2017). The inscription was composed by historian Ban Gu in 89 CE ensuing a bloody expedition to the North Xiongnu territory. The Han troops fatally defeated the nomadic North Xiongnu and dismantled its three-century threat to the agrarian Han. The troops were led by General Dou Xian, who invited Ban to join the expedition as staff officer. Upon the landmark win, the general asked Ban to compose a memorial. The piece narrated the expedition and ended with a short poem, which is quoted in the epigraph (Fan 2007, 245–46). The text was inscribed on a cliff surface facing southwest in a mountain local Mongolians now call Inil Hairhan.

144   *Praising and Criticizing as Entertainment*

In less than three hundred characters, the inscription tells an epic-like story. General Dou led the Han troops to the border commandery Shuofang. As his troops marched further north, he was joined by leaders of several tributary states and their armies. Together, thirty thousand cavaliers traversed wilderness and deserts. They defeated the North Xiongnu and brought its tribes to their knees. The story was narrated in the style of *fu*, or rhapsody, an esteemed genre in the Han. Specifically, Ban employed a variety of figures of speech, such as similes, metaphors, and parallelisms, to glorify the general's militarism. For example, he describes the Han troops as honorable as eagles and as brave as dragons and tigers, and he describes their armor shining bright under the sun and their scarlet banners filling the sky. When the troops launched attacks, they acted swiftly, like comets and lightening. All enemy troops were killed and the battleground turned deadly quiet (Fan 2007, 246). Mesmerized by the story, Chinese literati invented expressions such as 燕然勒功 (*yanran le gong*), literally meaning "inscribing achievements in Mt. Yanran," to anchor their imperial imagination and dreams of achieving stately honor.

The story was followed by a poem, written with features of the *Odes* and of the verse of Chu, genres prized in the aesthetic hierarchy of the Han. In the original inscription, every line of the poem contains six characters. When the poem circulated back to the Han, purportedly "to inspire ten thousand generations," each line was inserted with the character "兮" (*xi*) in the middle to mark a breath break. It helped to amplify the rhythms when the poem was sung. While "兮" was used sporadically in the *Odes*, it became popular in the verse of Chu and *fu*. In addition to the stylistic lineage, the poem inherited a cultural logic from the *Odes*. The poem starts with "鑠王師" (the grandiose kingly troops), an expression borrowed from one of the odes, which narrated a winning battle waged by King Wu of Zhou against King Zhou of Shang. King Wu was described as having received the Heavenly blessing and his troops as kingly.[1] Used to described the Han troops, the expression signifies the righteousness of their expedition.

The rhetorical power of the inscription comes additionally from a ritualistic spectacle. During the Shang and Zhou dynasties, the central states developed a tradition of inscribing texts in cooking vessels at events such as battles, sacrificial ceremonies, and the relocation of the capital city. The tradition evolved into inscribing texts in cliff surfaces and steles. In addition to their recording function, these texts mediated the ritual practice in which these material objects participated (Nylan 2005). There is little doubt that General Dou

Praising and Criticizing as Entertainment 145

had long planned the inscription because he recruited literati like Ban Gu, calligraphers, and handicraft men for his staff.[2] The inscription was part of a grand consecration ceremony joined by thousands of troops. Inscribing a Chinese text on a cliff surface deep in the Xiongnu territory was also symbolic. It symbolized the imposing power of the Han in military, cosmological, and linguistic terms. The memorial staged a long-lasting warning to the Xiongnu. As Xiongnu people gradually scattered and other peoples occupied the place, the memorial stood as a testament of the Han intrusion in this multilingual and multicultural space.

Therefore, the rhetorical power of the inscription came from a genre network involving human and nonhuman actors—a genre network as court historian Sima Qian had conceived. In contrast, Liu Xie's genre theory, grounded in literary criticism, suggests a different type of genre network in which the inscription participated. Liu proposed a hierarchy of genres, claiming that all genres of his day had evolved from Confucian classics, and, further, that genre boundaries were fluid. For illustration, he analyzed the verses of Chu as represented by Qu Yuan's "Li sao," to be discussed later in this chapter. He suggested that themes of the verses could be traced to those of the *Odes*, and their brilliant and dazzling language to the style used by members of the Vertical-Horizontal School. The inscription does show thematic and stylistic traces of the *Odes*. Liu's genre theory, with its attention to meanings, relations, and connections forged by texts as they traversed across a large temporal span, can complement Sima's theory. However, treating texts as literary artifacts by extracting them from genre networks as Sima conceived, Liu's genre theory has deprived texts of much of their sociohistorical agency.

In this chapter, in order to make a decolonial move, I will put literary genres, such as stories, odes, and rhapsody, back into their situated genre networks and examine how the networks helped to establish aesthetic and linguistic hierarchies in the Han. I will first survey the practice of storytelling that flourished in the Warring States period and furnished storytellers, historians, and *fu* writers of the Han with resources for developing character, plot, and setting. Performed in the palace, certain narrative forms were elevated from street art to courtly art. Next, I will consider the odes, the verses of Chu, and the rhapsodies. Depicting the lives of the commoners and the ruling class, the odes of the Zhou dynasty were often sung along with music, dance, or ritual practice in state events. Widely presented and quoted in political gatherings and used for the education of the elite, the odes became a prized literary form of the northern aristocracy. The verses of Chu, appearing in the late Warring States period, and *fu*, popularized during the Han dynasty, provided the literati with new forms for political participation and self-expression, in effect making *fu* the genre of the empire. Finally, I suggest that the elevated status of *fu* populated its writing style, making it instrumental in translating imperial lives, in that it allowed the literati to relate meaningfully to political, gendered, cultural, religious, and linguistic difference. The following is a list of literary works to be discussed in this chapter (see table 6.1).

The Trivial Talks

Court historians recognized the political power of story telling in the Han. They viewed the storytelling tradition as being deeply connected to the school of "trivial talks" (*xiaoshuo* 小說), one of the ten intellectual schools recorded in the *BH*. [3] Of the school, the book identified fifteen lineages, with more than one thousand and three hundred of their texts stored in the imperial libraries, the largest number for any school. The trivial talks refer to texts that originated from the street or in the marketplace, often with unverified substance ("街談 巷語, 道聽塗說者之所造也"). Although not as concerned about the serious topics of *dao* as the books of the other nine schools were, the trivial talks, in Ban Gu's opinion, were informative and engaging, thus proffered useful knowledge for a literatus ("閭裡小知者之所及, 亦使綴而不忘。 如或一言可采, 此亦芻蕘狂夫之議也"; Ban 2007, 338). Like adherents of some other schools, masters of the trivial talks often sought patronage from rulers and ranking officials. Some were recruited to serve in the palace. Working in the court, the trivial talkers elevated the practice of storytelling from local vernaculars to esteemed written forms.

A group of trivial talkers skilled in indirection (*yinyu* 隱語) were recorded in the *GSR*. The chapter "Memoires of Witty Courtiers" (滑稽列傳) included stories of nine individuals from both the Warring States period and the reign of Emperor Wu. Some of them served as court entertainers (*paiyou* 俳優) charged with the task of entertaining the ruler and his entourage through music, dance, and witty words. In these stories, they often used humorous analogies to create striking imaginations in the audience, leading the latter to smiling, musing, and then action. Chun Yu Kun (淳於髡) was one of those witty speakers, serving in the court of Qi. The king was indulging in drinking and women, paying no heed to threats from neighboring states. He was

Praising and Criticizing as Entertainment 147

TABLE 6.1 *Stories, Poetry, and Rhapsody*

Author	Works
Qu Yuan (屈原)	"Li sao" (離騷)
Sima Qian (司馬遷)	"Memoires of Witty Courtiers" (滑稽列傳)
Sima Xiangru (司馬相如)	"Zixü Fu" (子虛賦) "Shanglin Fu" (上林賦) "Announcement to the Ba and Shu Governors" (諭巴蜀檄)
Yang Xiong (楊雄)	"A Response to Mockery" (解嘲)
Ban Jieyu (班婕妤)	"A Concubine's Lament" (自悼賦)
Ban Gu (班固)	"Two Capital Cities" (兩都賦) "Mt. Yanran Inscription" (燕然山銘)
Kasyapa Matanga (迦葉摩騰) and Dharmaratna (竺法蘭)	"Sutra in Forty-Two Sections" (四十二章經)

approached by Chun with a story and a question: A giant bird landed in the king's courtyard and lingered for three years without making a sound. Why? Alerted, the king responded by completing the story: When the bird flies, it will shoot to the sky; when it makes a sound, it will appall others. Immediately, the king gathered his officials and started attending to state matters, eventually rising as a hegemon. The power of Chun's speech came from his story, in which he sets up an open-ended plot and leaves it to be perfected by the audience. Being invited into the story, into a form of cross-talk, the ruler was compelled to respond, to make a decision, and then to act upon it. Anecdotes of such witty speakers must have been told widely, as a similar plot was found across multiple sources in the Warring States period.[4]

The stories of Chun Yu Kun might have come from the marketplace. Miyazaki Ichisada argues that many stories told in the *GSR* originally came from oral forms. They included key elements of fiction, including a dramatic plot, prolonged dialogues, and detailed descriptions of bodily movements.[5] As a court historian, Sima Qian was undoubtedly exposed to historic fictions narrated or performed by storytellers (*ouyu zhe* 偶語者) in the marketplace (*shi* 市) and inside the palace. When he was young, he traveled in the former central states to examine historic events and persons, gaining access to their stories told locally. Miyazaki suggests that many of the stories told by Sima follow a narrative scheme, consisting of four moves: beginning, continuing, turning, and uniting (*qi cheng zhuan jie* 起承轉接).[6] The move "turning" resembles what is now being taught as crisis, or "the reversal of the protagonist's fortunes," in a typical fiction-writing course.[7] In the story of Chun Yu Kun, for instance, the evocation of a giant bird leads dramatically to persuasion, forming the "turning" point. Prolonged dialogues and detailed descriptions of bodily movements were other striking features in those stories. The dialogues often took place between two individuals, fitting for two or three storytellers to perform theatrically.

The narrative scheme was not only used by witty speakers and court historians, but also, to be illustrated later, writers of *fu*, the most esteemed literary form in the Han. The scheme also resonates with the form of the odes, which were used in entertainment and persuasion in preimperial court culture. That the scheme is found across genres supports Liu Xie's theory that genre boundaries are fluid.

The Odes

The odes represent the earliest Chinese poetry, and many of them were written with political motives. Largely produced in the Central Plains, the basin of the Yellow River in the northern part of China, between the eleventh and sixth century BCE, the odes depict the lives of both ordinary people and the ruling class. Many describe the hardship experienced by the commoners: they worked through the four seasons, planting and harvesting, picking mulberry and tea leaves, gathering firewood and hunting, and brewing wines and building houses. They provided service to the government in peaceful times and served as conscripts during wars. In contrast, officials enforced severe laws on the people and entertained themselves through hunting, dance, and banquets. Some events from the Zhou dynasty were recorded in the odes, where kings and their officials were either praised or criticized.

The compilation of the odes was also politically motivated. Multiple sources from the Han dynasty have attributed the work to Confucius, underscoring its political and rhetorical intents. In a preface to the collection by a Han scholar named Mao, for instance, the reader is introduced to a tripart organization emphasizing each part's political intents.[8] The collection was divided into *feng* (風), *ya* (雅), and *song* (頌). Literally meaning "wind" or "air," *feng* refers to the lower rank gently remonstrating the higher rank (*feng* 諷). The odes in the section of *feng*, according to the preface, represent the lives and feelings of the commoners. *Ya* means correction of errors. Composed by members of the ruling class, the pieces in this section are supposed to have captured their moods and to serve as a guide for the ruler. On the one hand, the authors criticized the ruler through satire (*ci* 刺) and offered him advice (*jian* 諫); on the other hand, they expressed discontent for the social reality. *Song* means praise. The poems in this section sing praise to the ruler's benevolence during the events of sacrifice for gods and ancestors. The tripart structure, as Mark Edward Lewis suggests, served as a literary model of empire: "Initially dispersed across the states, in poems which as 'wind' are identified with customs and the influence of locality, the verses ascend to kingly government in the center, and culminated in the temple where they rise up to the ancestral spirits" (Lewis 1999, 175). In the *Analects*, upon returning home from the state of Wei, Confucius was recorded as rearranging the pieces in the *ya* and *song* sections and adjusting their musical tunes (*Analects* 1998, 130).

This record about Confucius indicates two features of odes in his time. First, they were widely used in diplomacy. In the *ZT* and the *DS*, two collections of anecdotes dealing with statecraft in that period, odes were presented orally by the host and the visitor at state or private banquets several dozen times.[9] They were used to express personal feelings and aspirations and to make arguments. One draws on the shared interpretations of an ode to help make a point, often through the strategy of what Aristotle has called paradigm or example, treating an ode as representing historical precedents to illustrate or comment on the present. After visiting sixteen states and being poorly treated by them, Confucius keenly perceived the role of odes in political life and was probably inspired to rearrange them for educational purposes. Second, the odes were often sung or recited in company of music and dance during highly ritualistic events such as banquets and sacrificial ceremonies. In turn, music came to shape the form of the odes: consisting of several stanzas, an ode uses similar sentence patterns in each, forming parallelisms across stanzas.

These two features can be illuminated in a genre event from the *ZT* (Durrant, Li, and Schaberg 2016, 1041). In 557 BCE, Shusun Bao, a minister of Lu, visited the state of Jin, a hegemon among the central states. Shusun reported that the state of Qi was posing a grave threat to Lu, and he requested the assistance of Jin. Jin declined his request. At an audience with a ranking Jin official Zhong-hang Yan, Shusun presented the ode "Minister of War" (祈父). The ode was composed in the voice of Zhou's capital city guards, who complained that the Minister of War had sent them to the battlefield and kept them there for an unreasonably long time. They suffered from poor living conditions and failed to care for their parents. Juxtaposing a historical event with the present, implicitly Shusun remonstrated the Jin officials. As the hegemon, Jin was supposed to regulate the relations between the central states and to provide protection to small states such as Lu. However, it failed to do so, a failure that had caused a great danger to Lu. Immediately, Zhonghang apologized to Shusun. At another audience with the prime minister Fan Gai, Shusun recited the last stanza of the ode "Wild Geese" (鴻雁). The piece was composed in the voice of Zhou officials who were sent to help the people recuperate from wars. However, these officials were unappreciated or misunderstood by the people. Upon hearing the ode, Fan promised to provide the state of Lu with protection. The ode resonated with him probably because he was compared to those underappreciated officials.

In the story, the odes succeed at where arguments had failed. The odes were probably presented along with music. Most odes run four syllables (characters) in each line, but some use an uneven number. As the lines are short and not always rhyming, the use of the same syntactic patterns across stanzas is the key strategy to create rhythm. The music also helps with rhythm and rhyming in the odes' internal structures. In the ode "Minister of War," for example, the lines have an uneven number of syllables but use the same sentence patterns across stanzas. In contrast, the ode "Wild Geese" consistently uses four syllables in each line. Thus, the rhetorical power of the *Odes* in the *ZT* story becomes clear. First, it comes from the odes' interaction with arguments. The historical events or images they invoke in the audience enhance the ethical and affective appeals of Shusun's initial argument. Second, it comes from singing or reciting odes along with music, and probably with food and wine being served, all of which jointly create affection and sometimes affinity among the interlocutors.[10]

The power of odes also comes from their internal mechanism, which seems to resonate with the narrative scheme "beginning, continuing, turning, and uniting." In the preface to the *Odes*, Mao identifies three rhetorical devices used in the odes: *fu* (賦), *bi* (比), and *xing* (興). *Fu* means direct expression and elaboration. Specifically, a poet may enumerate a series of objects or details and make effusive use of parallelisms. In "Minister of War," for example, *fu* is used. To express his dissatisfaction with the military assignment, the narrator uses parallelisms across stanzas and raises three rhetorical questions. These devices helped him amplify his dreadful situation and his earnest feelings. *Bi* means

Praising and Criticizing as Entertainment

comparing *A* to *B* through the use of simile, metaphor, or analogy to create images. *Xing* literally means the beginning or rising, referring to the strategy of using a discussion of concrete objects, through the reader's imagination, to bring forth a particular theme. *Xing* seems to function similarly to the move of "turning" in narration: it brings a poetic narration or description to a climax, and then reveals the theme of the work. In the ode "Wild Geese," for instance, *bi* and *xing* are used. Wild geese are compared to the people displaced by war (*bi*). When the image of wild geese flying and making lamentable cries is juxtaposed with the mentioning of the "wise" and "foolish" men, the theme of the poem rises in the mind of the reader—people's miserable lives are caused by the government (*xing*).

The story of Shusun illustrates only one way that the odes were used in the political scene during the Spring and Autumn period; the more common way is to cite an ode in speeches. In the *ZT* narratives, when an ode was presented in the way that Shusun did at the banquet, only its title was named; when it was quoted as part of a speech, the quoted parts would be spelled out. Mark Edward Lewis suggests that presentation and quotation of a verse served distinct rhetorical functions. The former intended to elicit a particular action in the audience within the narrative by drawing on "the emotive or imagistic force of the ode and the bond created by the shared recognition of veiled meaning" (Lewis 1999, 166). In the latter, on the other hand, the ode is cited as an authority, as historical precedents and moral maxims, to reinforce an argument. While the meaning was generally veiled and subject to the interpretation in the presentation of a verse, it was fixed in the quotation of a verse. Either way, after the Zhou culture and political structure disintegrated, the odes provided politicians of the central states with a common code, or what Lewis called a "lingua franca," for political exchange and coded negotiation (158).

Recognizing the power of the *Odes* in political life, Confucius made them part of his teaching. In the *Analects*, he comments on the *Odes* when answering his students' questions dealing with the rich and the poor and with ritual and ornamentation, and when training a diplomat.[11] He sums up the *Odes*'s functions at home and in office: "Reciting the *Songs* [*Ode*] can arouse your sensibilities, strengthen your powers of observation, enhance your ability to get on with others, and sharpen your critical skills. Close at hand it enables you to serve your father, and away at court it enables you to serve your lord" (*Analects* 1998, 206). When masterfully used, the *Odes* could perform these social and rhetorical functions and enable a student to become a morally competent person. The example of Shusun using the odes in political suasion has clearly demonstrated these socio-rhetorical functions.

To sum up, the odes played a unique role in political discourse by participating in multigenre and multimodal communications. In turn, this role helped to elevate their aesthetic and linguistic status among the educated. In diplomacy in the Spring and Autumn period, they were often juxtaposed with arguments to achieve persuasion. Reasoning by example, the odes provided historical precedents for forming a comparison with the present. The odes were often presented orally in tune with musical performance, creating affection and reinforcing identification among the interlocutors. However, it's worth noting that these features of odes and political suasion are generalized based on stories from the *ZT* and the *DS*, both historiographic and literary works partly shaped by trivial talkers in the Warring States period.

Stories and poetry further converged toward the end of the Warring States period, giving rise to new art forms, such as *Chuci* (楚辭 the verses of Chu) and *fu* (賦 rhapsody), genres to be embraced by the Han literati for both political participation and self-expression.

The Voices of the *Shi* from Chu

A poem does not always truthfully express the poet's feelings and aspirations. The odes, as "Minister of War" and "Wild Geese" show, captured the voices of people of different walks and ranks. These voices may not belong to those who put them into written words. They were recorded, edited, recreated, and, through genre networks, reified by the literate, that is, the *shi* (士). *Shi* was a very small group in the Western Zhou, the dynasty in which the majority of the odes were produced. Serving as scribes during the royal family's sacrificial ceremonies, they carved words on animal bones for portending or kept records of events in bronze objects. As the Zhou government crumbled and states rose in the Central Plains, the *shi* dispersed into these polities. During the Spring and Autumn era, these states established their own bureaucratic system and staffed it with the *shi*. As the states fought against each other, the *shi* were coveted by the rulers as well as powerful families. In the Warring States era, the *shi* class grew and they turned poetry into a means of expressing their own feelings and aspirations.

The most known poet from the period was Qu Yuan (屈原), whose work best captured the feelings and aspirations of the *shi* and inspired generations

Praising and Criticizing as Entertainment

of imitators. According to the story told by Sima Qian, Qu lived in the state of Chu, a southern state historically viewed as barbaric and foreign by the central states, between 340 BCE and 278 BCE. Based on his poetic work and other historical records, like many *shi* of his times, Qu was deeply involved in statecraft. A counselor to the ruler, however, Qu's advice often fell on deaf ears. Feeling dejected, Qu expressed his frustration and sadness in a series of verse. At that time, Chu was in a tense rivalry with the state of Qin. When the capital of Chu was seized by the Qin troops, Qu committed suicide by drowning himself in a river. Qu's story, through his poetic work, resonated with a large number of *shi* whose counsel and loyalty were not readily appreciated either.

Compared with the odes, Qu's work performed two distinct political functions. First, he constructed a profound voice of a dejected *shi*. In his most renowned verse "Li sao" (離騷), for example, he recounts the origin of his family, reviews the government of early Chu rulers, contrasts his political ambitions with his dejection, exposes the dark side of the Chu political life, and sings praise to his ideal society. Qu's work painted an idealism for the *shi* and offered the group both a model and an outlet for self-expression. Second, Qu's voice is a distinctly southern one, filled with sensibilities of living in Chu—including its plants, myths, personalities, and language. In "Li sao," for example, Qu repeatedly draws on names of local plants to signify his qualities and personal values. This is the rhetorical device of *xing* (giving rise to a theme) also used in the odes. He draws on local myths and mythic figures as participants in his inner dialogues. He repeatedly employs *xi* (兮), an expression allegedly used in the Chu language for sighing. Compared with the odes, the sentence structures in his work are more varied, allegedly to match the music performed in local shamanic dances. Although Chu was conquered by Qin, Qu's work constructed a Chu identity and marked Chu as a politico-cultural center on par with the Central Plains.

Qu's lasting literary and political legacy comes from two features of the "Li sao," features that are derived from the *shi* culture. First, his work is marked by a *fu* style commonly employed by the *shi*. In the Warring States period, the *shi* served on government posts and sometimes took on diplomatic missions. They were noted for their eloquence. Eloquence means not only logical reasoning but also an elegant style, including extensive use of vivid and imagistic words, metaphors, and parallelisms. This style, called *fu* (賦), to be discussed in more detail in the later sections, is in full display across Qu's works, surpassing its use in the *Odes* in scale. In the following excerpt from the long verse "Li sao,"

154 *Praising and Criticizing as Entertainment*

through a *fu* style, Qu vows to remain upright in Chu society. He does so by first describing his gardening activities before turning to a description of Chu society, where, driven by greed and jealousy, people treat each other meanly.

> I grew nine *wan* of boneset,
> Planted one hundred *mu* of basil,
> Kept separate the plots of peonies and loose-strife,
> And mixed asarum with the scent-roots,
> Hoping for tall-standing stems and leaves bristling,
> Willing to wait for the reaping season.
> Why would I grieve if they withered and broke?
> Though I'd mourn if the fragrant fell to the weeds.
>
> The crowd for greed wrangles toward you,
> Unslakeable in their fury of seek and demand.
> Yes, each looks within for the standard to measure others,
> But a heart hopping with envy is all she finds.
> Everywhere at full gallop and nimbly they chase,
> But that is not my fret,
> For age sun-slow is on the way,
> My adornment's fame might not stand—*that* I fear.
>
> (Sukhu 2013, 185)

In this excerpt, Qu uses planting flowers and herbs (the first eight lines) as a lead to invoke his critique of Chu society (the last eight lines), a manifestation of the device *xing*. In terms of the *fu* style, Qu uses two parallelisms to introduce the flowers and herbs he planted (the first four lines). When describing the vices in Chu society, he uses an extended parallelism in line nine to line twelve. These parallelisms create rhythms, making the reading or singing pleasant to the ear; they stretch the reader's imagination, preparing them for the poet's exposition on the subject matter.

Second, the "Li sao" uses a discourse pattern commonly found in prose writing of the same period. In the Warring States period, the peripatetic *shi* were portrayed in texts of different schools as almost always engaging a ruler or other literati in dialogues as they tried to sell their political visions and strategies. The "Li sao" starts with an introduction to the context including the interlocutors (*xu* 序), and ends with some concluding remarks (*luan* 亂). In between, the verse is framed as dialogues. In the middle of the verse, for

Praising and Criticizing as Entertainment 155

example, an elder sister comes to remonstrate the poet, urging him to follow the mainstream Chu society rather than seeking unachievable ideals. Later, the poet seeks advice from a shaman, who suggests that he leaves behind Chu as well as his frustration. Dialogues like these take the reader into the poet's world or lead them to an in-depth exploration of a topic.

Thus, Qu Yuan's work achieves remarkable political and rhetorical significance. Politically, it foregrounded the *shi* by expressing their aspirations for serving an enlightened ruler and for maintaining uprightness. His work bolstered Chu as an important political and cultural center among the warring states and foreboded the rise of southern culture in the upcoming empire. Rhetorically, his work continued the tradition of the *Odes* by using *fu*, *bi*, and *xing* as devices to critique social ills and to express personal feelings and aspirations. Moreover, his work expanded the tradition by adding sensibilities of southern living, deploying the *fu* device on a large scale, and introducing a dialogical form into poetic invention. Inspired by Qu's achievements, as anthologized in the *Verses of Chu* (*Chuci* 楚辭), several generations of literati modeled after him in theme and technique.

Attributing the "Li sao" to Qu Yuan is now viewed by scholars as a deliberate political strategy to both glorify and contain Chu literature. The *Verses of Chu* was compiled by Liu An, the king of Huainan, part of the former state of Chu, and his patrons. Thus, as Mark Edward Lewis (1999) holds, on the one hand, the Qu Yuan of the "Li sao" should be viewed as "a set of attitudes, recurring images, and rhetorical tropes," and the narrative of the dejected man of virtue and martyr constructed by Sima Qian gave these attitudes, images, and tropes "a time, a place, and a human core to which (whom?) readers could attribute the stances and gestures in the text, and with which they could identify" (189). On the other hand, Sima's narrative was a strategy to domesticate the *Verses of Chu* and, by extension, Chu literature and culture by bringing its extravagant flights of language, the appeals to cult and religious practices, and the dangerous solipsism of the text into the imperial universe constructed by Mao in his preface to the *Odes*.[12]

Praise and Criticism in the Grand *Fu*

After Han was established, Chu culture rose to empire-wide prominence. The rise was captured by Sima Qian in his accounts of the rivalry between rebel leaders Xiang Yu and Liu Bang, both from the former state of Chu. When

156   *Praising and Criticizing as Entertainment*

Xiang's troops were rounded up by Liu's in Gaixia, in great desperation and sadness, Xiang composed a poem using "xi," the marker for breath breaks in Chu verse. Playing a string instrument called *zhu*, he sang it together with his concubine Yi.

> My strength uplifted a mountain (xi),
> My vigor shadowed the world.
> But the times do not favor me (xi),
> And Piebald can not gallop fast enough.
> Piebald can not gallop fast enough (xi).
> And what can I do about it?
> Oh, Yü (xi), Oh, Yü (xi)!
> What can I do about you?

> 力拔山兮氣蓋世。
> 時不利兮騅不逝。
> 騅不逝兮可奈何!
> 虞兮虞兮奈若何!

(Ssu-ma, 1994a, 205)

Shortly after, Xiang committed suicide and Liu Bang became the first emperor of Han. Before his death eight years later, Liu also composed a Chu-style poem when visiting his hometown. Playing *zhu*, he sang it together with a large group of children: "A great wind arose (xi), clouds flew up!/ My prestige increasing within the seas (xi), I return to my hometown./ But where will I find valiant warriors (xi) to hold the four directions!" ("大風起兮雲飛揚, 威加海內兮歸故鄉, 安得猛士兮守四方!"; Ssu-Ma 2002, 82). Depicting two strong men of their times, Sima used their verses to assert Chu culture in the empire.

The foreignness of Chu culture was strongly felt and finally contained in the large number of *fu*, or rhapsody, produced in the Han. Kong Deming, in examining historical records, has counted more than a thousand pieces with author names specified in the Han dynasty. Many of these pieces, as I will illustrate next, carried over the two rhetorical features manifested in Qu Yuan's work: the *fu* style and the dialogical form. The majority of renowned *fu* writers in the Western Han came from the Chu region (the former state of Chu), such as Sima Xiangru (司馬相如), Yang Xiong (楊雄), Mei Cheng (枚乘), Mei Gao (枚皋), Zou Yang (鄒陽), Wang Bao (王褒), and Liu An (劉安). According

Praising and Criticizing as Entertainment 157

to Ban Gu, in the preface of his renowned *fu* "Two Capital Cities" (二都賦), by his time, more than a thousand pieces were presented to the imperial court, a phenomenon that clearly indicates the imperial power's attempt to contain any threats posed by the "barbaric" Chu culture.

As many of the *fu* pieces were sanctioned by the court, *fu* became the literary genre of the state. In the reign of Emperors Wu and Xuan, the Han enjoyed political stability and economic development. The state was able to render more support to the cultural domain, such as creating posts to oversee ritual practice and hiring officials through essay exams, building an academy for studying Confucian classics and a library for storing books, and opening an office for collecting folk songs and adjusting musical tunes. The government hoped to recover old laws, regulations, and other types of cultural heritage. It hired court attendants who were specialized in letters, such as Sima Xiangru, Yiqiu Shouwang, Dongfang Shuo, Mei Gao, Wang Bao, and Liu Xiang, to compose *fu*. Other officials sometimes also presented their *fu* work. Continuing the *ya* and *song* tradition of the odes, the *fu* pieces, particularly the so-called grand *fu* written for the consumption of the sovereign, served both to praise and remonstrate the ruler.

An examination of Sima Xiangru's "*Zixü Fu*" (子虛賦) and "*Shanglin Fu*" (上林賦) can reveal the challenges in performing criticism amid the political wrangling between the kingdoms and the central government, and between glorifying and containing the Chu culture. Sima composed "*Zixü Fu*" to entertain King Xiao of Liang, a vassal kingdom, during his sojourn there (Ssu-ma 2020, 155). In *fu*, Sima constructs a story involving Chu and Qi, two major states during the Warring States period (Ssu-ma 2020, 158–85). The southern part of Liang used to belong to Chu. The story follows the scheme "beginning, continuing, turning, and uniting." *Beginning*: Chu sends an emissary called Zixü (Master Empty) to visit Qi. After a hunting trip with the ruler of Qi, Zixü discusses the trip with a teacher named Wuyou (Master Nonexistent). He tells Wuyou that the ruler boasted to him about the hunting expedition and asked whether Chu had land for such an event. *Continuing*: Zixü responds by giving a speech, elaborating on a hunting expedition that he witnessed in one of the Chu water regions called Yunmeng. The long-winded speech is filled with objects, animals, and actions described in a *fu* style. Praising the riches of Chu in the context of warring states would sound not only reasonable but also pleasing to the King of Liang, who owns the water region described in the story.

158 *Praising and Criticizing as Entertainment*

After the pleasing speech, the piece turns into a gentle criticism of the King of Liang. *Turning*: After hearing the details of the Chu water region, Wuyou explains that the ruler of Qi did not mean to boast his hunting expedition, but rather took the opportunity to learn about the achievements of Chu in educating its people. Further, Wuyou comments on Zixü's speech: "However, you did not celebrate the grand moral achievements made by the King of Chu but boasted the riches of the Yunmeng region. You focused on the grandiose hunting and entertainment events and showed off wasteful spending. I think you should not have done that" (Ban 2007, 576). Undoubtedly, this criticism was directed at the King of Liang, who was known for his extravagance. However, the rather short criticism was embedded in a profuse description of the riches of the water region and the actions during the hunting expedition, thus losing much of its critical thrust. *Uniting*: Wuyou enumerates the rich resources of Qi and suggests that the king of Qi was humble enough not to boast them.

Impressed by the piece, a few years later, Emperor Wu requested that Sima compose a *fu* for him. Adopting a similar storyline and a similar narrative scheme, Sima produced a sequel to "*Zixü Fu*" by adding another figure named Wushigong (Lord There Is No Such Thing) to the dialogue. *Beginning*: Siding with the imperial power, Wushigong first criticizes both Chu and Qi: The fiefs submit gifts to the Son of Heaven on a regular basis, a practice which gives them an opportunity to report their work; their fiefdoms are clearly marked geographically so they would act lawfully. However, Qi has crossed its borders, secretly making contact with the barbaric Shusheng people and going on fishing expeditions in the East Sea. And by competing against each other on hunting expeditions, both Chu and Qi have ignored the proper relationship expected between the King of Zhou and the fiefs or between the fiefs. Although Wushigong comments on Chu and Qi from the perspective of the Zhou court, this setup unequivocally reiterates the supreme power of the Han emperor, who demands respect and submission from the vassal kingdoms. *Continuing*: Along with this praise for the imperial power, Wushigong goes on to describe the riches of the royal forest named Shanglin and an imperial hunting expedition therein.

The highly anticipated criticism, the *turning*, comes at the end of Wushigong's profuse speech on the expedition. The expedition ends with an extravagant banquet, where the emperor suddenly comes to recognize his pompous lifestyle. He halts the feast and orders a series of reforms declaring that: the hunting ground be turned into arable land; the imperial gardens and ponds be opened for public use; poor people and those who have no kin and cannot support themselves be provided for; laws be enforced leniently; and regulations and calendars be revised. After these reforms, the imperial Way prevails, people treat each other like family members, and penalty and punishments are abandoned. The criticism is clear: the emperor has led an extravagant life, setting up a poor model for the fiefs and government officials. However, Sima creates a twist, making the emperor an enlightened ruler who is capable of correcting his errors. *Uniting*: Wushigong goes back to criticizing the kings of Qi and Chu for focusing on entertainment rather than on their people's lives. This literary feat, a blend of praise and criticism, pleased the emperor, who then awarded Sima with a court attendant position.

Sima's two pieces helped to establish the grand *fu* genre, which was composed by the emperor's literary attendants for his consumption. In general, this genre centers around the lives of the royal family, dealing with such topics as the imperial palace, gardens, capital cities, sacrificial tours, hunting expeditions, and banquets. Composed at these events, the genre praises the ruler's benevolence by numerating his material possessions and his political, economic, agricultural, and educational achievements. As the genre was to entertain the most powerful, if there was any criticism, it had to be nuanced, sugarcoated, and sometimes framed in a dialogue between imaginative figures. Occasionally, this genre might respond to a serious political issue. For example, in "*Changyang Fu*" (長楊賦), Yang Xiong (楊雄) criticized the emperor for sending people to hunt down animals for entertaining foreign visitors, an act that would exhaust the people and harm agriculture (Ban 2007, 867–68). Ban Gu composed his "Two Capital Cities" (兩都賦) to dismiss a proposal that the state capital of the Eastern Han be relocated to Chang'an from Luoyi. Arguing against the proposal, Ban reviewed the reasons previous dynasties chose capital city sites and praised the current dynasty for its moral achievements.[13]

The grand *fu* writers' efforts in blending in criticism marked the trailing influence of the Vertical-Horizontal School. Some of the renowned writers were either students or practitioners of the Vertical-Horizontal School, such as Yan Zhu, Mei Cheng, and Zou Yang, who once advised those such as the kings of Wu, Liang, and Huainan in brokering power with the Han court (see chapter 5). Unsurprisingly, their *fu* and non-*fu* texts shared similar stylistic features, including the profuse use of parallelisms, metaphors, and similes for emotive and imagistic effects. After the kingdoms declined, these individuals were recruited by the emperor as court attendants, both to employ talents for imperial service and to contain the literati. These literati had to heed Han Fei's warnings on the difficulties of persuasion in a unified state.[14] Sima's "*Zixü Fu*" and "*Shanglin Fu*" exemplify a literatus's strategies of suasion when caught in the struggle between the kingdoms and the central government. Relegated to the role of entertainers, these court attendants blended praise and criticism as a necessary compromise in order to assert their worth in the political structure.

Translating Imperial Lives Through the *Fu* Style

The elevated status of *fu* helped to populate the *fu* style, making it instrumental in translating imperial lives. Translation can be understood as the practice of trying to relate meaningfully to difference, including political, cultural, gendered, religious, and linguistic difference. It is a living process to be carried out with both arguments and emotions (Santos 2016). The genre networks archived in dynastic histories indicate that the *fu* style was extensively used in such a process in contexts such as personal expression, bureaucratic communication, and religion.

Fu was used by the *shi* group to forge a distinct identity in a political structure where they were marginalized, like what Qu Yuan did with the "Li sao." After Emperor Wu endorsed Confucian classics as state orthodox and established an official-selection mechanism based on local recommendation and court exams, the *shi* group grew significantly large. Officialdom was their shared goal, but not within everyone's reach. Even officials might feel underappreciated and become disillusioned. *Fu* or the *fu* style often enabled a *shi* to express these sentiments forcefully, giving rise to a critical ethos. After composing several renowned grand *fu* pieces as a literary attendant, for instance, Yang Xiong perceived the genre's limitations as a critical tool and turned to scholarly writings. Not being promoted for some years, Yang was ridiculed by some for wasting time. Yang composed a *fu* titled "A Response to Mockery" (解嘲) to justify his approach to officialdom (Ban 2007, 869–70). Also marginalized in the political structure, Zhao Yi (趙壹) of the Eastern Han used *fu* to voice his criticisms of the government. In his renowned "A Mockery on Social Ills" (刺世嫉邪賦), he accused the government for causing discontent and suffering in the people (Fan 2007, 770–71). In their writings, the *fu* style helped to create a series of images in the reader, strengthen the author's points, and construct a *shi* persona with critical consciousness.[15]

Fu also gave elite women a means for expressing their feelings of marginalization, although few such voices have survived. One of them came from Ban Jieyu (班婕妤), Ban Zhao's aunt. Known for her conversance with the classics and her observance of ritual propriety in the court, Ban was one of Emperor Cheng's favorite concubines. When she lost favor with the sovereign, she composed a *fu* to describe and reflect upon her palace life. In the second half of the piece, she expresses her feelings in an elaborate way. To capture the feelings of a deserted concubine, Ban employs strategies traceable to the odes. She first describes her residence with effusive details (*fu*), making them expressions of her desolation. She then goes into a description of her acts, giving rise to an explicit note of her longing and sadness (*xing*). At the end of the piece, she criticizes the sovereign for his obsession with wicked women by mentioning the titles of two odes "Green Robe" and "White Jade" ("綠衣兮白華, 自古兮有之"; Ban 2007, 997). The two poems dealt with lamentations of court ladies as well, who criticized kings in ancient times. Thus, Ban served as the mouthpiece of the Han court ladies who suffered desertion and loneliness in the harem.[16]

The *fu* style made its way into bureaucratic genres. When serving as court attendant, for instance, Sima Xiangru was once asked to compose an announcement called *xi* (檄), to clarify the emperor's intention on the southwestern frontiers. One general had used martial law to recruit soldiers for transporting government supplies, an act which caused unrest in Ba and Shu regions. The emperor wanted to make it known to the locals that no military actions were planned. In the announcement, Sima first reviews military actions the state took to stop foreign states and tribes from harassing the Han people, and then explains the general's intentions. In reviewing the military actions, a *fu* style is adopted: four-character phrases are extensively used, forming parallelisms with adjacent ones (e.g. "存撫天下, 輯安中國") or with ones across sentence boundaries (e.g. "單於怖駭, 交臂受事, 屈膝請和。康居西域, 重譯請朝, 稽首來享"; Ban 2007, 579). When read aloud, these phrases and the parallelisms they form would overwhelm the reader with a series of images and rhythms. These images then cluster to form an image of the empire: The emperor sent kingly troops to pacify the realms. Being overpowered, foreign states and peoples presented tributes to the court to show their submission and respect. The elaboration of the military actions serves as a praise for the Han's imposing political and military power. In turn, this praise helps to explain that military actions were not planned and the local unrests not warranted.

The authority of the announcement was further strengthened by its materiality. Archaeological findings from the Han dynasty indicate that a *xi* was often written on a polygonal rod twice as long as regular slips and without any cover and are therefore called "exposed polygonal rod of notification" by Tomiya Itaru. This generic function was corroborated at the end of Sima's announcement, where the governors of Ba and Shu were urged to make it public: "Upon arrival, pass the *xi* down to counties and daos immediately. Make His Majesty's intent widely known. No neglect! ("檄到, 亟下縣道, 咸諭陛下意, 毋忽!"; Ban 2007, 580). As a common practice, after the *xi* arrived, the text would be copied onto regular slips and hung up for public display with guards watching.[17] Because the literacy level was extremely low in the Han, a translingual spectacle was thus created: the text would be read out loud to a viewing public in a local accent, sometimes followed by explications in a local dialect. Put up for public display, and similar to the "Mt. Yanran Inscription," the *xi* asserted the authority of the Han court two thousand *li* away and inspired awe and fear in the locals.

As an esteemed style, *fu* was adopted to introduce Buddhist thoughts into the Han. In 76 CE, inspired by a dream, Emperor Ming sent an envoy to the west to seek Buddhist teachings. When the envoy returned, they brought back two Yuezhi monks, Kasyapa Matanga (迦葉摩騰) and Dharmaratna (竺法蘭), as well as sutras. Residing in the capital city Luoyi, the two monks allegedly translated six sutras into Chinese. However, only one, titled *Sutra in Forty-Two Sections* (四十二章經), has survived. A compilation of Buddha's words drawn from other sutras, the text was rendered through two translingual choices with political significance.[18] First, the translator adopted a four-syllable sentence pattern in some sections. This feature would appeal to the Han literati because of its prevalence in *fu*. This familiar style, along with borrowed Daoist vocabulary, might put the reader at ease and reduce the foreignness of the message. The style might also be an attempt to accommodate music played in Buddhist gatherings. Second, the translator made extensive use of similes. They appear in twenty-one out of the twenty-four sections; and a few sections contain multiple similes. The use of similes seems to have as much to do with the way Buddha preaches as it is a strategy to make the Buddhist ideas more accessible to the literati.

While translating the text under the auspice of the emperor could be viewed as an attempt to contain a foreign culture, the scholar-officials used the text to develop critical discourse against the court culture. In 166 CE,

Praising and Criticizing as Entertainment 163

as first discussed in chapter 2, in a memorial submitted to Emperor Huan advising him not to indulge in women and entertainment, Xiang Kai referred to this scripture multiple times (Fan 2007, 320). For example, Xiang claims that "The Buddha did not pass three nights under the [same] mulberry tree; he did not wish to remain there long," which is a reference to section 3 of the scripture. The scripture says, "Satisfied with alms food, he takes only one meal a day at noon and passes the night beneath the same tree only once, careful to curb his desires" ("日中一食, 樹下一宿, 慎勿再矣"!; *Sishier* 2010, 15). Furthermore, Xiang also refers to section 26 of the scripture, when he tells the story of a deity presenting a beautiful maiden to the Buddha, to which the Buddha replies, "This is nothing but a leather sack filled with blood." The scripture says, "O skin bag, full of all kinds of filth! What have you come here for?" ("革囊眾穢, 爾來何為?"; *Sishier* 2010, 54). This example demonstrates that, circulating among Han officials, the sutra joined the odes, the verses of Chu, and *fu* to form a shared textual repertoire in court communications.

Conclusion

Along with other Confucian classics, the circulation of the *Odes* inculcated in the Central Plains both an imperial imagination and prized aesthetic values. During the Spring and Autumn and Warring States periods, thanks to the odes, notions such as the Kingly Way (王道), the sovereignty (皇土), All-under-Heaven (天下), and the Heavenly Mandate (天命) made their way into political discourse in states historically viewed as barbaric, such as Chu, Qin, Yue, and Wu. In the Han, as illustrated by the "Mt. Yanran Inscription" and Sima Xiangru's *xi*, these concepts were frequently invoked to suggest the Han's moral superiority and to justify its military and cultural incursions in neighboring states. The literary devices of the odes, such as *fu*, *bi*, and *xing*, were adopted in the verses of the Chu and the Han rhapsody, becoming the key to encoding and decoding meanings of the empire. By treating the *Odes* as the fountainhead of all rhymed genres, Liu Xie's genre network theory acknowledges and endorses the imperial imaginary and these aesthetic values.

While Liu's theory has accounted for a genre hierarchy of the empire, the court historians' genre theory has accounted for the establishment of an aesthetic and linguistic hierarchy. All the texts discussed in this chapter have been extensively studied in literary criticism for their aesthetic and political power. However, as they were often not examined in their original genre networks, their sociohistorical agency was overlooked. This chapter suggests that these texts played multiple rhetorical functions within their genre networks—praising, criticizing, and entertaining in the court, expressing personal feelings, and translating imperial lives. In performing these functions, these texts helped to establish an aesthetic and linguistic hierarchy: odes, verses of Chu, and *fu* as the prized genres; beginning, continuing, turning, and uniting as the favored narrative form; *fu*, *bi*, *xing* as popular poetic devices; and classical Chinese as the esteemed language of the empire.

CONCLUSION

Limits of the Genre Network

Ban Gu was known as a court historian and a *fu* writer of the Han empire. His work the *Book of Han* was sponsored by the monarch and became the standard dynastic history upon its completion; his *fu* piece "Two Capital Cities" was an invested disposition on the imperial styles of government; and his "Mt. Yanran Inscription" provided generations of literati with an anchor for dreaming of stately honor. Nevertheless, when tracing his works across genre networks, one would have to pause in 92 CE, the year that he died while imprisoned for siding with the powerful Dou family (He had infamously sung praise to General Dou in the "Mt. Yanran Inscription"). While tragic, Ban's case was not singular. In Emperor Wu's reign, counselor Yan Zhu, general Wang Hui, and prince of Huainan Liu An deeply shaped foreign policy decisions. In the famous court debate on the state monopoly over salt, iron, and liquor, Imperial Counselor San Hongyang successfully defended economic and foreign relations measures inherited from Emperor Wu. However, these shapers of state policies were all sentenced to death in the wake of factional strife in the court. In narrating the stories of these power brokers, Sima Qian, Ban Gu, and Fan Ye strove to fulfill an onerous obligation expected of historians: to provide moral and political lessons for the ruling class. In the end, however, they could not evade the same fate as that of the historical characters whose lives they chronicled.

The tragic endings of these eloquent individuals suggest not only the extremely contested nature of political deliberation but also that violence was inherent in the imperial matrix of power. While the court-centered genre activities shaped policy decisions, the network processes were punctuated by fluid and often pernicious tensions among the ruling elites. When speaking to the monarch or the regent, as Han Fei warned in his renowned treatise, "Difficulties of Remonstration," the ministers must act with extreme caution

166 *Conclusion*

lest they lose their lives.[1] While recognizing the power of genre networks in imperial government, we must therefore also consider their limits, not only on political but also epistemological terms.

In this conclusion, I will reflect upon what the study reveals about the nature of genre networks in the Han dynasty, what it tells us about imperial government and political deliberation, and what affordances and limits genre networks have as an epistemic construct. Further, I will offer thoughts for decolonizing studies of ancient rhetorics in terms of the network approach, historiography, border thinking, and recovering non-Western epistemologies for decoloniality.

While studies of rhetoric in early imperial China have examined modes of advice to the monarch, this book demonstrates that genre networks were both a political institution and an epistemic construct, hence a central means for understanding rhetoric and government. Genre networks operated in imperial government in ways that Sima Qian and Liu Xie theorized. On the one hand, manifesting an agentive ontology of genre, dynastic historians like Sima perceived discourses as performing political actions within a network of actors and unfolding events. Thus, they portrayed discourses as call and response, as a nexus of actors, and as a mediator of interlocking events. Informed by this network approach, their historical narratives came to provide both moral and administrative guidance to the ruling class. On the other hand, literary critic Liu Xie introduced a network approach to genre studies by establishing a hierarchy of genres, privileging *jing* (classics and their derivatives) and deprecating *wei* (apocrypha). The circulation of Confucian classics not only supported the training of the ruling elite but also provided them with resources for political deliberation—ideas, historical precedents, and discursive forms. It was from the interweaving of these resources with the individual's exegetical efforts in reoccurring and interlocking events that new genres formed and stabilized.

While excavated materials have revealed governmental practice in the far reaches of the empire, the genre networks examined in this book focus on deliberation and negotiation in the political epicenter that caused ripple effects felt in the peripheries. The study has revealed the power of genres, both written and oral, as an essential technology of imperial government. Genre networks were the very form of government which possessed its regularities, logic, tactic, self-evidence, and reason. The court-centered genre networks worked to sustain and enact the Confucian concept of government, including

Conclusion 167

cultivating the self, managing the family, and governing the state—a concept that was aligned with the imperial matrix of power.

The genre networks encouraged self-cultivation based on Confucian morality, working to foster imperial subjects. As the proclaimed Son of Heaven, the emperor was pressured to assess his governance through theories of history, five phases, *yin-yang*, and Heaven that were developed or appropriated by Confucian literati. These theories undergirded the genre networks that were spurred by natural disasters and anomalies, which often included the emperor issuing edicts to invite officials and scholars to interpret these natural occurrences and the latter submitting commentaries in response. These genre networks mobilized theories, ideologies, texts, and human bodies. The officials' commentaries often led to their own self-examination and the promotion or demotion of their peers. Scholars were nominated for court exams in the names of "the morally and culturally cultivated" or "the filial and uncorrupted." The appeals of civil service inspired classics-based education at the local level, including the studies of the Confucian classics and their theories of self-cultivation. Encouraging self-cultivation among the imperial subjects, the genre networks became a means of government.

The genre networks also regulated elite families. The emperor used edicts to offer suggestions and warnings to the empress and concubines and, when they died, to award them with posthumous titles. The court women responded with memorials to petition, to explain, and to argue. Their exchanges were mediated by court officials through memorials, women's biographies, and essays. In these exchanges, ancient texts such as the *Rites of Zhou* and the *Record of Rites* were cited to formulate theories of obedience and womanly virtues, which in turn came to undergird the reasoning for regulating the family. As these networks worked to regulate the elite families, in effect, they encouraged literacy among elite women and improved their ability to negotiate with men on matters of the inner court, or even to gain political power in the cases of the empress dowagers who ruled the state. The genre networks created a space for all parties, though with power differentials, to address matters of the domestic sphere and to formulate rules of conduct.

The genre networks also enabled the ruler and officials to actuate the imperial myth. Responding to a sociopolitical exigency, a genre network might rise from a cabinet meeting or a court gathering of literati recruited from commanderies and kingdoms. Often involving contending arguments, the meeting might elicit

168 *Conclusion*

memorials from officials near and far in the ensuing discussions. The arguments tended to develop along the lines of the Kingly Way and the Despotic Way, with evidence drawn from the past or the present. Once a decision was made by the monarch or his court, it would turn into an edict directed at certain officials to initiate actions. When interacting with a contending power outside the sovereignty, confidential letters were often used. The edict or letter would be sealed in the process of transport; it might be accompanied by envoys, who would explicate the imperial intent. When the edict or any documents reached the local and the periphery, as the unearthed written materials demonstrate, the imperial myth was perpetuated and realized.

This book demonstrates that genre networks created numerous spaces for literati to participate in political deliberation, and that scholar-officials played an indispensable role in decision-making at every node of the network. The networks examined in this book have amply shown the exchanges among the emperors, the kings, and the officials, which led to policy decisions to affect the far reaches of the empire. Each discourse in the network was a social action involving push-and-pull processes of argument and persuasion. Contrary to previous understanding of disputation in China as mainly taking place in the preimperial period and being "relatively short-lived" compared to the West (van Els and Sabattini 2012, 9), disputation continued in the court and was structured, extended, and complicated by genres in the imperial period. Genre networks created opportunities in which the imperial subjects could have a voice, thus gaining political power in an autocracy.

Genre networks foregrounded by dynastic historians thus become the central means to understanding how discourses enabled a Confucian moral universe to form and to operate. On the one hand, the genre conventions established by the court stipulated the textual and material processes for one to speak at each node. These stipulated processes imparted the imperial myth and hailed the interlocutors as imperial subjects. Within the textual and social spaces prescribed by these conventions, on the other hand, the imperial subjects spoke back to those in power. The four types of memorials established by the court allowed not only officials but also commoners to submit reports and requests and to express feelings to the sovereign. These voices were heard and often responded to by the bureaucrats, if not by the monarch. The genre network perspective allowed the dynastic historians to portray how a chain of discursive actions performed by individuals helped to forge or undermine a Confucian empire.

Conclusion

169

While the networked approach to genre enables us to examine rhetoric, epistemology, and government from ancient Chinese perspectives, these perspectives have limitations. They are male dominant, Confucianism centered, ethnocentric, and couched in the imperial power. At the same time as they undergirded the historical accounts that men constructed and the genre networks that they featured, these perspectives marginalized and erased certain voices, such as those of women, commoners, and the ethnic other. Therefore, these historical accounts and genre networks were triangulated in the book with other sources, including archaeologically discovered materials, both to gain alternative perspectives and to reveal a fuller picture of each genre network. Further, these ancient Chinese perspectives were enriched in the study by including contemporary understandings of genre and transnational sensitivities. These understandings view genres as rhetorical events and have provided the study with an analytical parameter.

Finally, I would like to offer a few thoughts on studies of classical rhetorics. To study rhetoric and imperial government, this book has developed a framework by integrating two approaches that originated from ancient Chinese historiography and literary criticism. Sima Qian theorized and historicized the role genres played as agents in shoring up a Confucian moral universe. Combining Buddhist and Confucian ontology, epistemology, and stylistics, Liu Xie provided an antidote to literary ailments by mapping and analyzing the corpus of Chinese writing. In studies of classical Chinese and other rhetorical traditions, it is worth exploring what other network approaches to genre were also developed, what ontological and epistemological assumptions undergirded these approaches, and further, to what extent genre networks could be a useful construct for studying classical rhetorics.

Another implication of the study is that rhetorical studies needs to pay attention to ancient Chinese historiography.[2] The field continues to pay lip service to inclusivity when it comes to understanding historiographies of rhetoric or the rhetoric of historiographies.[3] There has already been a sizable amount of scholarship on the rhetoric of ancient Chinese historiography.[4] In studies of the historiography of the Han dynasty, for instance, Dorothee Schaab-Hanke (2012) analyzed the rhetorical strategies that Sima Qian adopted to handle the accounts of his contemporary, Emperor Wu, in the GSR. Garret Olberding examined issues of evidentiality in dynastic histories, including the tensions between the historians' moralistic comments and their descriptive accounts of events, and further, tensions involving narrative contradictions, ironic voices, and dramatic devices employed both by historical figures and by historians. This book has highlighted a network approach to genre that was practiced by the dynastic historians. This network approach allowed these chroniclers not only to construct "truthful" and engaging narratives but also to theorize and demonstrate how genre networks could function as a form of imperial government.

This book has contributed to studies of government by accentuating the mediation of genre networks. In studies of the imperial government in early China, scholars have examined institutions, theories, and ideologies concerning rulership. When it comes to studies of institutions, they have examined government documents and communications as part of the political establishment, and they tend to focus on the formal, textual aspects of this institution (Giele 2006; Loewe 2006; Tomiya 2010; Ye Qiuju 2016). Indraccolo and Behr recognize that rhetoric in the Chinese tradition is often understood as an effective tool for "social engineering," with the ultimate aim of "achievement of a successful government" (2014, 908). Further, Olberding suggests that court addresses "offer unique insight into the everyday developments of [government] policy" (2012, 3). Highlighting the social actions enabled by genre networks across various political concerns, this study suggests that examining court addresses alone is far from enough. These addresses need to be studied as discourses within specific genre networks consisting of both human and nonhuman actors. We need to expand our studies of rhetorical and political power from that realized in single addresses to that achieved through genre networks.

By simultaneously drawing on scholarship from decoloniality and Chinese studies to study rhetoric, epistemology, and government, the book demonstrates the importance of practicing interdisciplinarity and developing "border thinking" in rhetorical studies. Academic disciplines are legacies of coloniality, established under the influence of European modernist epistemology and operating to sustain the colonial matrix of power. To decolonize means to decompartmentalize knowledge making. Previous studies on Chinese rhetoric and government mostly took place in the fields of Chinese history and literature. The last decade saw a spike of rhetorical scholarship in early Chinese history, focusing on government documents and communications as part of the political establishment and the modes of advice proffered to the monarch. Further, history has studied imperial discourse along with other institutional forms of power, such as art (music), ritual (mourning, witchcraft), and warfare.[5] It could inform rhetorical studies on how rhetoric worked through not only language but also other semiotic forms and embodiments. Literary studies have examined genres that were deeply connected to the court, such as poetry, rhapsody, and essays. They could inform rhetorical studies on how identification and persuasion were achieved through aesthetic experiences among the ruling elites.[6]

Responding to colonial ideologies and Western biases in studies of ancient Chinese rhetoric, this book has worked toward the decolonial option on two fronts. First, it has built a hybrid conceptual frame for studying genre networks by centering ancient Chinese perspectives to genre and putting them in dialogue with contemporary rhetorical genre perspectives. Rhetorical studies must practice respectful, dialogical engagement with different rhetorical traditions and perspectives in knowledge making. Second, the book has scrutinized how patriarchal thoughts, ethnocentric perceptions, and colonial impulses materialized in early imperial China through rhetoric. With colonial impulses, every empire has established a colonial matrix of power. Certainly, not all empires are identical, and all colonial impulses across the globe cannot be conflated. For example, the Aztec Empire never committed genocide leading to a 90 percent population decline. Western colonial expansion did that.[7] It is the responsibility of rhetoricians to expose and critique such impulses and such a power matrix in the study of empire.[8]

In exploring ancient Chinese epistemologies, this book has revealed the limits of such an effort for decoloniality. Decoloniality means delinking from European modernist epistemology and relinking with historically marginalized or border epistemologies. By studying how rhetoric, genre networks, scholar-officials, and Confucian academies helped establish and maintain the imperial matrix of power, the book reveals not only the knowledges (the enunciated) but also the epistemological mechanisms (the enunciation) of early Chinese empire. However, while Chinese epistemologies were distinct, we have to recognize that epistemic constructs such as Heaven, ritual, history, *yin-yang*, and five phases were appropriated by the state to bolster its imperial rule and control.[9] This kind of appropriation was certainly not unique to the Chinese empire. While seeking non-Western epistemologies does aid decoloniality by allowing us to think, feel, understand, and live otherwise, we must keep in mind the histories of their appropriation by the colonial and imperial powers.

172 *Conclusion*

Along the same line, this book reveals the ability of imperial powers to appropriate rhetorical resources for control and conquest. Comparative and cultural rhetoricians have been keen in retrieving indigenous modes of representation as alternatives to alphabetic script, which they view as the foundation of Eurocentric epistemology (Baca 2008, 2009; Cushman 2012). This study reminds us that not only alphabetic script but also other scripts, such as Chinese logograms, Egyptian hieroglyphs, and Mayan glyphs, have functioned as a technology of spatial rationality and political control for empires. While retrieving other ways (languages, media, and modes) of representation serve to decenter Western epistemology (Cushman 2016), it is equally important to examine how these ways may have been employed to establish ethnic, racial, gendered, colonial, and aesthetic hierarchies in a specific society or culture.

While pursuing the decolonial option, this study has insisted on a transnational and dialogical stand. Decolonial scholarship tends to underscore a unidirectional quest for delinking Western epistemology and ideologies in pursuit of "thinking" and "writing" otherwise, and in pursuit of "writing [that is] no longer limited by Eurocentric foundations" and a global reality that is "no longer determined by imperial, Eurocentric horizons" (Ruiz and Baca 2017, 227–28).[10] While sympathetic with this ethical intent, I argue that a full epistemic delinking not only is impossible but also unproductive for actuating a more equal and just academic and social future. Complete delinking is impossible because of the interlocking nature of cultures, of rhetorical traditions, and of academic discourses, which developed historically by engaging and learning from one another. It is unproductive because an aggressive version of epistemic delinking could encourage nationalism, isolationism, racism, and xenophobia, as seen in the foreign policy debates in the Han dynasty, during the Cold War era, and now in the struggles of de-Westernization.[11] In their narratives of genre networks, ancient Chinese historians such as Sima Qian and Ban Gu all spoke as imperial subjects. While working within the imperial power, they were also critical of it. With imperial impulses being felt strongly in the contemporary world, it is imperative that scholars not only examine genre networks of empire but also ask how their work will contribute to a more egalitarian academic and social future.

Appendix

Notes

Works Cited

Index

APPENDIX

Genres Discussed in the Book

Cross-talk: *ouyu* 偶語

Discussion: *yi* 議, *tingyi* 庭議, *chaoyi* 朝議

Dissenting opinion: *boyi* 駁議

Edict: *zhao* 詔

Enigma: *yingyu* 隱語

Exam essay: *dui* 對, *duice* 對策

Humor: *xie* 諧

Inscription: *ming* 銘

Lesson: *jie* 戒

Letter: *shu* 書

Memoir: *zhuan* 傳

Memorial: *zou* 奏

Poetry: *shi* 詩

Presentation: *shu* 疏, *biao* 表

Prophecy: *chen* 讖

Rhapsody: *fu* 賦

Sovereign answers: *bao* 報

Verse of Chu: *Chuci* 楚辭

War proclamation: *xi* 檄

NOTES

Introduction

1. Mignolo (2011) sees border epistemology as emerging "from the exteriority of the modern/colonial world, from bodies squeezed between imperial languages and those languages and categories of thought negated by and expelled from the house of imperial knowledge" (20).

2. See Baca (2008, 2010) for the challenges of decolonization in rhetorical studies.

3. My proposal shares a resonance with the work of Baca and Cortez. Baca (2008) has critiqued multiple patriarchies and heteronormativeities in mestiza consciousness. Cortez (2016) argues that minority rhetoricians need to take a critical stance towards their own tradition. Recognizing a hegemonic logic in their attempts to represent non-Western rhetorics as distinct from Greco-Roman rhetoric, he suggests, "historiographic disruptions to hegemonic orders of meaning and writing may now require one to subvert one's own cultural allegiances" (59).

4. See Yameng Liu ("To Capture the Essence"), You ("A Comparative-Rhetoric View"), and You and Liu for a critique of the racial *différance* constructed by scholars of rhetoric and writing in the West.

5. See Geaney; and Xiao, for discussions on how ancient Chinese viewed "language as bodily practice," You ("The Way") for the role of language in the multimodality of ritual practice, and Boltz for the performative role of texts in ceremonial and religious rites and ancestral worship practices.

6. Among the many issues examined in the recent shift to the manuscript culture in early China, Lai and Wang list the following: "How were these texts produced, used, and transmitted," "What were the material forms of the texts," and "How did these changing formats affect the reading and understanding of the texts?" (169). See also Kern for issues related to text and ritual practice (ix).

7. See a discussion on how American rhetorics influenced Chinese rhetorical studies in the 1920s and thereafter in You, *Writing in the Devil's Tongue*, 49-50, 52; and Wu, "Lost and Found."

8. Zheng Ziyu, Zhou Zhenfu, and their colleagues published a few histories of Chinese rhetoric in the 1980s and 1990s. Like Oliver, they surveyed Confucian, Daoist, Moist, and Legalist perspectives to language use, focusing on Chinese

concepts. Zheng published his work, 中國修辭學史稿, in 1984; Zhou his work, 中國修辭學史, in 1991; Zheng et al. their work, 中國修辭學通史, in 1998. However, as Wu ("Lost and Found") and I (You "Conflation," *Writing in the Devil's Tongue*) have pointed out, most scholars of Chinese rhetoric in mainland China adopted a narrow definition of rhetoric, perceiving it as mainly dealing with arrangement and style in written discourse.

9. A liberal internationalism was introduced by US president Woodrow Wilson after World War I as a way to end the incessant wars among European states. Reflecting Anglo-Saxon Hegelianism, this ideology holds that the mix of free markets, free government, and rule of law (democracy) will transform the rest of the world and bring it peace and prosperity. Scholars have increasingly recognized liberal democracy as a European and North American ideology, and it is now being resisted by enduring civilizational states such as China, India, Russia, and Turkey (Mead).

10. Modes of advice in the early Chinese court are examined across multiple genres in collections of essays edited by Behr and Indraccolo; Gentz and Meyer; Olberding (2013a); and van Els et al. Cutter and Knechtges ("The Rhetoric of Imperial Abdication") analyzed several bureaucratic genres at the end of the Han dynasty and the beginning of the Wei dynasty, including edict, order, and a type of memorial called *biao* (表). In several histories of Chinese rhetoric (see note 8), scholars have also surveyed the rhetorical thinking and practices of several influential literati in the Han dynasty. For example, Zheng introduced Dong Zhongshu (董仲舒), Jia Yi (賈誼), Wang Yi (王逸), Wang Fu (王符), Liu Xiang (劉向), Sima Qian (司馬遷), Huang Kuang (恒寬), Yang Xiong (楊雄), Ban Gu (班固), and Wang Cong (王充). However, Olberding has viewed the Chinese scholarship as "encyclopedias of rhetorical terminology, often containing later terminology anachronistically applied to documents written centuries, or even millennia, earlier" (2013a, 7).

11. The Western fascination with the discursive wrangling in the Warring States period, following Hum and Lyon, could be attributed to colonialist and patriarchal ideologies. The colonialist ideology makes scholars claim Western values "as ideal, both as the best and as most transcendent" (159). The patriarchal ideology encourages scholars to focus on "work that silences the specifics of the other's cultures, meanings, and intentions" (159).

12. In a study of the emergent manuscript culture, Krijgsman posits that developments in the textual culture itself were a necessary condition for explaining the changes in the intellectual discourse of the period. The key developments of textual culture in this period, as he notes, include the rise of collecting materials into compilations, the emergence of genre classification, the development of new authorship functions, an increase in textual structuring, the integration of lore about

Notes to Pages 9–13

the past, the development of commentarial traditions, the emergence of an explicit, self-reflexive understanding of writing and transmission, and advances in material structuring of manuscript-texts that interrelate form and content.

13. See Li Zhenhong, *Juyan hanjian yu handai shehui* 居延漢簡與漢代社會; Oba, *Qin han fazhishi yanjiu* 秦漢法制史研究; Tomiya, *Bunsho gyōsei no Kan teikoku* 文書行政の漢帝國.

14. Yu Xuetang, 先秦兩漢文體研究; Ye, 秦漢詔書與中央集權研究; Olberding, "How did Ministers Err?"; Queen, "The Rhetoric"; Nylan, "Yang Xiong's Final *Fayan* Chapter"; Sabattini, "'People as Root' (*min ben*) Rhetoric"; van Els, "Tilting Vessels and Collapsing Walls"; Schaab-Hanke, "'Waiting for the Sages of Later Generations'"; Cutter, "Personal Crisis"; Knechtges, "The Rhetoric of Imperial Abdication."

15. The *Rites of Zhou* (周禮) has noted six genres that *dazhu* (大祝) performed when serving various government roles: "作六辭, 以通上下、親疏、遠近: 一曰祠, 二曰命, 三曰誥, 四曰會, 五曰禱, 六曰誄" 《周禮·春官·大祝》 (*Zhouli zhushu* 777). Schaberg suggests that during the Spring and Autumn era, certain classes of *shi* (史) were at times sent across the borders as emissaries (*shi* 使; "Functionary Speech").

16. Efforts to theorize classical genres might have occurred much earlier than the Han dynasty. For example, it was mentioned in the *Rites of Zhou* that ancient teachers taught six features of the *Odes*: "大師……教六詩: 曰風, 曰賦, 曰比, 曰興, 曰雅, 曰頌" (周禮·春官·大師; *Zhouli zhushu* 717). These features refer to three subcategories of odes and three rhetorical devices. However, other than knowing that the *Rites of Zhou* first emerged in the Han dynasty, scholars have not agreed upon when it was written.

17. See Wai-Yee Li ("Traditional Genre Spectrum") and Yao for an overview of the concept 體 (*ti*) in ancient Chinese genre studies.

18. While the prevailing interpretations of *The Literary Mind and the Carving of Dragons* in China and overseas have viewed it as a treatise on literature, focusing on either creative writing, literary criticism, literary aesthetics, or history of literature, Zhao argues instead that the text was the first systematic treatment on the rhetoric of written discourse in China. He substantiates his argument by pointing out that the text introduces a study of thirty-two types of genre patterns, the process of writing, and the art of organization.

19. Mair suggests that Liu Xie obtained his basic epistemological model, his analytical methods, his organizational schemes, and many key concepts from Buddhist sources ("Buddhism in *The Literary Mind*").

20. See Kang-I Sun Chang.

21. See Plato's *Phaedrus* for an illustration of how his dialectic of collection and division was used in philosophical reasoning and rhetorical criticism.

180   Notes to Pages 13–18

22. Contemporary studies of classical Chinese genres (中國古代文體學) have not fundamentally departed from the theory and methodology laid out by Liu Xie. For instance, Yao has offered a survey of studies of classical Chinese genres conducted over the last century, a survey which confirms the lasting influence of Liu Xie's network theory of genre, particularly of the *jing* threads in understanding genres. Most studies published in the recent book series "Studies in Chinese Classical Genres" (中國古代文體學研究叢書) edited by Wu Chengxue and Peng Yuping, for instance, very much followed the four steps suggested by Liu Xie in studying a genre.

23. See a discussion of Sima Qian's attempt to create a Confucian moral universe through history writing in Hardy (1999).

24. It is useful to consider the use of speeches in ancient historiography across cultures. After discussing the histories by Herodotus and Thucydides, Carey suggested that speeches were used in Greek histories not only because of the centrality of oratory in Greek politics but also that speeches could add artistry to historical inquiry and to provide a means to get into psychology and policy: "Any attempt to reach beyond the dry narrative of events into psychology or policy without simple assertion of motives needed speeches" (67).

25. An activity system is defined in Bawarshi and Reiff as "a system of mediated, interactive, shared, motivated, and sometimes competing activities. . . . Context, when viewed with a focus on activity systems, is 'an ongoing, dynamic accomplishment of people acting together with shared tools, including—more powerfully—writing'" (Russell, quoted in Bawarshi and Reiff, 210).

26. Sima Qian described the moral universe using another network metaphor involving *jing* and *wei* (the network of the humanly Way, or *rendao jingwei*; 人道經緯) when he discussed rites. The network of the humanly Way was forged through rites and genre networks alike. See "Treatise on Rites" (禮書) in *GSR*.

27. Various metaphors have been proposed in literacy studies to capture the travel of meanings, such as "chronotopic lamination" (Prior and Shipka), "scale jumps" (Blommaert), "text trajectories" (Silverstein and Urban), "literacy networks" (Leander and Lovvorn), "traffic of texts" (Kell "Inequalities and Crossings"), and "meaning making trajectories" (Kell "Ariadne's Thread").

28. See 隗囂公孫過列傳; 竇融列傳; 馬援列傳, *BLH* (Fan 2007).

29. A revealing case in point is Chinese scholars' debates on the role of Buddhism in Liu Xie's *The Literary Mind and the Carving of Dragon* that took place in the 1980s. As Mair observes, whether these scholars saw Buddhism as playing a crucial or a negligible role in this masterpiece, their judgements were tainted by national pride and cultural prejudice ("Buddhism in the *Literary Mind and Ornate Rhetoric*").

30. Elsewhere I have argued for and demonstrated a transnational approach to studying literacy practice (*Writing in the Devil's Tongue*; *Cosmopolitan English and*

Transliteracy; Transnational Writing Education). Cushman (2016) also demonstrates that the translingual perspective holds a potentially transformative power for leveling hierarchies of thoughts and languages fostered by modernity's colonial matrix of power and for generating pluriversal understandings, values, and practices.

31. Compare the imperial matrix of power with a Western colonial matrix of power identified by Mignolo (2011), which includes racial, class, labor, politico-military, gender, sexual, religious, aesthetic, epistemic, and linguistic hierarchies (17–19).

32. Mignolo warns of the danger of using Western categories in studying ancient Chinese civilization: "Today, however, we tend to look at ancient China and ancient Mesoamerica and ask questions . . . based on our own categories of knowledge and being, because asking such questions and providing such answers is a consequence of being embedded and living in a Western imaginary enveloped in the process of becoming itself" (Mignolo and Walsh 147).

33. In the *Analects*, Confucius regarded one's understanding of the will of heaven or the Heavenly Mandate (*ming* 命) as essential to becoming a gentleman-leader (*junzi* 君子; 229). The genre networks dealing with the Heavenly Mandate served the purpose of educating the Han emperor and his officials, enabling them to become what Confucius had envisioned as gentleman-leaders.

1. Genre Networks as a Political Institution

1. The passage from the *Record of Rites* states, "於是有進膳之旅, 有誹謗之木, 有敢諫之鼓, 瞽史誦詩, 工誦正諫, 士傳民語; 習與智長, 故切而不攘; 化與心成, 故中道若性" (大戴禮記·保傅; Huang Huaixin). The passage from *Discourses of the States* says, "所以天子聽政, 應該使公卿至於列士獻詩, 瞽獻曲, 史獻書, 師箴, 瞍賦, 矇誦, 百工諫, 庶人傳語, 近臣盡規, 親戚補察, 瞽、史教誨, 耆艾修之, 而後王斟酌焉" (邵公諫厲王弭謗, *DS*). The passage from *Zuo Tradition* says, "自王以下, 各有父兄子弟, 以補察其政, 史為書, 瞽為詩, 工誦箴諫, 大夫規誨, 士傳言, 庶人謗, 商旅於市, 百工獻藝, 故夏書曰, 遒人以木鐸徇于路, 官師相規, 工執藝事以諫" (左傳·襄公十四年; Durrant, et al. 1024).

2. As explained in the *Rites of Zhou*, the master musician performs a number of musical instruments and recites songs dealing with the royal family lineages ("瞽蒙: 掌播鞀、柷、敔、塤、簫、管、弦、歌。諷誦詩, 世奠系, 鼓琴瑟。掌《九德》、六詩之歌, 以役大師"; 周禮·春官·宗伯; *Zhouli zhushu* 705).

3. Efforts to upend the dominance of Greco-Roman rhetoric in rhetorical studies have been made in a series of edited collections such as Lipson and Binkley (*Rhetoric Before and Beyond the Greeks*), Lipson and Binkley (*Ancient Non-Greek Rhetorics*), and Keith Lloyd (*The Routledge Handbook of Comparative World Rhetorics*).

182 *Notes to Pages 26–44*

4. Yakobson suggests that even in imperial Rome where the emperors held absolute power like their Chinese counterparts, they and their advisers addressed each other in senatorial sentiments and conventions inherited from the Republic period.

5. Yan points out that the literati (*shi* 士、*yu* 儒) consciously distanced themselves from the relatively larger number of government bureaucrats (*wenfali* 文法吏) in early China. While the former aspired to join the latter, it viewed itself as different in that it occupied a high moral ground and held political visions. In contrast, it viewed the latter as purely technocrats competent in handling office work and conversant in laws and regulations (see Yan 33–36). Yan's assertation can be supported by the conscientious efforts made by officials and literati to construct distinct identities for themselves when they debated government policies concerning salt, iron, and liquor industries in 81 BCE (see chapter 4).

6. According to Liu Xia, Jia Yi and the author or compiler of the *Record of Rites*, Dai De, might have drawn from the same sources produced in the Warring States era.

7. In recent years, scholars have identified the text with the "Daoist," "Huang-Lao," or "Eclectic" school. However, Queen argues that its authors did not ally themselves with any single school and to impose such an identification would negate all that they sought to achieve ("Inventories of the Past").

8. See Lu (*Rhetoric in Ancient China*) and You ("The Way, Multimodality of Ritual Symbols") for analyses of the rhetorical theory contained in the *Analects*.

9. Scholars have long debated the dating of the *Guiguzi*. After studying the evolution of the text, its relation to transmitted and excavated texts, its thoughts, and its phonological features, Xu Fuhong concluded that the text was written in the pre-Qin period.

10. Gentz has offered a different reading of these two treatises, suggesting that the *Guiguzi* does not offer advice to rulers about how to protect themselves against the *shi*'s manipulation; therefore, "the *Hanfeizi* appears like a response to the first part of the *Guiguzi* written from the perspective of the ruler" (1014).

11. In several Warring States era texts excavated in 1993 from a tomb in Guodian, located in the former state of Chu, Pines noted similar perceptions of ruler-minister relations expressed by the occupant, who was either a high-ranking *shi* or a low-ranking noble (*dafu*) ("Friends or Foes").

12. I interpreted the original Chinese passage "故與陽言者, 依崇高。與陰言者, 依卑小。以下求小, 以高求大" differently from Wu and Swearingen. They translate it as "Speeches in the *yang* category begin with lofty topics, while those in the *yin* category rely on low and small matters. Bring yourself down to accomplish small matters; elevate yourself to accomplish lofty causes" (42).

13. See details of these government positions in Xu Tianlin; and An and Xiong.

14. Hou has examined the political influences exercised by bureaucrats who worked in proximity of the emperor and gained the latter's favor in the Western

Han. See those bureaucrats favored by the Western Han emperors in the *BH*, 佞幸列傳 (Ban).

15. See biographies of the empresses in the "Memoires of In-Laws" (外戚傳), *BH* (Ban) and "Memoires of Empresses" (皇后紀), *BLH* (Fan 2007).

16. An example of the emperor shuttling between the three quarters can be found in the memoire of Dongfang Shuo (東方朔傳) in the *BH* (Ban). See the functionality of the palaces in the capital city in Li Yufang. Watanabe Masatoshi proposed the concept of "political spaces" (政治空間) and studied the political decision-making units and processes within each space in the Eastern Han.

17. See Giele for an English translation of the passages dealing with the eight bureaucratic genres described in Cai Yong's *Duduan* (獨斷 Independent Assessment; 306–11).

2. Reading the Heavenly Mandate

1. In the *Analects*, Confucius also used the term "Heavenly Mandate" to refer to one's life attitude and destiny.

2. While imperial edicts on natural anomalies and disasters became the most common means to recruit scholars in the Western Han, the first recorded edict on recruiting talents was issued by the first emperor, Emperor Gaozhu, in 194 BCE, who did not appeal to the Heaven-and-government epistemology. See Ban 17.

3. See examples of Confucius commenting on historical figures such as Taibo in the *Analects* 120 and Duke Wen of Jin and Duke Huan of Qi in the *Analects* 175.

4. Intricately connected, both the Huang-Lao philosophy and the Yin-Yang school emerged in the middle of the Warring States era. The Huang-Lao philosophy, according to Peerenboom, is a syncretic political philosophy that draws heavily on Daoism and Legalism. It holds that the way of humans is predicated on the normative way of the natural order, and that laws governing society are objective laws of a predetermined natural order discoverable by humans. The Yin-Yang School, allegedly headed by Zou Yan (鄒衍), developed a cosmology based on the concepts of *yin*, *yang*, and five phases. It construed *yin* and *yang* as the primal pair of cosmical forces underlying the natural processes.

5. Dong was not the first person making this shift in interpreting Chinese history. See Allan for the precedents during the Warring States era (*The Heir and the Sage*).

6. See Allan for how legends of kings and ministers, heirs and sages, ministers and recluses, and regents and rebels were invoked during the Warring States era (*The Heir and the Sage*).

7. See Takao.

184 *Notes to Pages 63–80*

8. The court exam that Dong Zhongshu participated in in 134 BCE has been generally viewed as the starting point of the scrutiny and recommendation model for selecting officials (察舉制). This model placed emphasis on the recommendation of aristocrats and local officials, with the court exam serving as a sorting tool. In general, all recommendees would be assigned government posts. The scrutiny and recommendation model would evolve into the Confucian-classics-centered exam model (科舉制), starting from the Tang dynasty (581–618 CE) and ending in 1905.

9. Dialectal differences in the Han dynasty were captured in Yang Xiong's 輶軒使者絕代語釋別國方言, which gathered the expressions used in different commanderies and kingdoms. See Serruys for a study of this dialectal work and Knechtges for a translation of Yang Xiong's account of the origin of the work ("The Liu Hsin/Yang Hsiung Correspondence on the Fang Yen"). See Yuying Ye for a discussion on the formation of regional dialects in the Warring States period based on her study of excavated manuscripts.

10. In both the *BH* and *The Literary Mind and the Carving of Dragons*, exam essays and officials' commentaries were all labelled as "answer" (*dui* 對) because they were responses to the imperial queries. I view them as two genres because they were produced in remarkably distinct rhetorical situations with different textual forms.

11. In their commentaries on natural anomalies, Dong tended to blame ill portents on the ruler while Liu did so on those surrounding the throne, including palace ladies, consort kinsmen, and eunuchs. See Hinsch for a review of the criticism of powerful women by portent experts.

12. Emperor Zhao was described by Ban Gu as having mastered the *Book of Education* (保傅傳), *Book of Piety*, *Analects*, and *Documents* (Ban 54); Emperor Xuan as having studied the *Odes*, the *Analects*, and the *Book of Piety* (Ban 58); and Emperor Yuan as good at the *Annals* and the *Documents* (Ban 74).

13. See Gu (chapter 22) and Knechtges ("The Rhetoric of Imperial Abdication") for detailed analyses of the arguments and genre networks that were constructed surrounding the power transition at the end of the Eastern Han dynasty.

3. Regulating the Inner Court

1. A few edicts were briefly recorded in the *BH* about revoking empresses' titles because they demonstrated substandard moral character.

2. See a discussion of the position Empress Xu took in the court politics in Kinney xxii.

3. These stories of woman came originally from historical and philosophical writings produced in the preimperial era. As anecdotes, they were short,

Notes to Pages 98–104

freestanding accounts of particular events in the lives of actual persons. As literary constructs, they served didactic and other rhetorical functions in the original narrative or expository structures. See rhetorical studies of anecdotes in early China in van Els and Queen.

4. Weighing the Ways of Government

1. See Liu Pak-Yuen for an overview of the practice of court discussions in the Qin and Han dynasties. While court discussion or debate was called *yi* (議) in the Western Han, the term *boyi* (駁議) was used in the Eastern Han to refer to a dissenting opinion presented by an official as opposed to the position held by the majority.

2. Liu Xie, for example, placed court speeches alongside exam essays and officials' commentaries in the same chapter, "discussion and answer" (*yidui* 議對), in *The Literary Mind and the Carving of Dragons* because these genres were all produced during court consultations. In two recent books studying speeches delivered in the early Chinese court, one written by and one edited by Olberding, scholars treated these speeches as written genres without considering their oral, embodied, and performative features.

3. However, Confucius criticized Guan Zhong on other occasions. Sima Qian surmised that Confucius did so probably because Guan assist the king of Qi to rise as a hegemon rather than as the king of the Middle Kingdom ("豈以為周道衰微, 桓公既賢, 而不勉之至王, 乃稱霸哉?"; Ssu-ma, Vol. VII, 16). In making this supposition, Sima not only offered his take on the Kingly Way and the Despotic Way but also expressed a desire for a unified Middle Kingdom like many historians before him.

4. "Treatise on the Balanced Standards" (平准書), *GSR*.

5. "過秦論" (Jia Yi); "The Lord of Shang" (Ssu-ma, Vol. VII, 87–96)

6. Shang Yang; "The Lord of Shang" (Ssu-ma, Vol. VII, 87–96).

7. While Shang emphasized loving or caring the people as the purpose of law making ("法者, 所以愛民也"; 109), the Qin laws were penal laws rather than laws serving to protect rights.

8. See the formation of the genre network and the new law in 刑法志, *BH* (Ban 152), and a discussion of this bureaucratic deliberation process in Oba Osamu's study of laws and regulations in the Qin and Han dynasties (*Qin Han* 147–48).

9. See chapter 1, "Revising the Laws," in Shang.

10. See Olberding for an analysis of evidentiality in the Wang-Han debate in 134 BCE as well as in other addresses related to military campaigns in the Han dynasty (*Dubious Facts*). In these addresses, he identifies a series of moral premises shared

among the scholar-officials (134), premises that had become common sense in their construction of arguments.

11. In *Yantielun*, Huan Kuan suggested that the polarization between the Kingly Way and the Despotic Way is key to understanding this court debate. In his authorial note, he disparaged the previous readings of the debate as a struggle for morality (仁義) versus for political and financial powers (權利) and suggested that the two parties—officials and the literati—stood for the Kingly Way and the Despotic Way, as embodied by the long-lived House of Zhou and the short-lived House of Qin, respectively. Further, when he commented on the two parties' oratorical performance, he praised a scholar from the kingdom of Zhongshan for advocating the Kingly Way and criticizing the *Dafu* for celebrating the Despotic Way (*Yantielun* 616).

12. See "公孫劉田王楊蔡陳鄭傳第三十六": "推衍鹽鐵之議, 增廣條目, 極其論難, 著數萬言, 亦欲以究治亂, 成一家之法焉," *BH* (Ban 668); and "雜論第六十", *Yantielun*.

13. *Yantielun* represented the officials by their job titles. In total, the Dafu spoke 114 times, the Yushi 19 times, the Chengxiangshi 15 times, and the Chengxiang occasionally.

14. Wenxue and Xianliang are not names of individual literati but nomination categories based on which the literati were summoned. These categories placed emphasis on the nominees' esteemed learning in rulership. For example, in an earlier edict that was exclusively addressed to the Xiangliang nominees in 134 BCE, the nominees were described as having demonstrated a masterly understanding of imperial rulership of the past and the present. They were asked to submit essays in response to the emperor's queries ("賢良明于古今王事之體, 受策察問, 鹹以書對, 著之於篇, 朕親覽焉"; *BH* 40). In *Yantielun*, the Wenxue spoke 123 times and the Xianliang 26 times.

15. According to Jiang Jianshe, legal training in the Han dynasty existed outside of the state academy in three forms: students studied the thoughts of the Legalist school and laws and regulations with a master in private academies, with senior family members as a family tradition, or with senior officials in the government. In private academies, in addition to the Legalist school, the master might also teach the thoughts of other schools.

16. See Pines for a survey of the attitudes towards aliens expressed by the elites of the central states during the Spring and Autumn and Warring States periods ("Beasts or Humans").

17. Thanks to the arguments invoked by the literati, the state monopoly over salt and iron industries was ceased in 44 BCE but restored four years later (Ban 71, 72, and 163); it was ceased again in 88 CE.

Notes to Pages 118–144   187

18. In *Yantielun*, the literati were recorded as having been awarded the governmental rank of Dafu. Some scholars believed that the record was inaccurate. Instead, the literati might have received Dafu as the title of nobility rather than as the governmental rank. See note 2 in *Yantielun*, 473.

5. Defending Imperial Integrity

1. Once, Mencius was approached by Jing Chun, who asked him a rhetorical question: "Truly, Gongsun Yan and Zhang Yi [two members of the Vertical-Horizontal school] were great men, were they not? When they were angry, the lords would tremble in fear; when they dwell in peace, the fires of conflict throughout the world were extinguished." Mencius answered, "How can they be considered as great men?" and then he went on to elaborate what a truly great man meant for the Confucius school (*Mencius* 62).

2. See Giele for an analysis of the formal features of these two genres.

3. Not only recognizing *Yin-Yang* as the dominant philosophy of *Guiguzi's* rhetorical theory, Wu took a step further by suggesting that it constitutes *the* philosophical foundation of Chinese rhetoric ("Yin-Yang").

4. According to the *BH*, the five exegetical lineages for the *Spring and Autumn Annals* are *zuo shi* 左氏, *gong yang* 公羊, *gu liang* 穀梁, *zhou shi* 鄒氏, and *jia shi* 夾氏 (Ban 329).

5. Zou Yang and Mei Cheng were portrayed by Ban Gu in a positive light because they guarded the imperial authority and contributed to the imperial integrity. In contrast, Kuai Tong (蒯通) and Wu Bei (伍被), who were also practitioners of the Vertical-Horizontal school in the formative years of the Western Han, were depicted in a pejorative tone because they advised Han Xin (韓信) and Liu An to rebel against the emperor (漢書, 蒯伍江息夫傳; Ban 466–71).

6. In Zou's biography, Sima Qian praised him for a memorial submitted to the king of Liang because "his metaphors and comparisons are enough to move men" ("比物連類, 有足悲者"; Ssu-ma, Vol. VII, 292). I view this comment as one of Sima's efforts in historizing and theorizing memorials.

7. See 隗囂公孫過列傳; 竇融列傳; 馬援列傳 in *BLH* (Fan 2007).

6. Praising and Criticizing as Entertainment

1. The ode is one of the Zhou hymns: "于鑠王師, 遵養時晦。時純熙矣, 是用大介。我龍受之, 蹻蹻王之造。載用有嗣, 實維爾公允師"《周頌·酌》.

188   *Notes to Pages 145–155*

Arthur Waley's translation reads: "Oh, gloriously did the king lead; / Swift was he to pursue and take. / Unsullied shines his light; / Hence our great succor, / We all alike receive it. / Valiant were the king's deeds; / Therefore there is a long inheritance. / Yes, it was your doing; / Truly, you it was who led" (*The Book of Songs*, 306).

2. See an analysis of the types of labor involved in constructing the "Mt. Yanran Inscription" in Xin.

3. See an account of the Chinese narrative tradition in Fu Xiuyan.

4. A similar plot, set in an earlier era involving a different king (King Zhuang of Chu) and a different advisor, appeared in *Hanfeizi* (韓非子·喻老). It was then rehearsed in *Lü's Annals* (*Lüshi chunqiu*; 呂氏春秋·重言) as well as in *GSR* (史記·楚世家). Appropriating a similar plot across sources suggests that their authors, or perhaps the *Shi* in general, admired creative ways of persuasion. See more about Chun Yu Kun in 田敬仲完世家 (*GSR*). The most well-known witty speaker from the Han was probably Dongfang Shuo (東方朔) during Emperor Wu's reign. See his stories recorded in both 滑稽列傳 in the *GSR* and 東方朔傳 in the *BH* (Ban).

5. Miyazaki illustrates the oral and theatrical features of these stories with the examples of Jingke (荊軻) assassinating the King of Qin (刺客列傳), a banquet at Hongmen (鴻門宴) (項羽本紀), and Li Si's (李斯) biography (李斯列傳), all from the *GSR*. See more discussions of the oral and theatrical genres in the Han in Ren Huifeng; Kang.

6. 起承轉接, or 起承轉合; the analytical pattern used by Miyazaki for narratives is generally believed to have arisen in the civil service exam culture. It was first proposed in treatises on poetics in the Yuan dynasty (1279–1368) and thereafter widely used in primers for teaching prose and poetry. See a historical overview of this analytical pattern in Jiang Yin.

7. See Burroway (2019).

8. The tri-part organization of the *Odes* along with their three key literary devices was recorded much earlier in the *Rites of Zhou*. See note 16 to the Introduction.

9. See Wang Fuhan (1989, 1990); Liu Liwen; and Lewis (*Writing and Authority*).

10. In the classic *Rites* (儀禮 *yili*), written during the Warring States period, two chapters, "Banquet Rite" (燕禮 *yanli*) and "Diplomacy Rite" (聘禮 *pinli*), have detailed the complex ritual practices during a diplomatic mission in the Zhou dynasty. They include having an audience with the ministers and attending banquets occasioned by musical performance. See Peng.

11. *Analects* 1.15 75; 3.8 83; 13.5 163; 17.9 206.

12. Luo has identified two strategies that Sima Qian used to contain the "Li sao" within the imperial aesthetic universe (110–13). First, following Liu An, he compared the verse with the *Odes* for its stylistic features, hinting at a lineage and

Notes to Pages 159–166 189

subordinating southern (Chu-Yue) culture to that of the Central Plains. Second, Sima depicted Qu Yuan as striving to express his thoughts and feelings of being dejected in the verse, a narrative reflecting more of his own life story. This narrative frame was then used by Sima to interpret the title "Li sao" as meaning "feelings of being dejected." Sima's two strategies helped to chart a genre trajectory from the *Odes* to the "Li sao," a trajectory that later was taken up by Liu Xie in his chapter on verse "辨騷" for developing his network theory of genre.

13. The proposal was made by Du Du (杜篤) in the early years of the Eastern Han in a *fu* submitted to Emperor Guangwu titled "論都" ("On Capital City"; 文苑列傳, Fan 762–64). The proposal then inspired a series of *fu* pieces throughout the dynasty, one of which was Ban's "Two Capital Cities" (班彪列傳, Fan 396–403).

14. In "答客難," Dongfang Shuo (東方朔) explicated the differences between acting as a political adviser in the Warring States and in the Western Han; in "非有先生," he discussed the difficulties of persuasion in his times (東方朔列傳, Ban 656–59).

15. In addition to Yang Xiong and Zhao Yi, other renowned literati who composed *fu* pieces for expressing personal feelings and forging a distinct identity in the political structure include Sima Xiangru, Dong Zhongshu ("士不遇賦," Fei 112), Dongfang Shuo ("答客難", 東方朔列傳, Ban 656–57), Feng Yan ("顯志", 馮衍列傳, Fan 295–98), Ban Gu ("答賓戲", 班彪列傳, Fan 403), Cui Ying ("達旨", 崔駰列傳, Fan 504–6), Zhang Heng ("應間", 張衡列傳, Fan 559–61), and Cai Yong ("設誨", 蔡邕列傳, Fan 573–75).

16. See Knechtges for a detailed analysis of Ban Jieyu's *fu* piece ("The Poetry").

17. Instructions for copying and displaying the *Xi* text are found in archeological discoveries. See Tomiya, 81.

18. Of equal political significance, these translations also marked the rise of written vernacular not only in China but also in East Asia. Working with Chinese assistants, these foreign translators of Buddhist sutras developed what Mair has called Buddhist Hybrid Sinitic, a style that blends Literary Sinitic (*wenyan*) and Vernacular Sinitic (*baihua*), to spread the Buddhist teaching to uneducated people, particularly those marginalized in Chinese society ("Buddhism and the Rise of the Written Vernacular").

Conclusion

1. Han Fei was executed while serving the king of Qin. In Han's biography, Sima Qian inserted the text "The Difficulties of Remonstration" to show his admiration for this rhetorical treatise, and he lamented that someone who was perceptive of remonstration could not survive the strife of court politics ("餘獨悲韓子為

《說難》而不能自脫耳"; Ssu-ma, Vol. VII, 29). This could be an indirect comment on his own fate as court historian.

2. Studies of rhetoric in ancient Western historiography are numerous. See two surveys of these studies in Carey; and Ash. Two foundational studies are Woodman's book *Rhetoric in Classical Historiography: Four Studies* and Marincola's book *Authority and Tradition in Ancient Historiography*.

3. In a recent book, *Landmark Essays on Historiographies of Rhetorics*, although the editor, Vitanza, nodded to non-Western rhetorics (3), the landmarks he identified were all centered on Greco-Roman rhetorics.

4. Book-length studies of rhetoric in ancient Chinese historiography include: Hardy, *Worlds of Bronze and Bamboo: Sima Qian's Conquest of History*; Ng and Wang, *Mirroring the Past: The Writing and Use of History in Imperial China*; Wai-Yee Li, *The Readability of the Past in Early Chinese Historiography*; Pines, *Foundations of Confucian Thought: Intellectual Life in the Chunqiu Period 722-453 B.C.E*; and Schaberg, *A Patterned Past: Form and Thought in Early Chinese Historiography*.

5. Allan, *The Shape of the Turtle: Myth, Art, and Cosmos in Early China*; Brindley, *Music, Cosmology, and the Politics of Harmony in Early China*; Cai, *Witchcraft and the Rise of the First Confucian Empire*; Brown, *The Politics of Mourning in Early China*; Lewis, *Sanctioned Violence in Early China*.

6. While studies of rhetoric and government in early China conducted in the discipline of history have drawn on rhetorical studies, cross-pollination seems less obvious in literary studies. In a recent Oxford handbook on classical Chinese literature (Denecke, Li, and Tian), for instance, rhetoric was hardly mentioned. Certainly, there are exceptions. For example, Knechtges has long drawn on rhetorical studies to examine the strategies of persuasion in the Han rhapsody.

7. Baca pointed out the crucial distinctions between empires in his reading of this manuscript.

8. In her recent study of Greek rhetoric in the Roman empire, Jarratt also proposes that "there is need to recognize empire not only as an empirical historical fact but also an analytical frame for rhetorical studies, and to put ancient and contemporary discourses in critical contact with each other" (xv). Baca put Jarratt's proposal to action in his book *Mestiz@ Scripts* (2008).

9. Mignolo introduced Chinese concepts *qi* and *yin-yang* as alternative to European conceptions of nature (Mignolo and Walsh 167).

10. In their search for decolonial options and possibilities, Ruiz and Baca propose the need for reclaiming erased histories, delinking from Western philosophical canon, and dismantling cultural hierarchies.

11. In a *Newsweek* cover story published in June 2020, for instance, Powell describes the US attempts to start a new Cold War by decoupling its economic, financial, and technological ties with China.

WORKS CITED

Allan, Sarah. 1991. *The Shape of the Turtle: Myth, Art, and Cosmos in Early China*. Albany: SUNY Press.

———. 2016. *The Heir and the Sage: Dynastic Legend in Early China*. Albany: SUNY Press.

An Zuozhang, and Xiong Tieji 安作璋、熊鐵基. 1985. *Qinhan guanzhi shigao* 秦漢官制史稿, Vol. 1 and 2. Jinan: Qilu shushe.

Analects of Confucius: A Philosophical Translation. 1998. Translated by Roger T. Ames and Henry Rosemont, Jr. New York: Random House.

Ash, Rhiannon. 2017. "Rhetoric and Historiography." In *The Oxford Handbook of Rhetorical Studies*, edited by Michael J. Macdonald, 195–204. Oxford University Press.

Baca, Damián. 2008. *Mestiz@ Scripts, Digital Migrations, and the Territories of Writing*. New York: Palgrave Macmillan.

———. 2009. "The Chicano Codex: Writing Against Historical and Pedagogical Colonization." *College English* 71 (6): 564–83.

———. 2010. "Te-ixtli: The 'Other Face' of the Americas." In *Rhetorics of the Americas: 3114 BCE to 2012 CE*, edited by Damián Baca and Victor Villanueva, 1–14. New York: Palgrave Macmillan.

Baca, Damián, and Romeo García, eds. 2019. *Rhetorics Elsewhere and Otherwise: Contested Modernities and Decolonial Visions*. Champaign, IL: National Council of Teachers of English.

Ban Gu 班固. 2007. *Han shu* 漢書. Beijing: Zhonghua shuju.

Bawarshi, Anis S., and Mary Jo Reiff. 2010. *Genre: An Introduction to History, Theory, Research, and Pedagogy*. West Lafayette, IN: Parlor Press and the WAC Clearing House.

Bazerman, Charles. 1997. "The Life of Genre, the Life in the Classroom." In *Genre and Writing: Issues, Arguments, Alternatives*, edited by Wendy Bishop and Hans Ostrom, 19–26. Portsmouth, NH: Heinemann.

———. 1999. *The Languages of Edison's Light*. Cambridge, MA: MIT Press.

Berkenkotter, Carol, and Thomas N. Huckin. 1993. "Rethinking Genre from a Sociocognitive Perspective." *Written Communication* 10 (4): 475–509.

Biinn, Sharon Bracci, and Mary Garrett. 1993. "Aristotelian Topoi as a Cross-Cultural Analytical Tool." *Philosophy and Rhetoric* 26 (2): 93–112.

Binkley, Roberta. 2009. "The Gendering of Prophetic Discourse: Women and Prophecy in the Ancient Near East." In *Ancient Non-Greek Rhetorics*, edited by Carol S. Lipson and Roberta Binkley, 67–93. West Lafayette, IN: Parlor Press.

Blommaert, Jan. 2010. *The Sociolinguistics of Globalization*. Cambridge: Cambridge University Press.

———. 2013. *Ethnography, Superdiversity, and Linguistic Landscapes: Chronicles of Complexity*. Bristol, UK: Multilingual Matters.

Boltz, William G. 2005. "The Composite Nature of Early Chinese Texts." In *Text and Ritual in Early China*, edited by Martin Kern, 50–78. Seattle: University of Washington Press.

Book of Songs: The Ancient Chinese Classic of Poetry. 1996. Translated by Arthur Waley. New York: Grove Press.

Brindley, Erica Fox. 2012. *Music, Cosmology, and the Politics of Harmony in Early China*. Albany: SUNY Press.

Brown, Miranda. 2007. *The Politics of Mourning in Early China*. Albany: SUNY Press.

Burroway, Janet. 2019 *Writing Fiction: A Guide to Narrative Craft*. With Elizabeth Stuckey-French, and Ned Stuckey-French. Chicago: Universtity of Chicago Press.

Cai Yong 蔡邕. 1985. "*Duduan* 獨斷." *Han liqi zhidu (ji qita wuzhong)* 漢禮器制度 (及其他五種). Beijing: Zhonghua shuju.

Cai, Liang. 2014. *Witchcraft and the Rise of the First Confucian Empire*. Albany: SUNY Press.

Cai, Zong-Qi, ed. 2001. *A Chinese Literary Mind: Culture, Creativity, and Rhetoric in Wenxin Diaolong*. Stanford: Stanford University Press.

Canagarajah, Suresh. 2019. *Translingual Practice: Global Englishes and Cosmopolitan Relations*. London: Routledge.

Carey, Chris. 2017. "Rhetoric and Historiography." In *The Oxford Handbook of Rhetorical Studies*, edited by Michael J. Macdonald, 63–72. Oxford: Oxford University Press.

Ch'en, Kenneth. 1964. *Buddhism in China: A Historical Survey*. Princeton: Princeton University Press.

Chang, Kang-I Sun. 2001. "Liu Xie's Idea of Canonicity." In *A Chinese Literary Mind: Culture, Creativity, and Rhetoric in Wenxin Diaolong*, edited by Zong-Qi Cai, 17–32. Stanford: Stanford University Press.

Chang, Su-ching. 2013. "Three Rhetorical Modes in Pre-Qin Court Remonstrances." In *Facing the Monarch: Modes of Advice in the Early Chinese Court*, edited by Garret P. S. Olberding, 42–68. Cambridge, MA: Harvard University Asia Center.

Chen Wangdo 陳望道. 1932. *Xiucixue fafan* 修辭學發凡. Shanghai: Dajiang shupu.

Chen, Yu-Shih. 1996. "The Historical Template of Pan Chao's *Nü Chieh.*" *T'oung Pao* 82, 4/5 (October): 229–57.

Combs, Steve. 2000. "Sun-zi and the 'Art of War': The Rhetoric of Parsimony." *Quarterly Journal of Speech* 86 (3): 276–94.

Confucius. 1971. "The Great Learning." In *Confucian Analects, The Great Learning and The Doctrine of the Mean,* translated by James Legge. Dover Publications, 355–81.

Connell, Raewyn. 2007. *Southern Theory: The Global Dynamics of Knowledge in Social Science.* Crows Nest, AU: Allen and Unwin.

Cortez, José. 2016. "History." In *Decolonizing Rhetoric and Composition Studies: New Latinx Keywords for Theory and Pedagogy,* edited by Iris D. Ruiz and Raúl Sánchez, 49–62. New York: Palgrave Macmillan.

Crump, James I., Jr. 1964. *Intrigues: Studies of The Chan-Kuo Ts'e.* Ann Arbor: University of Michigan Press.

———. 1996. *Chan-kuo Ts'e.* Ann Arbor: University of Michigan Press.

Cushman, Ellen. 2012. *The Cherokee Syllabary: Writing the People's Perseverance.* Norman: University of Oklahoma Press.

———. 2016. "Translingual and Decolonial Approaches to Meaning Making." *College English* 78 (3): 234–42.

Cutter, Robert Joe. 2005. "Personal Crisis and Communication in the Life of Cao Zhi." In *Rhetoric and the Discourses of Power in Court Culture,* edited by David R. Knechtges and Eugene Vance, 149–68. Seattle: University of Washington Press.

De Weerdt, Hilde. 2015. *Information, Territory, and Networks: The Crisis and Maintenance of Empire in Song China.* Cambridge, MA: Harvard University Asia Center.

De Weerdt, Hilde, Chu Ming-Kin, and Ho Hou-Ieong. 2016. "Chinese Empires in Comparative Perspective: A Digital Approach." *Verge: Studies in Global Asias* 2 (2): 58–69.

Denecke, Wiebke, Wai-Yee Li, and Xiaofei Tian, eds. 2017. *The Oxford Handbook of Classical Chinese Literature (1000 BCE–900 CE).* Oxford: Oxford University Press.

Dong Zhongshu. 2016. *Luxuriant Gems of the Spring and Autumn.* Translated by Sarah A. Queen and John S. Major. New York: Columbia University Press.

Durrant, Stephen, Wai-Yee Li, and David Schaberg, trans. 2016. *Zuo Tradition/ Zuozhuan: Commentary on the "Spring and Autumn Annals."* Seattle: University of Washington Press.

Elman, Benjamin A. 2000. *A Cultural History of Civil Examinations in Late Imperial China.* Berkeley: University of California Press.

Fan Ye 範曄. 2007. *Houhan shu* 後漢書. Beijing: Zhonghua shuju.

Fei Zhengang 費振剛. 1993. *Quan Han fu* 全漢賦. Beijing: Peking University Press.

Fraiberg, Steve, Xiqiao Wang, and Xiaoye You. 2017. *Inventing the World Grant University: Chinese International Students' Mobilities, Literacies, and Identities.* Logan: Utah State University Press.

Fu Xiuyan 傅修延. 1999. *Xianqin xushi yanjiu* 先秦敘事研究. Beijing: Dongfan chubanshe.

Gao Ping, and An Shenglan 高平、安勝藍. 2017. "Lijing jin 2000 nian Ban Gu suozhuan yanranshang ming moya shike zhaodao le 歷經近 2000 年班固所撰《燕然山銘》摩崖石刻找到了." *Guangming ribao* 光明日報, 16 August, 3.

García, Romeo, and Damián Baca. 2019. "Introduction." In *Rhetorics Elsewhere and Otherwise: Contested Modernities, Decolonial Visions,* edited by Romeo García and Damián Baca, 1–48. Champaign, IL: National Council of Teachers of English.

García, Romeo, and José M. Cortez. 2020. "The Trace of a Mark That Scatters: The Anthropoi and the Rhetoric of Decoloniality." *Rhetoric Society Quarterly* 50 (2): 93–108.

Garrett, Mary. 1993a. "Classical Chinese Rhetorical Conceptions of Argumentation and Persuasion." *Argumentation & Advocacy* 29 (3): 105–15.

———. 1993b. "Pathos Reconsidered from the Perspective of Classical Chinese Rhetorical Theories." *Quarterly Journal of Speech* 79 (1): 13–39.

———. 1999. "Some Elementary Methodological Reflections on the Study of the Chinese Rhetorical Tradition." *International and Intercultural Communication Annual* (22): 53–63.

———. 2012. "'What Need is There of Words?': The Rhetoric of Lü's Annals (Lü shi chun qiu)." *Rhetorica* 30 (4): 354–74.

Geaney, Jane. 2018. *Language as Bodily Practice in Early China: A Chinese Grammatology.* Albany: SUNY Press.

Gentz, Joachim. 2014. "Rhetoric as the Art of Listening: Concepts of Persuasion in the First Eleven Chapters of the *Guiguzi*." *Asiatische Studien* 68 (4): 1001–17.

Gentz, Joachim, and Dirk Meyer, eds. 2015. *Literary Forms of Argument in Early China.* Leiden, NL: Brill.

Giele, Enno. 2006. *Imperial Decision-Making and Communication in Early China: A Study of Cai Yong's Duduan.* Wiesbaden, DE: Otto Harrassowitz.

Graham, A. C. 1989. *Disputers of the Tao: Philosophical Argument in Ancient China.* Chicago: Open Court.

Gu Jiegang 顧頡剛. 2005. *Qin han de fangshi yu rusheng* 秦漢的方士與儒生. Shanghai: Shiji chuban jituan.

Guoyu 國語. 2014. Translated by Chen Tongsheng. Beijing: Zhonghua shuju.

Hall, David, and Roger Ames. 1995. *Anticipating China: Thinking through the Narratives of Chinese and Western Culture.* Albany: SUNY Press.

Han Feizi: Basic Writings. 2003. Translated by Burton Watson. New York: Columbia University Press.

Hardy, Grant. 1994. "Can an Ancient Chinese Historian Contribute to Modern Western Theory? The Multiple Narratives of Ssu-Ma Ch'ien." *History and Theory* 33 (1): 20–38.

———. 1999. *Worlds of Bronze and Bamboo: Sima Qian's Conquest of History*. New York: Columbia University Press.

Hinsch, Bret. 2006. "The Criticism of Powerful Women by Western Han Dynasty Portent Experts." *Journal of the Economic and Social History of the Orient* 49 (1): 96–121.

Hou Xudong 候旭東. 2018. *Cong: xinren xing junchen guanxi yu xihan lishi de zhangkai* 寵: 信任型君臣關係與西漢歷史的展開. Beijing: Shifan daxue chubanshe.

Huang Huaixin 黃懷信. 2019. *Dadai liji yizhu* 大戴禮記譯註. Shanghai: Shanghai guji chubanshe.

Hum, Sue, and Arabella Lyon. 2008. "Recent Advances in Comparative Rhetoric." In *The Sage Handbook of Rhetorical Studies*, edited by Andrea A. Lunsford, Kirt H. Wilson, and Rosa A. Eberly, 153–65. Thousand Oaks, CA: Sage.

Indraccolo, Lisa, and Wolfgang Behr. 2014. "Introduction." *Asiatische Studien* 68 (4): 889–913.

Jarratt, Susan C. 2019. *Chain of Gold: Greek Rhetoric in the Roman Empire*. Carbondale: Southern Illinois University Press.

Jia Yi 賈誼. 2017. *Xinshu jiaozhu* 新書校注, collated and annotated by Yan Zhengyi and Zhong Xia (閻振益、鐘夏). Beijing: Zhonghua shuju.

Jiang Jianshe 蔣建設. 2020. "Pochu bachu baijia de huangxiang: lianghan lüxue jiaoyu xingtai de zai tantao 破除 "罷黜百家" 的幻象: 兩漢律學教育形態的再探討." *Shixue yuekan* 史學月刊 (3): 126–32.

Jiang Yin 蔣寅. 1998. "Qicheng zhuanhe jixie jiegou lun de xiaozhang, jianlun bagu wenfa yu shixue de guangxi 起承轉合機械結構論的消長—兼論八股文法與詩學的關係." *Wenxue yichan* 文學遺產 (3): 66–76.

Kang Baocheng 康寶成. 2003. "Lun handai xiju xingtai 論漢代戲劇形態." *Zhonghua xiqu* 中華戲曲 (1): 19–36.

Kaplan, Robert B. 1966. "Cultural Thought Patterns in Intercultural Education." *Language Learning* 16 (1): 1–20.

Kell, Catherine. 2011 "Inequalities and Crossings: Literacy and the Spaces-In-Between." *International Journal of Educational Development* 31 (6): 606–13.

———. 2013. "Ariadne's Thread: Literacy, Scale and Meaning Making across Space and Time." Tilburg Papers in Culture Studies, no. 81, https://www .tilburguniversity.edu/sites/default/files/download/TPCS_81_Kell_2.pdf

Kennedy, George A. 1998. *Comparative Rhetoric: An Historical and Cross-Cultural Introduction*. Oxford: Oxford University Press.

Kern, Martin, ed. 2005. *Text and Ritual in Early China*. Seattle: University of Washington Press.

Kinney, Anne Behnke, trans. 2014. *Exemplary Women of Early China: The Lienü Zhuan of Liu Xiang*. New York: Columbia University Press.

Kirkpatrick, Andy. 1995. "Chinese Rhetoric—Methods of Argument." *Multilingua* 14 (3): 271–95.

———. 2005. "China's First Systematic Account of Rhetoric: An Introduction to Chen Kui's *Wen ze*." *Rhetorica* 32 (23): 103–52.

Knechtges, David, R. 1976. *The Han Rhapsody: A Study of the Fu of Yang Hsiung (53 B.C.–A.D. 18)*. Cambridge: Cambridge Univerity Press.

———. 1977–78. "The Liu Hsin/Yang Hsiung Correspondence on the Fang Yen." *Monumenta Serica* (33): 309–25.

———. 993. "The Poetry of an Imperial Concubine: The Favorite Beauty Ban." *Oriens Extremus* 36 (2): 127–44.

———. 2002. *Court Culture and Literature in Early China*. Farnham, UK: Ashgate.

———. 2005. "The Rhetoric of Imperial Abdication and Accession in a Third-Century Chinese Court: The Case of Cao Pi's Accession as Emperor of the Wei Dynasty." In *Rhetoric and the Discourses of Power in Court Culture*, edited by David R. Knechtges and Eugene Vance, 3-35. Seattle: University of Washington Press.

Kong Deming 孔德明. 2013. *Hanfu de shengchan yu xiaofei yanjiu* 漢賦的生產與消費研究. Beijing: Guangming ribao chubanshe.

Krijgsman, Rens. 2016. "The Rise of a Manuscript Culture and the Textualization of Discourse in Early China." PhD diss., Oxford University.

Lai, Guolong, and Q. Edward Wang. 2017. "Manuscript Culture in Early China: Editors' Introduction." *Chinese Studies in History* 50 (3): 167–71.

Leander, Kevin M., and J. F. Lovvorn. 2006. "Literacy Networks: Following the Circulation of Texts, Bodies, and Objects in the Schooling and Online Gaming of One Youth." *Cognition and Instruction* 24 (3): 291–340.

Lewis, Mark Edward. 1989. *Sanctioned Violence in Early China*. Albany: SUNY Press.

———. 1999. *Writing and Authority in Early China*. Albany: SUNY Press.

Li Yufang 李毓芳. 1997. "Han Chang'an cheng de buju yu jiegou 漢長安城的佈局與結構." *Kaogu yu wenwu* 考古與文物 (5): 71–74.

Li Zhenhong 李振宏. 2003. *Juyan hanjian yu handai shehui* 居延漢簡與漢代社會. Beijing: Zhonghua shuju.

Li, Wai-Yee. 2008. *The Readability of the Past in Early Chinese Historiography*. Cambridge, MA: Harvard University Press.

Liang Xiao 梁效, 1974. "Du yan tie lun: xihan zhongqi rufa liangjia de yichang da lunzhan 讀鹽鐵論: 西漢中期儒法兩家的一場大論戰." In Huan Kuan, *Yan tie lun* 鹽鐵論, 1–14. Shanghai: Shanghai renmin chubanshe.

Lipson, Carol S., and Roberta Binkley, eds. 2004. *Rhetoric Before and Beyond the Greeks*. Albany: SUNY Press.

Lipson, Carol S., and Roberta Binkley, eds. 2009. *Ancient Non-Greek Rhetorics*. West Lafayette, IN: Parlor Press.

Liu An. (2010). *The Huainanzi*. Translated by John S. Major, Sarah A. Queen, Andrew Seth Meyer, and Harold D. Roth. New York: Columbia University Press.

Liu Pak-Yuen 廖伯源. 1995. "Qin han chaoting zhi lunyi zhidu 秦漢朝廷之論議制度." *Zhongguo wenhua yanjiusuo xuebao* 中國文化研究所學報 (4): 141–72.

Liu Xia 劉霞. 2012. *Cong dadai liji baofu kan zhoudai baofu zhidu* 從《大戴禮記‧保傅》看周代保傅制度. Master's thesis, Qufu Normal University.

Liu, Hsieh. 2015. *The Literary Mind and the Carving of Dragons*. Translated by Vincent Yu-Chung Shih. Hong Kong: Chinese University of Hong Kong Press.

Liu, Liwen 劉麗文. 2004. "Chunqiu shiqi fushi yanzhi de lixue yuanyuan ji xingcheng de jizhi yuanli 春秋時期賦詩言志的禮學淵源及形成的機制原理." *Wenxue yichan* 文學遺產 (1): 33–43.

Liu, Lydia H. 2015. "Scripts in Motion: Writing as Imperial Technology, Past and Present." *PMLA* 130 (2): 375–83.

Liu, Yameng. 1995. "Disciplinary Politics and the Institutionalization of the Generic Triad in Classical Rhetoric." *College English* 57 (1): 9–26.

———. 1996. "To Capture the Essence of Chinese Rhetoric: An Anatomy of a Paradigm in Comparative Rhetoric." *Rhetoric Review* 14 (2): 318–35.

Lloyd, Keith, ed. 2020. *The Routledge Handbook of Comparative World Rhetorics*. New York: Routledge.

Loewe, Michael. 2006. *The Government of the Qin and Han Empires: 221 BCE–220 CE*. Indianapolis: Hackett.

Lu, Xing. 1998. *Rhetoric in Ancient China, Fifth to Third Century B.C.E.: A Comparison with Classical Greek Rhetoric*. Colombia: University of South Carolina Press.

Luo Genze 羅根澤. 2015. *Zhongguo wenxue piping shi* 中國文學批評史. Beijing: Shangwu chubanshe.

Lyon, Arabella. 2008. "Rhetorical Authority in Athenian Democracy and the Chinese Legalism of Han Fei." *Philosophy and Rhetoric* 41 (1): 51–71.

Mair, Victor H. 1994. "Buddhism and the Rise of the Written Vernacular in East Asia: The Making of National Languages." *Journal of Asian Studies* 53 (3): 707–51.

———. 2001. "Buddhism in the *Literary Mind and Ornate Rhetoric*." In *A Chinese Literary Mind: Culture, Creativity, and Rhetoric in Wenxin Diaolong*, edited by Zong-Qi Cai, 63–82. Stanford: Stanford University Press.

Mann, Susan. 2001. "Preface." In *Pan Chao: Foremost Woman Scholar of China* by Nancy Lee Swann. Ann Arbor: University of Michigan Press

Mao, LuMing. 2013. "Beyond Bias, Binary, and Border: Mapping out the Future of Comparative Rhetoric." *Rhetoric Society Quarterly* 43 (3): 209–25.

Mao, Zedong. 1961. *Selected Works of Mao Tse-tung: Volume IV*. Beijing: Foreign Languages Press.

Marincola, John. 1997. *Authority and Tradition in Ancient Historiography*. Cambridge: Cambridge University Press.

Mead, Walter Russell. 2021. "The End of the Wilsonian Era: Why Liberal Internationalism Failed." *Foreign Affairs* 100 (1): 123–37.

Mencius. 2009. Translated by Irene Bloom and edited by Philip J. Ivanhoe. New York: Columbia University Press.

Meyer, Dirk. 2012. *Philosophy on Bamboo: Text and the Production of Meaning in Early China*. Leiden, NL: Brill.

Mignolo, Walter D. 2011. *The Darker Side of Western Modernity: Global Futures, Decolonial Options*. Durham, NC: Duke University Press.

Mignolo, Walter D., and Catherine E. Walsh. 2018. *On Decoloniality: Concepts, Analytics, and Praxis*. Durham, NC: Duke University Press.

Miller, Carolyn R. 1984. "Genre as Social Action." *Quarterly Journal of Speech* 70 (2): 151–67.

Miyazaki Ichisada 宮崎市定. 2018. *Dongyang de gudai: Cong dushi guojia dao qin han diguo* 東洋的古代: 從都市國家到秦漢帝國. Beijing: Zhongxin chubangjituang.

Ng, On-Cho, and Q. Edward Wang. 2005. *Mirroring the Past: The Writing and Use of History in Imperial China*. Honolulu: University of Hawai'i Press.

Nylan, Michael. 2005. "Toward an Archaeology of Writing: Text, Ritual, and the Culture of Public Display in the Classical Period (475 B.C.E.–220 C.E.)." In *Text and Ritual in Early China*, edited by Martin Kern, 3–49. Seattle: University of Washington Press.

———. 2013. "Yang Xiong's 楊雄 Final *Fayan* 法言 Chapter: Rhetoric to What End and for Whom?" In *Facing the Monarch: Modes of Advice in the Early Chinese Court*, edited by Garret P.S. Olberding, 237–72. Cambridge, MA: Harvard University Asia Center.

Oba Osamu 大庭脩. 1988. "Yuankang wunian (61 BCE) zhaoshuce de fuyuan yu yushi dafu de yewu 元康五年 (前61年) 詔書冊的復原和御史大夫的業務." Qilu xuekan 齊魯學刊 3 (2): 3–8.

———. 2017. *Qin han fazhishi yanjiu* 秦漢法制史研究. Translated by Xu Sihong 徐世虹. Shanghai: Zhongxi shuju.

Olberding, Garret P. S. 2012. *Dubious Facts: The Evidence of Early Chinese Historiography*. Albany: SUNY Press.

———, ed. 2013a. *Facing the Monarch: Modes of Advice in the Early Chinese Court*. Cambridge, MA: Harvard University Asia Center.

————. 2013b. "How did Minister Err?" In *Facing the Monarch: Modes of Advice in the Early Chinese Court*, edited by Garret P. S. Olberding, 133–65. Cambridge, MA: Harvard University Asia Center.

Oliver, Robert T. 1971. *Communication and Culture in Ancient Indian and China*. Syracuse: Syracuse University Press.

Pang-White, Ann A., trans. 2018. *The Confucian Four Books for Women: A New Translation of the Nü Sishu and the Commentary of Wang Xiang*. Oxford: Oxford University Press.

Peerenboom, R. P. 1993. *Law and Morality in Ancient China: The Silk Manuscripts of Huang-Lao*. Albany: SUNY Press.

Peng Lin 彭林, trans. 2001. *Yili* 儀禮. Changsha: Yuelu shushe.

Pines, Yuri. 2002a. *Foundations of Confucian Thought: Intellectual Life in the Chunqiu Period 722–453 B.C.E.* Honolulu: University of Hawai'i Press.

————. 2002b. "Friends or Foes: Changing Concepts of Ruler-Minister Relations and the Notion of Loyalty in Pre-Imperial China." *Monumenta Serica* 50 (1): 35–74.

————. 2005. "Beasts or Humans: Pre-imperial Origins of the 'Sino-barbarian' Dichotomy." In *Mongols, Turks, and Others: Eurasian Monads and the Sedentary World*, edited by Reuven Amitai and Michal Biran, 59–102. Leiden, NL: Brill.

————. 2013. "From Teachers to Subjects: Minsters Speaking to the Rulers, from Yan Ying to Li Si." In *Facing the Monarch: Modes of Advice in the Early Chinese Court*, edited by Garret P. S. Olberding, 69–99. Cambridge, MA: Harvard University Asia Center.

Plato. 2003. *Phaedrus*. Translated by Robin Waterfield. Oxford: Oxford University Press.

Powell, Bill. 2020. "America Is in a New Cold War and This Time the Communists Might Win." *Newsweek*, June 18, 2020. https://www.newsweek.com/2020/06/05/america-new-cold-war-this-time-communists-might-win-1504447.html.

Pratt, Mary Louise. 1992. *Imperial Eyes: Travel Writing and Transculturation*. New York: Routledge.

Prior, Paul, and Jody Shipka. 2003. "Chronotopic Lamination: Tracing the Contours of Literate Activity." In *Writing Selves/Writing Society: Research from Activity Perspectives*, edited by Charles Bazerman and David R. Russell, 180–238. N.p.: WAC Clearinghouse.

Queen, Sarah A. 1996. *From Chronicle to Canon: The Hermeneutics of the Spring and Autumn, According to Tung Chung-Shu*. Cambridge: Cambridge University Press.

————. 2001. "Inventories of the Past: Rethinking the 'School' Affiliation of the 'Huainanzi.'" *Asia Major, Third Series* 14 (1): 51–72.

———. 2013. "The Rhetoric of Dong Zhongshu's Imperial Communications." In *Facing the Monarch: Modes of Advice in the Early Chinese Court*, edited by Garret P.S. Olberding, 133–65. Cambridge, MA: Harvard University Asia Center.

Quint, David. 1993. *Epic and Empire: Politics and Generic Form from Virgil to Milton*. Princeton: Princeton University Press.

Raphals, Lisa. 1998. *Sharing the Light: Representations of Women and Virtue in Early China*. Albany: SUNY Press.

Ren Huifeng 任慧峰. 2007. *Handai xiju yanjiu* 漢代戲劇研究. Master's thesis, Ocean University of China.

Ren Jiyu 任繼愈. 1985. *Zhongguo fojiao shi* 中國佛教史. 3 vols. Beijing: Zhongguo shehui kexue chubanshe.

Ruiz, Iris, and Damián Baca. 2017. "Decolonial Options and Writing Studies." *Composition Studies* 45 (2): 226–29.

Ruiz, Iris D., and Raúl Sánchez, eds. 2016. *Decolonizing Rhetoric and Composition Studies: New Latinx Keywords for Theory and Pedagogy*. New York: Palgrave Macmillan.

Russell, David. 1997. "Rethinking Genre in School and Society: An Activity Theory Analysis." *Written Communication* 14 (4): 504–54.

Sabattini, Elisa. 2012. "'People as Root' (*min ben*) Rhetoric in the *New Writings* by Jia Yi (200-168)." In *Political Rhetoric in Early China*, edited by Paul van Els, Romain Graziani, Yuri Pines, and Elisa Sabattini, 167–93. Saint-Denis, FR: Presses Universitaires De Vincennes.

Sanft, Charles. 2014. *Communication and Cooperation in Early Imperial China*. Albany: SUNY Press.

Santos, Boaventura de Sousa. 2016. *Epistemologies of the South: Justice Against Epistemicide*. New York: Routledge.

Saussy, Haun. 1995. *The Problem of a Chinese Aesthetic*. Stanford: Stanford University Press.

Schaab-Hanke, Dorothee. 2012. "'Waiting for the Sages of Later Generations': Is there a Rhetoric of Treason in the *Shiji*?" In *Political Rhetoric in Early China*, edited by Paul van Els, Romain Graziani, Yuri Pines, and Elisa Sabattini, 111–40. Saint-Denis, FR: Presses Universitaires De Vincennes.

Schaberg, David. 2002. *A Patterned Past: Form and Though in Early Chinese Historiography*. Cambridge, MA: Harvard University Press.

———. 2013. "Functionary Speech: On the Work of *Shi* 使 and *Shi* 史." In *Facing the Monarch: Modes of Advice in the Early Chinese Court*, edited by Garret P. S. Olberding, 19–41. Cambridge, MA: Harvard University Asia Center.

Serruys, Paul Leo Mary. 1959. *The Chinese Dialects of Han Time According to Fang Yen*. Berkeley: University of California Press.

Works Cited

Shang Yang. 2019. *The Book of Lord Shang: Apologetics of State Power in Early China*. Abridged edition. Edited and translated by Yuri Pines. New York: Columbia University Press.

Shih, Heng-ching, trans. "The Sutra of Forty-Two Sections." In *Apocryphal Scriptures*, 27–44. Moraga, CA: BDK America.

Silverstein, Michael, and Greg Urban, eds. 1996. *Natural Histories of Discourse*. Chicago: University of Chicago Press.

Sima Qian 司馬遷. 2006. *Shiji* 史記. Zhonghua jingdian puji wenku 中華經典普及文庫. Beijing: Zhonghua shuju.

Sishier zhang jing 四十二章經. 2010. Beijing: Zhonghua shuju.

Spinuzzi, Clay. 2003. *Tracing Genres Through Organizations: A Sociocultural Approach to Information Design*. Cambridge, MA: MIT Press.

———. 2008. *Network: Theorizing Knowledge Work in Telecommunications*. Cambridge: Cambridge University Press.

Ssu-ma, Ch'ien. 1994a. *The Grand Scribe's Records, Vol. I: The Basic Annals of Pre-Han China*. Edited by William H. Nienhauser, Jr., and translated by Tsai-fa Cheng, Zhongli Lu, William H. Nienhauser, Jr., and Robert Reynolds. Bloomington: Indiana University Press.

———. 1994b. *The Grand Scribe's Records, Vol. VII: The Memoirs of Pre-Han China*. Edited by William H. Nienhauser, Jr., and translated by Tsai-fa Cheng, Zhongli Lu, William H. Nienhauser, Jr., and Robert Reynolds. Bloomington: Indiana University Press.

———. 2002. *The Grand Scribe's Records, Vol. II: The Basic Annals of Han China*. Edited by William H. Nienhauser, Jr., and translated by Weiguo Cao, Scott W. Galer, William H. Nienhauser, and David W. Pankenier. Bloomington: Indiana University Press.

———. 2011. *The Grand Scribe's Records, Vol. IX: The Memoirs of Han China*, Part II. Edited by William H. Nienhauser, Jr., and translated by J. Michael Farmer, Enno Giele, Christiane Haupt, Li He, Elisabeth Hsu, William H. Nienhauser, Jr., Marc Nurnberger, and Ying Qin. Bloomington: Indiana University Press.

———. 2019. *The Grand Scribe's Records, Vol. XI: The Memoirs of Han China*, Part IV. Edited by William H. Nienhauser, Jr., and translated by Guilia Baccini, Maddalena Barenghi, Stephen Durrant, Kathrin Leese-Messing, Clara Luhn, Jakob Pöllath, Jr. Nienhauser William, Edward Shaughnessy, and Hans van Ess. Bloomington: Indiana University Press.

———. 2020. *The Grand Scribe's Records, Vol. X: The Memoirs of Han China*, Part III. Edited by William H. Nienhauser, Jr. and translated by Chiu Ming Chan, Thomas D. Noel, Marc Nürnberger, Jakob Pöllath, Andreas Siegl, and Lianlian Wu. Bloomington: Indiana University Press.

Sukhu, Gopal. 2013. *The Shaman and the Heresiarch: A New Interpretation of the Li sao*. Albany: SUNY Press.

Swann, Nancy Lee. 2001. *Pan Chao: Foremost Woman Scholar of China*. Ann Arbor: University of Michigan Press.

Takao Hirase 平勢隆郎. 2014. *Cong chengshi guojia dao zhonghua: Yin zhou chunqiu zhanguo* 從城市國家到中華: 殷周春秋戰國. Guilin: Guangxi Shifan daxue chubanshe.

Tomiya Itaru 冨穀至. 2010. *Bunsho gyōsei no Kan teikoku* 文書行政の漢帝國. Nagoya: Nagoya daigaku shuppankai.

Tuck, Eve, and K. Wayne Yang. 2012. "Decolonization is not a Metaphor." *Decolonization: Indigeneity, Education, and Society* 1 (1): 1–40.

van Els, Paul. 2012. "Tilting Vessels and Collapsing Walls—On the Rhetorical Function of Anecdotes in Early Chinese Texts." In *Political Rhetoric in Early China*, edited by Paul van Els, Romain Graziani, Yuri Pines, and Elisa Sabattini, 141–66. Saint-Denis, FR: Presses Universitaires De Vincennes.

van Els, Paul, and Elisa Sabattini. 2012. "Introduction: Political Rhetoric in Early China." In *Political Rhetoric in Early China*, edited by Paul van Els, Romain Graziani, Yuri Pines, and Elisa Sabattini, 5–14. Saint-Denis, FR: Presses Universitaires De Vincennes.

van Els, Paul, and Sarah A. Queen, eds. 2017. *Between History and Philosophy: Anecdotes in Early China*. Albanyy: SUNY Press.

van Els, Paul, Romain Graziani, Yuri Pines, and Elisa Sabattini, eds. 2012. *Political Rhetoric in Early China*. Saint-Denis, FR: Presses Universitaires De Vincennes.

Vitanza, Victor, ed. 2016. *Landmark Essays on Historiographies of Rhetorics*. New York: Routledge, 2016.

Wang Fuhan 王扶漢. 1989. "Zuozhuan suoji fushi li fawei, lun shi zai chunqiu shiqi yizhong dute de shehui gongneng 《左傳》所記賦詩例發微—論 《詩》在春秋時期一種獨特的社會功能." *Beijing sifa xueyuan xuebao* 北京司法學院學報 (2): 118–26.

———. 1990. "Fushi duanzhang bian, zuozhuan suo ji fushi li fawei zhier "賦詩斷 章" 辯—《左傳》所記賦詩例發微之二." *Guyuan shizhuan xuebao* 固原師 專學報 (3): 9–15.

Wang Ruoshui 王若水. "Wang dao hu? ba dao hu? Mao Zedong yuan he liangci tidao han yuandi 王道乎? 霸道乎? 毛澤東緣何兩次提到漢元帝." http://www.wangruoshui.net/CHINESE/hanyuandi.HTM.

Wang, Robin R. 2005. "Dong Zhongshu's Transformation of Yin-Yang Theory and Contesting of Gender Identity." *Philosophy East and West* 55 (2): 209–31.

Watanabe Masatoshi 渡邊將智. 2014. *Gokan seiji seido no kenkyū* 後漢政治制度 の研究. Tokyo: Waseda daigaku shuppan-bu.

Woodman, Anthony. 1988. *Rhetoric in Classical Historiography: Four Studies*. London: Croom Helm.

Wu, Hui. 2009. "Lost and Found in Transnation: Modern Conceptualization of Chinese Rhetoric." *Rhetoric Review* 28 (2): 148–66.

———. ed. and trans. 2010. *Once Iron Girls: Essays on Gender by Post-Mao Chinese Literary Women*. Lanham, MD: Lexington Books.

———. 2018. "Yin-Yang as the Philosophical Foundation of Chinese Rhetoric." *China Media Research* 14 (4): 46–55.

———. 2020. "Reinventing Yin-Yang to Teach Rhetoric to Women." In *Reinventing Rhetoric Scholarship: Fifty Years of the Rhetoric Society of America*, edited by Roxanne Mountford, Dave Tell, and David Blakesley, 186–94. West Lafayette, IN: Parlor Press.

Wu, Hui, and C. Jan Swearingen. 2016. *Guiguzi, China's First Treatise on Rhetoric: A Critical Translation and Commentary*. Carbondale: Southern Illinois University Press.

Wu Chengxue, and Peng Yuping 吳承學、彭玉平 (eds). 2012. *Zhongguo gudai wenti xue yanjiu congshu* 中國古代文體學研究叢書. Beijing: Peking University Press.

Xiao, Yang. 2007. "How Confucius Does Things with Words: Two Hermeneutic Paradigms in the *Analects* and Its Exegeses." *Journal of Asian Studies* 66 (2): 497–532.

Xin Deyong 辛德勇. 2018. *Faxian yanranshan ming* 發現燕然山銘. Beijing: Zhonghua shuju.

Xu Fuhong 許富宏. 2008. *Guiguzi yanjiu* 《鬼穀子》研究. Shanghai: Shanghai guji chubanshe.

Xu Tianlin 徐天麟. 1963a. *Donghan huiyao* 東漢會要. Taipei: Shijie Shuju.

———. 1963b. *Xihan huiyao* 西漢會要. Taipei: Shijie shuju.

Yakobson, Alexander. "Political Rhetoric in China and in Imperial Rome: The Persuader, the Ruler, and Audience." In *Political Rhetoric in Early China*, edited by Paul van Els, Romain Graziani, Yuri Pines, and Elisa Sabattini, 195–208. Saint-Denis, FR: Presses Universitaires De Vincennes.

Yan Buke 閻步克. 2017. *Bofeng yu bogu, qin han wei jin nanbei chao de zhengzhi wenming* 波峰與波谷: 秦漢魏晉南北朝的政治文明. Beijing: Peking University Press.

Yantielun jiaozhu 鹽鐵論校注. 1992. Collated and annotated by Wang Liqi (王利器). Beijing: Zhonghua shuju.

Yao Aibin 姚愛斌. 2012. *Zhongguo gudai wenti lun sibian* 中國古代文體論思辨. Beijing: Peking University Press.

Ye Qiuju 葉秋菊. 2016. *Qin han zhaoshu yu zhongyang jiquan yanjiu* 秦漢詔書與中央集權研究. Beijing: Zhongguo shehui kexue chubanshe.

Ye, Yuying. 2017. "Variant Speech Sounds in the Warring States Period and Variant Characters in the Chu Manuscript: On the Nature of the Chu Dialect in the Warring States Period." *Chinese Studies in History* 50 (3): 213–34.

You, Xiaoye. 2005. "Conflation of Rhetorical Traditions: The Formation of Modern Chinese Writing Instruction." *Rhetoric Review* 24 (2): 150–69.

———. 2006. "The Way, Multimodality of Ritual Symbols, and Social Change: Reading Confucius's Analects as a Rhetoric." Rhetoric Society Quarterly 36 (4): 425–48.

———. 2010a. "Building Empire through Argumentation: Debating Salt and Iron in Western Han China." *College English* 72 (4): 367–84.

———. 2010b. *Writing in the Devil's Tongue: A History of English Composition in China*. Carbondale: Southern Illinois University Press.

———. 2014. "A Comparative-Rhetoric View of Contrastive Rhetoric." *Journal of Second Language Writing* 25 (4): 116–17.

———. 2016. *Cosmopolitan English and Transliteracy*. Carbondale: Southern Illinois University Press.

———. ed. 2018. *Transnational Writing Instruction: Theory, History, and Practice*. New York: Routledge.

You, Xiaoye, and Yichun Liu. 2009. "Confucians Love to Argue: Policy Essays in Ancient China." *College Composition and Communication* 60 (4): W56–W65.

Yu Xuetang 於雪棠. 2012. *Xianqin lianghan wenti yanjiu* 先秦兩漢文體研究. Beijing: Beijing shifan daxue chubanshe.

Zaleski, Michelle. 2020. "Recontextualizing Comparative Rhetoric." In *The Routledge Handbook of Comparative World Rhetorics*, edited by Keith Lloyd, 268–76. New York: Routledge.

Zang Rong 臧嶸. 1997. *Zhongguo gudai yizhan yu youchuang* 中國古代驛站與郵傳. Beijing: Shangwu yinshuguan.

Zhao, Heping. 1990. *Wen Xin Diao Long: An Early Chinese Rhetoric of Written Discourse*. PhD diss., Purdue University.

Zheng Ziyu 鄭子瑜. 1984. *Zhongguo xiucixue shigao* 中國修辭學史稿. Shanghai: Shanghai jiaoyu chubanshe.

Zheng Ziyu, Zong Tinghu, and Chen Guanglei 鄭子瑜、宗廷虎、陳光磊. 1998. *Zhongguo xiucixue tongshi* 中國修辭學通史. Changchun: Jilin jiaoyu chubanshe.

Zhongyang yanjiu yuan lishi yuyan yanjiu suo 中央研究院歷史語言研究所. "Yuankang wunian zhaoshu 元康五年詔書." Juyan hanjian ziliao ku 居延漢簡資料庫. https://wcd-ihp.ascdc.sinica.edu.tw/woodslip/.

Zhou Zhenfu 周振甫. 1991. *Zhongguo xiucixue shi* 中國修辭學史. Beijing: Shangwu yinshuguan.

Zhouli zhushu 周禮注疏. 2000. Beijing: Peking University Press.

INDEX

activity system, 15, 25, 180n25

Analects: evoked in court discussions, 110, 127, 138–39; on ontology and epistemology, 57–58, 149, 151, 181n33, 183n1; on rhetorical education, 27–29, 33–35, 182n8

ancient Chinese rhetoric. *See* rhetoric

argumentation: Confucius on, 33–34; in Ban Zhao's writings, 93–95; in court discussions, 98, 104–18, 167–68; on Heavenly Mandate, 68–70, 73; poetry as, 149–51; in political intrigues, 54–55; styles of, 120–21, 124–25, 127, 131, 133–34, 138–40; theory of, 38–39

astrology, 69–70, 76, 85–88, 90

astronomy, 15

Ban Gu: biography of, 85, 165; on the genre *fu*, 12, 143, 157, 159; historiographic practice, 50, 72, 88, 119, 120, 129, 135, 142, 146, 172, 187n5

Ban Zhao: and *Lessons for Women*, 92–95; on Heavenly Mandate, 85–92

bao (報). *See* sovereign answers

biao (表). *See* presentation

Biographies of Eminent Women (*lienü zhuan* 烈女傳), 80, 94

Book of Changes, 11, 66, 68–70, 136–37

Book of Han, 20, 165

Book of Songs. See *Odes*

border epistemology. *See* epistemology

boyi (駁議). *See* dissenting opinion

Buddhism, 67–71, 162–63, 179n19, 180n29, 189n18

Cai Yong, 9, 11–12, 46, 193n17

Changes. See *Book of Changes*

chaoyi (朝議). *See* discussion

Chen Wangdao, 6

chuci (楚辭). *See* verse of Chu

Chunqiu fanlu (春秋繁露). See *Luxuriant Gems of the Spring and Autumn*

classics: evoked in court discussions, 52, 63–67, 79, 109–10, 117, 121, 135–37, 139–41, 161; overview of, 10–14; scholarship on, 145, 166; used in education, 26, 58, 71, 84, 95, 167

colonialism, xv, 2, 16

comparative rhetoric, xv, 1–2, 4

conduct book, 79, 85

correlative thinking, 19, 75, 78, 82, 88, 96

cross-talk (*ouyu* 偶語), 147

Crump, James, 7, 124–25

Dao, 12, 32, 56

Daoism, 31, 40, 69–71, 95–96, 116, 136–37, 183n4

debate: in the court, 7, 23, 98, 103–6, 135–36, 186n11; as embodied practice, 117–18; training in, 34–35, 110

206   *Index*

decolonial option, 1–2, 171–72, 190n10

Despotic Way: conceptual evolution of, 99–102, 126; evoked in court debates, 22–23, 102–5, 108, 111–12; evoked in historiography, 118–19, 185n3, 186n11

Discourses of the States (*guoyu* 國語), 14, 25, 29, 35

Discourses on Salt and Iron (*yantielun* 鹽鐵論), 105–6, 107–19, 186n11–14, 186n18discussion (*yi* 議, *tingyi* 庭議, *chaoyi* 朝議), 98

dissenting opinion (*boyi* 駁議), 121

Dong Zhongshu: and gender relations, 75–76, 93–94; on government, 126–27; on Heavenly Mandate, 56, 58–62, 68, 73, 115

dui (對). *See* exam essay

duice (對策). *See* exam essay

dynastic history: construction of, 50, 64, 72, 75, 77, 85, 102, 114, 119, 142; and genre networks, 13–15, 160, 165–66, 168–70; as research data, 20–21

edict (*zhao* 詔), 19, 46, 49, 55

education: rhetorical, 8, 26–36, 95–96; women's, 81, 83, 84, 93–96

embodiment, 52–53, 57–58, 82, 96, 117–18, 144–45

Emperor Cheng, 67, 75–77, 82, 88, 161

Emperor Guangwu, 17, 52, 54–55, 72, 189n13

Emperor Wen, 30, 55–56, 102–103

Emperor Wu: and classical studies, 64, 120, 126–27; and foreign relations, 104–5, 135–36, 138–40; and literary culture, 146, 158; inquiring about Heavenly Mandate 58–63

empire: communications across, 47–50; government of, 59–60, 71–73; and

its integrity, 112, 114, 121; literary representation of, 149, 155–60, 161–64, 165–66; study of, 2–5, 9, 18, 171–72 and women, 84, 89–92

Empress Dowager Deng, 83–85, 90–91

Empress Dowager Ma, 81–83

Empress Xu, 79–80

enigma (*yingyu*隱語), 146–47

entertainment, 25–26, 146–48, 157–60, 163–64

epistemic delinking, 21, 172

epistemology: border, 1–2, 170–72, 177n1; Buddhist, 69, 73; Confucian, 53, 56–57, 169, 183n2; modernist, xv, 19, 21

exam essay (*dui* 對, *duice* 對策), 53, 58–64, 72–74, 77

filial piety, 30, 53, 69, 82–84, 90, 124

Five Phases, 68, 88, 171

fu (賦). *See* rhapsody

Garrett, Mary, 7

gender, 18, 61, 75–76, 86–87, 91, 94, 96

genre network: as an epistemic construct, 5, 10, 12–16, 20, 72–73, 96, 129, 135, 142, 163, 166, 167; limits of, 165–66, 169, 171–72; as a political institution, 4, 21–24, 25–26, 35–36, 47–50, 166–68; study of, 5, 10, 13, 17–20, 168–69

genre studies: a decolonial perspective to, 5, 10–16; in early China, 10–16, 166, 177n17; as a field of study, 3, 5, 16–17, 166; a transnational perspective to, 5, 16–21

government: criticism of, 160; debating the way of, 103–5, 119; and gender, 79–80, 83–84, 89–90; and genre networks, 166–67; genre practice related to, 10–11, 18–20, 43–50; Kingly Way and Despotic Way to, 97–98, 100–102; officials, 25, 30–32, 40, 44–46, 49–50, 106, 182n5, 182n13, 184n8, 186n15, 187n18; and rhetoric, 3–4, 8–9

Greco-Roman rhetoric. *See* rhetoric

Gu Yong, 65, 75–77

Guiguzi (鬼穀子). *See Master of the Ghost Valley*

Guoyu (國語). *See Discourses of the States*

Han Fei, 36, 39–43, 108, 160, 165, 189n1

Heavenly Mandate, 19, 54, 58–60, 62–64, 67–68, 73, 86–89, 181n33, 183n1

historiography. *See* Ban Gu; dynastic history; Sima Qian

Huainanzi (淮南子), 31, 137

Huang-Lao school, 59, 61, 69–71, 182n7, 183n4

humor (*xie* 諧), 15, 146

inner court, 19, 22, 45, 75–77

inscription (*ming* 銘), 143–45

Itaru, Tomiya, 9, 162

Jia Juanzhi, 138–40

Jia Yi, 25, 30, 35, 182n6

jie (戒). *See* lesson

jing-wei (經緯), 12, 180n26

Kennedy, George, xv

Kingly Way: conceptual evolution of, 97–102, 126; evoked in court debates, 22–23, 103–5, 110, 116; evoked in historiography, 118–19, 185n3, 186n11; evoked in the *Odes*, 136–37

Knechtges, David R., 7–8, 184n9, 184n13, 189n16, 190n6

Legalism, 98, 106, 108, 110, 183n4

lesson (*jie* 戒), 19, 92

Lessons for Women (*nüjie* 女戒), 85, 92–96

letter (*shu* 書), 21, 102, 114, 168

Lewis, Mark Edward, 8, 149, 151, 155

liberal democracy, 6, 178n9

Lienü zhuan (烈女傳). *See Biographies of Eminent Women*

listening, 8, 31–32, 35, 43

Literary Mind and the Carving of Dragons (*wenxin diaolong* 文心雕龍), 12–13, 36

Liu An, 31–32, 35, 135–37, 155, 187n5, 188n12

Liu Xiang, 68, 76, 80, 94

Liu Xie: influenced by Buddhism, 179n19, 180n29; influences on later scholars, 180n22; on genre networks, 12–13, 15, 145, 148, 163, 166, 169, 185n2, 188n12

long and short art, 124–25, 129

Lu, Xing, 8, 11

Luxuriant Gems of the Spring and Autumn (*chunqiu fanlu* 春秋繁露), 63

Mao Zedong, 1–2, 119

Master of the Ghost Valley (*Guiguzi* 鬼穀子), 31, 36–39, 43, 51, 91

materiality, 4, 9–10, 46, 117, 142, 162

Mei Cheng, 129–35, 142, 159, 187n5

memoir (*zhuan* 傳), 19, 80

memorial (*zou* 奏): as court ritual, 46, 48–49; 167; dealing with imperial integrity, 129–33, 135–37, 139–42, 168; dealing with the inner court, 75, 78–79, 86, 90–92, on education, 30

208 Index

Mencius, 33–34, 100, 187n1
ming (銘). *See* inscription
music: in classical education, 27–29, 57, 181n2; and government, 25, 89–90, 127, 145–46, 149–50, 152–53

narrative: as a literary form, 145, 146–48, 150–51, 158, 188n3, 188n6 in historiography, 119, 155, 170, 172, 180n24, 188n12; as research data, 20
network: as an approach to genre studies, 2–5, 10, 17–20; in genre theory, 12–13, 15. *See also* genre network; theory
nonaction, 39–40, 69–70, 116
non-Western rhetoric. *See* rhetoric
Nüjie (女戒). *See Lessons for Women*

Odes: evoked in court discussions, 52, 66, 80, 91, 93, 112, 140, 144–45; influences on literary creativity, 152–53, 155, 161, 163; scholarship on, 11–12, 179n16; in the Spring and Autumn period, 148–52; used in rhetorical education, 24–25, 28–19, 58, 188n12
Oliver, Robert T., 6, 8
omen, 53–55, 64–68, 71–73, 75–79, 86–88
Osamu, Oba, 9, 47, 185
ouyu (偶語). *See* cross-talk

poetry (*shi* 詩). See *Odes*
postal system, 47, 121, 135
presentation (*shu* 疏, *biao* 表), 78, 86
prophecy (*chen* 讖), 54

Qin Shi Huang, 3, 7
Qu Yuan, 152–56, 160, 189n12

Record of Rites, 19, 25, 30, 31, 79, 92–94, 167, 181n1, 182n6

rectification of names, 110–12, 116
rhapsody (*fu* 賦), 7–8, 19, 89, 92, 144, 156–61
rhetoric: ancient Chinese, 6–7, 170–71, 177n7, 177n8, 178n10; Greco-Roman, xv, 1, 5–6, 26, 177n3, 181n3, 190n3; non-Western, xv-xvi, 1–2, 6, 177n3, 190n3
rhetorical education. *See* education
rhetorical theory. *See* theory; *yin-yang*
ritual: education, 27–30, 57–59, 94, 151; genre practices as, 9–10, 12, 25, 46–50, 53, 144, 149, 177n6; as practiced in the court, 62–63, 77, 188n10; suasive power of, 89–90, 112–15, 177n5

Sanft, Charles, 8
shi (詩). *See Odes*
shu (書). *See* letter
shu (疏). *See* presentation
Sima Qian: on genre networks, 13–16, 169, 180n26, 187n6, 188n12, 189n1; historiographic practices, 72, 86–88, 100–101, 114, 124, 147, 155, 166, 172, 180n23, 185n3
Sima Xiangru, 15, 157, 161
sovereign answers (*bao* 報), 121, 137
Spring and Autumn Annals: evoked in policy debates, 108, 120–21, 126–28, 134, 139; evoked to elucidate Heavenly Mandate, 58, 62, 68; overview of, 11, 14
Su Qin, 15, 120–23, 125

theory: western rhetorical, xv, 6; on genre networks, 12–13, 15, 145, 163; on Heavenly Mandate, 59, 68, 73; on political persuasion, 36–43, 51, 123–24; on *yin-yang*, 75–76

tingyi (庭議). *See* discussion

translation, 7–8, 17, 20–21, 136, 160–63

translingualism, 18, 21, 53, 68, 162, 180n30

trivial talks (*xiaoshuo* 小說), 146–48

verse of Chu (*chuci* 楚辭), 144, 152–55

Vertical-Horizontal school, 36–37, 120–25, 128–35, 141, 159, 187n1, 187n5

war proclamation (*xi* 檄), 161–62

Wenxin diaolong (文心雕龍). *See Literary Mind and the Carving of Dragons*

Wu, Hui, 8, 20, 94, 96

xi (檄). *See* war proclamation

Xiang Kai, 70, 163

xiaoshuo (小說). *See* trivial talks

xie (諧). *See* humor

Xiongnu, 90, 104, 107, 109, 113–15, 141, 143–45

Yan Zhu, 120, 127, 137–38, 141–42, 159

Yang Xiong, 8, 159–60, 184n9

Yantielun (鹽鐵論). *See Discourses on Salt and Iron*

yi (議). *See* discussion

yingyu (隱語). *See* enigma

yin-yang: evoked in court debates, 115–16; for decoloniality, 190n9; and gender, 75–76, 93–94, 96; and Heavenly Mandate, 61–62; in rhetorical theory, 8, 37–39, 43, 123, 187n3

Zhang Yi, 15, 122–23, 125

Zhang Yu, 67

zhao (詔). *See* edict

zhuan (傳). *See* memoir

zou (奏). *See* memorial

Zou Yang, 129–31, 133–35, 141–42, 159

Zuo Tradition (*zuozhuan* 左傳), 14, 25, 35, 181n1

Zuozhuan (左傳). See *Zuo Tradition*

Xiaoye You is Liberal Arts Professor of English and Asian Studies at Pennsylvania State University and formerly Yunshan Chair Professor at Guangdong University of Foreign Studies. He is the author and editor of several books, including *Writing in the Devil's Tongue: A History of English Composition in China* and *Cosmopolitan English and Transliteracy*, also published by Southern Illinois University Press.